Literature Circles
and
Response

Literature Circles
and
Response

Edited by
Bonnie Campbell Hill
Nancy J. Johnson
Katherine L. Schlick Noe

Foreword by
Kathy G. Short

Christopher-Gordon Publishers 1995
Norwood, MA

Credits

Every effort has been made to contact copyright holders for permission to reproduce borrowed material where necessary. We apologize for any oversights and would be happy to rectify them in future printings.

The authors would like to gratefully acknowledge all student work which is included with permission.

Christopher-Gordon Publishers, Inc.
480 Washington Street
Norwood, MA 02062

Printed in the United States of America

10 9 8 7 6 5 4 3 2   99 98 97 96
ISBN: 0-926842-48-X

/

Contents

Chapter 1
**Treasures in the Attic: Building the Foundation for
   Literature Circles** 1
Sarah Owens

   Defining Literature Circles 2
   Rationale for Literature Circles 3
   Literature Circles and Teaching Reading 8
   Conclusion 10
   References 10

Chapter 2
**A Delightful Journey: Literature Circles in First
   Grade** 13
Christy Clausen

   Planning the Journey: Literature Circle Goals for Beginning
      Readers 13
   Daily Reading Program (First Grade) 14
   Getting Started: The Five-Day Schedule 15
   Weekly Schedule 15
   Journal Prompts 19
   Stepping Stones: Literature Circle Teaching Strategies 21
   Looking Back: Reflections on Literature Circles in First
      Grade 23
   References 23
   Literature Circles: Parental Involvement 24

Chapter 3
**Learning Together: Sharing Control with Emergent
   Readers** 27
Margee Morfitt

   Trusting Student Choice 28
   Developing Independence in Reading 28
   Encouraging and Extending Journal Response 29
   Creating a Climate for Discussion 30
   Spotlighting Students' Use of Strategies 33
   Allowing Students to Lead 33
   Responding to Literature 34
   Questions That Remain 38
   References 40

Chapter 4
Nurturing Response with Emergent Readers 41
Katherine L. Schlick Noe

How Readers Differ in Literacy Development 42
Questions Teachers Ask 45
Summary 52
References 53

Chapter 5
Finding a Balance: Literature Circles and "Teaching Reading" 55
Penny Redman

Daily Schedule 55
Reading Workshop Structure 56
Mini-Lessons 57
Literature Study Choices 61
Literature Circle Discussions 62
Debriefing 65
Independent Reading and Conferences 66
Management Issues 66
Literature Circle Extensions 67
Conclusions 67
References 67

Chapter 6
Sparking a Love for Reading: Literature Circles with Intermediate Students 71
Anne Klein

Getting Ready 71
Beginning the Year 72
Homelessness: A Sample Literature Circle 75
Final Thoughts 80
References 81

Chapter 7
Going with the Flow: Getting Back on Course When Literature Circles Flounder 85
Kary Brown

Getting My Feet Wet 86
Jumping In 86
Calm Waters 87
Treading Water 88
Swimming with the Current 90
Smooth Sailing 91
References 93

Literature Circles: Good Intentions 94
Carolyn Callaghan

Chapter 8
Invisible Scaffolding: Fostering Reflection 97
Patricia Kamber

    Examining Genuine Conversations 98
    Building Relationships and Establishing Trust 99
    Setting the Stage for Literature Circles 101
    Beginning Literature Circles 102
    Encouraging Positive Group Dynamics 103
    Nurturing Reflective and Thoughtful Response 108
    Benefits of Literature Circles 110
    References 111

Chapter 9
Choosing Books for Literature Circles 113
Dianne Monson

    Selecting Traditional Literature 114
    Looking at the Structure of Traditional Literature 116
    Selecting Fantasy 117
    Structure of Fantasy 119
    Selecting Realistic Fiction 121
    Structure of Realistic Fiction 122
    Selecting Informational Books 123
    References 127

Chapter 10
Deepening Response Through the Arts 131
Lisa F. Norwick

    Introducing Writing and the Visual Arts 132
    Weaving in the Performing Arts 139
    Celebrating Through Writing, Visual Arts, and Performing
        Arts 142
    Literature Circle Extension Possibilities 143
    Closing Thoughts 148
    References 148

Chapter 11
**Drawing on the Artist's Perspective: Ventures into
    Meaning Making** 153
Barry Hoonan

    Articulating a Personal Definition of Literacy 155
    Responding Through the Arts: Literature Study with Artists . 156

Implications for the Classroom 161
Final Thoughts 165
References 166

Chapter 12
Literature Circles: Assessment and Evaluation 167
Bonnie Campbell Hill

Assessing Oral Response 168
Assessing Extensive Reading 175
Assessing Participation 178
Assessing Written Response 185
Assessing Artistic and Dramatic Response 188
Evaluation and Portfolios 194
Assessment Challenges and Celebrations 197
References 198

Chapter 13
Goals and Assessment: How They Go in Circles 199
Sam Sebesta

Authentic Assessment in Literature Circles: The Beginnings 201
Wide Reading 202
Reader Response 203
Another Look at Achievement Testing 207
Summary 208
References 209

Chapter 14
Time Changes Everything: One Teacher's Story 211
Nancy J. Johnson

Year One—Surviving and Feeling Secure 212
Year Two—Experiencing Cognitive Dissonance 213
Year Three—Beginning to Let Go 215
Year Four—Stepping Back 218
Year Five—Fine Tuning and Trusting the Community ... 220
Year Six—Looking Forward 222
Final Reflections 222
References 223

Closing Remarks 225

About the Authors 227

Books for Literature Circles:
   A Selected Annotated Bibliography 231

Author and Title Index 277
General Index 280

Foreword

Kathy G. Short

The current swing of the pendulum in the field of education has focused attention on literature-based curriculum and literature discussion groups. Books, articles, and conferences extol the benefits of children reading "real" books and talking and writing about their responses to those books. Many educators fear, however, that this focus on literature will soon be replaced by a swing back to basal readers and skill-based approaches to reading instruction.

Already, publishers have taken over the rhetoric of literature-based curriculum. Instead of basal readers, they now have literature anthologies and "real" books. Instead of workbooks, there are literature logs with questions for students to answer. Literature-based curriculum has been reduced to a new set of materials and a few new practices with no real change in understandings about the reading process, learning or inquiry.

While I am pessimistic about much of what I see happening, there are also many positive signs that more substantive changes are being made. One of those signs is that the focus on literature in the curriculum has come about through a collaboration of educators in schools and universities. Traditional innovations are imposed from experts outside the school context. The interest in literature, however, has been both a grass roots movement within classrooms and a focus of attention within universities and in the broader field. The authors of *Literature Circles and Response* exemplify this collaboration of teachers and researchers from university and school settings who come together because of their shared interests in literature and its role in children's learning and thinking. Specifically, the authors of this book have worked together to pursue their interest in literature circles, small group discussions about books.

Literature circles fit within a broader theoretical and curricular framework. That broader framework needs to be acknowledged given the field's tendency to take one part and make it the whole. Literature circles are not the entire curriculum, but function within a cycle of authoring and inquiry.

The term "literature circle" grew out of my work with Jerry Harste and Carolyn Burke on the authoring cycle (Short, 1986). Initially the authoring cycle was developed as a curricular framework for the writing process which focused on the importance of building from children's life experiences, writing for a wide variety of purposes, taking new perspective on some pieces of writing by sharing them with peers, revising and editing those pieces, publishing them for a broader audience, reflecting on strategies of writing, and continuing the cycle through new invitations and actions. One of the most powerful aspects of the cycle were authors circles where

[handwritten margin note: based on Her dissertation]

students brought rough draft pieces of writing to a small group for their response. Those drafts were "in-process" pieces of writing that the author wanted to think more about with a group of peers. As I sat in authors circles, I was impressed with the talk that occurred as students worked to collaboratively think and explore together as authors.

The authoring cycle allowed us to take our beliefs about learning and language and put them into action through a curricular framework. We quickly realized that the authoring cycle was a metaphor for learning, not just writing. In any learning context, children author meaning through reading, writing, speaking, drawing, singing, and dancing their way into understandings about the ideas they are considering. As they author meaning, they build from their own life experiences and are involved in many authentic engagements with meaning. They consider some of these engagements more intensively by collaborating with other learners, revising their understandings, presenting these understandings publicly, reflecting on their learning, and taking new actions and invitations (Harste & Short with Burke, 1988, Short & Burke, 1991).

Initially, many of us who were exploring literature in the curriculum focused on using literature extensively in the classroom. We flooded the classroom with books. We read aloud, provided time for independent reading, and engaged students in activities related to the books that filled the classroom. My major goal as a teacher was to have my students become fluent readers who loved books. I accomplished that goal but quickly realized that students can read extensively without thinking deeply and critically about what they read. Through conversations with educators such as Karen Smith, I became convinced that what was missing was the counterpart to authors circles and so began to explore literature circles.

Literature circles provide a curricular structure to support children in exploring their rough draft understandings of literature with other readers. Literature circles encourage children to expand and critique their understandings about their reading through dialogue with other readers. These circles are based on the belief that reading is a transactional process where students actively construct understandings by bringing meaning to as well as taking meaning from a text (Rosenblatt, 1978). Students' primary focus is not on extracting information from a text, figuring out the interpretation the teacher wants to hear, or learning about literary elements. They enter the world of literature to learn about life and to make sense of the world.

In literature circles, readers must think collaboratively with each other, not simply work together cooperatively. Cooperative learning formats where tasks and roles are divided among the members of the group shut down the thinking and talk which is at the hear to dialogue. Children do not simply contribute their part of completing a task; they listen carefully and think deeply with other group members to create understandings that go beyond those of individual members. The dialogue in these groups leads children to new perspectives on literature and their lives.

Literature circles are not a variation on reading groups. They are not a better way to teach reading. They are a place to think and inquire. This is not to say that students do not learn about language and explore reading strategies during these groups. They do, but the primary focus of a literature circle is not on the reading process but on life and inquiry.

Students may not be able to independently read the books they are discussing in literature circles because these books must support children's indepth consideration of many layers of meaning. When I worked with first graders, the predictable books they could read independently did not support this indepth consideration and so I read aloud powerful picture books. In older classrooms, students often partner read with each other. The issue is not whether they can read the books, but whether they can productively think together about the books.

Literature circles, therefor, must exist within a broader curricular framework that includes opportunities for students to read widely from high interest books that supports their development as fluent readers. There must also be opportunities to engage in shared reading and strategy lessons where they examine language and reading strategies. Literature circles cannot serve all of these purposes without losing its own key purpose in encouraging children to become reflective and critical thinkers and readers.

Literature circles are most powerful when they are part of an inquiry-based classroom. The heart of curriculum is not books, but inquiry. Through inquiry, students search for the questions that are significant in their lives and become problem-posers as well as problem-solvers (Short & Harste, 1995). Although literature circles play a key role in supporting students in personal and class inquiries, inquiry, not the literature itself, drives the learning process. I have come to realize that literature-based curriculum is a misleading term. What we really want is an inquiry-based curriculum where literature plays a key role in that inquiry.

Too often curricular innovations such as literature circles remain at an abstract theoretical level or are packages as a program with a specific set of procedures. The authors of *Literature Circles and Response* have tried to resist the temptation to reduce literature circles to steps and procedures. Instead, they share their struggles to think with each other and with their students as they work through the difficult tasks of creating curriculum, of putting their beliefs into practice. Their chapters end with the questions they are continuing to pursue in classroom settings. They have not "arrived" at some final point, but are continuing to think with each other.

Through this book, the authors not only provide practical suggestions about literature circles, but an example of how to support professional growth. Their process as a study group of learning and thinking together is more powerful and transforming than the traditional model of "training" teachers in a curricular innovation through a series of inservice presentation. They have built from the earlier work of other educators who shared their thinking in books such as *Cycles of Meaning* (Pierce & Gilles, 1993), *Grand Conversations* (Peterson & Eeds, 1990), *Talking about Books* (Short & Pierce, 1990), and *Creating Classrooms for Authors* (Harste & Short, with Burke, 1988). The ideas and strategies they share from their own teaching in this book add to the conversation and provide another point of connection for educators who are exploring literature circles. Inquiry is not just the heart of the curriculum for children, but the heart of our own growth as educators.

References

Harste, J. & Short, K. with Burke, C. (1988*). Creating Classrooms for Authors*. Portsmouth, NH: Heinemann.

Peterson, R., & Eeds, M. (1990). *Grand Conversations*. New York: Scholastic.

Pierce, K. & Gilles, C., Eds. (1993*). Cycles of Meaning: Exploring the Potential of Talk in Learning Communities*.

Rosenblatt, L. (1978). *The Reader, the Text, the Poem: The Transactional Theory of the Literary Work*. Carbondale, IL: Southern Illinois University Press.

Short, K. (1986). *Literacy as a Collaborative Experience*. Unpublished doctoral dissertation. Bloomington, IN: Indiana University.

Short, K. & Burke, C. (1991) *Creating Curriculum*. Portsmouth, NH: Heinemann.

Short, K. & Pierce, K., Eds., (1990). *Talking about Books*. Portsmouth, NH: Heinemann.

Preface

This book tells the stories of teachers and children who love books. The inspiration for the book grew out of our common pursuit of authentic ways to deepen children's engagement with literature. We came together over the past three years to fine-tune, revise, and re-think our ideas about literature circles and response.

Together, we began writing to articulate the ideas that were flying around in our heads and tried to make clear, for ourselves and for others, what we had learned. We wanted to be able to share our stories and insights with other teachers.

As we talked and wrote, we noticed the common threads in our classrooms. We all treasure children's voices and have faith in what young readers can accomplish. We all consume children's books and "Have you read . . . ?" is one of our favorite questions. Despite these commonalities, however, the patterns of how we weave literature into our particular classrooms are quite varied. As we wrote this book, we wrestle with how best to capture pictures of various classrooms, yet avoid being prescriptive. We hope our pedagogical stories will show that there are no "right answers" or "one way" to structure literature circles or respond to books. Our goal is to honor the variations and urge you to adapt these ideas, weaving them into the fabric of your own teaching.

Acknowledgments

One of the greatest joys of writing this book was getting together with colleagues who shared a common passion for books, teaching, and learning. The warm, collegial relationships that developed as we wrote together both inspired us and nourished our hearts. Working together has been the most joyful part of the process as the pieces of the book began to take shape. Dr. Sam Sebesta's tips on writing and pithy insights helped us focus and inspired us as writers. We'd also like to thank our editor, Sue Canavan, whose faith in our project was unswerving, and our reviewers, John Warren Stewig, Karen Bromley, Kathy Short and Susan Hepler, for their helpful suggestions.

We would like to thank the administrators and colleagues who supported us, listened to drafts, and added a "hooray" or pat on the back in the hall or late in the afternoon after everyone else had gone home. Most important, all of us feel deeply indebted to the students who have been our teachers. The words, art, and writing of these young people are the heart of this book.

Finally, we thank our families. They put up with our long phone calls, piles of drafts on the dining room table, our addiction to children's books, and our many late evenings at the computer.

Chapter 1

Treasures in the Attic:
Building the Foundation for Literature Circles

Sarah Owens

"Hey, Mom, when we get to Oma's house, can we go to the attic?"

"Sure," I reply, "but why?" The attic of my mother's hundred-something-year-old house can be sweltering hot in mid-August.

"I want to look at Oma's old books—books you read. You know—the classics."

Am I *that* old? Well, classics do weather the test of time!

Mark's persistence pays off as our three generations climb the narrow stairs to the attic. Vintage prom gowns hang from exposed beams. Antique furniture and piles of memorabilia spanning several lifetimes clutter the dark room.

Mark makes a beeline for the books, wiping off a thick film of dust. Worn faces of old friends peer out—*The Wizard of Oz* (Baum, 1900), Nancy Drew mysteries, and *Little Women* (Alcott, 1868). Childhood memories of happy times spent with books sweep over me—excursions to the library with friends followed by ice cream sundaes at the drug store, presents of books on Christmas morning, and escapes to our basement to curl up with adolescent romances.

Just as my mother and I shared our favorite books with my son, I also love to share books with my students. So, too, do the teachers whose stories make up the rest of this book.

This book began two years ago when classroom teachers and university professors formed a literature circles study group. We met once a month to explore different issues related to literature circles, such as how to select books that elicit response. We swapped titles for books on particular themes. We exchanged schedules and ideas about how literature circles fit into our total reading program. Teachers took turns sharing their students' artistic responses, revealing engaging possibilities. Throughout the year, we grappled with our evolving roles as facilitators of literary discussions. Some of the richest conversations sprang from sharing problems we encountered, as well as our successes. These meetings sustained our enthusiasm for literature circles and response to literature and inspired our teaching.

The chapters in this book were written by teachers who have been involved with literature circles in elementary classrooms for several years. We have all wrestled with both philosophical and practical issues in the process of building programs around literature and response. In this chapter, I'll begin with a definition of literature circles and then give a rationale for their use. Subsequent chapters will provide detailed glimpses into a variety of classrooms in order to focus on specific practical issues.

Defining Literature Circles

Literature circles are discussion groups in which children meet regularly to talk about books. Despite numerous variations in structure and organization, literature circles contain several common threads. Groups are determined by book choices; literature circles are heterogeneous and include a range of interests and abilities. A whole class may read one book in common, or groups of students may read different titles connected by a theme, genre, or author. During literature circles, students meet in small groups to discuss their books. Teachers find that groups of four to six participants are most effective. In primary grades, students may meet once a week to talk about the book. Intermediate students determine how many pages they will read and gather two or three times each week in their literature circle. They may share a favorite passage, raise a question, express a personal reaction, or talk about literary elements.

You'll often see students huddled in groups on the floor or around a table, leaning forward and listening intently. Children read questions from their dialogue journals, make predictions, and ask for clarification. Ideas are tossed around—sometimes quietly, at other times with great animation. The level of passion is often tied directly to how much they love the book. Children discuss a wide range of topics—from an author's craft, to a character's motivation, to connections to their own lives. When a question sparks keen interest, students' voices compete for attention; at other times their voices rise and fall, or are even hushed. Students flip pages to find a passage to prove a point. What strikes the casual observer most are students' involvement and their obvious enthusiasm.

Students are not just "on task"; they are engaged and eager to discuss their ideas. While the depth and quality of students' insights vary with their age and experience, at all levels you can observe students helping each other understand books. When I asked one of my fourth graders what he liked about literature circles, he replied, "Well, if you don't understand something in the story, you have four other people who can help you." Students become teachers and learners simultaneously.

Rationale for Literature Circles

Given the myriad of demands on teachers today, why should you consider adding to your already-stretched curriculum? A review of professional literature provides an impressive rationale for literature circles. In this section, I'll explore nine points in more depth. See Figure 1-1.)

Rationale for Literature Circles

Literature Circles:

- promote a love for literature and positive attitudes toward reading
- reflect a constructivist, child-centered model of literacy
- encourage extensive and intensive reading
- invite natural discussions that lead to student inquiry and critical thinking
- support diverse response to texts
- foster interaction and collaboration
- provide choice and encourage responsibility
- expose children to literature from multiple perspectives
- nurture reflection and self-evaluation

Figure 1-1. Rationale for Literature Circles

Literature circles promote a love for literature and positive attitudes toward reading.

A literature-based reading program should foster a spirit of curiosity and appreciation of literature. As teachers, we endeavor to create an atmosphere in which children are eager to turn to books to escape to an enchanted kingdom, absorb beautiful pictures and words, and to unravel a mysterious plot. Donna Norton (1991) lends support when she writes, "When children discover enjoyment in books, they develop favorable attitudes toward them that usually extend into a lifetime of appreciation" (p. 2).

Experts agree that helping children *want* to read is an essential part of helping children *learn* to read (Cullinan, 1987; Weaver, 1988). Children's experiences as they learn to read may affect their feelings about learning in general (Bettelheim & Zelan, 1981). A child's love for reading begins at an early age as families share literary experiences together. Teachers also play an important role in influencing positive attitudes about reading. According to Regie Routman, "The way students are asked to respond to literature in school influences their development as readers, writers, and thinkers as well as their enjoyment of literature" (1991, p. 133). Literature circle books frequently become catalysts for independent reading. Teachers see daily evidence of children's delight in reading as they clamor to share responses and eagerly exchange book titles.

Literature circles reflect a constructivist, child-centered model of literacy.

Readers don't *take* meaning from texts; they *construct* meaning. Louise Rosenblatt (1978) describes reading as a transaction, a dynamic interaction among author, text, and reader. Understanding of literature is enriched when students share their experiences and interpretations through authentic reading and writing events. Kathryn Au (1993) underscores this when she writes, "Constructivist models of literacy instruction generally include discussions of literature, either in small, teacher-led groups or in literature circles" (p. 43). Opportunities to talk about books help readers construct an understanding that begins with their own experience and reaches beyond.

Taking a constructivist perspective helps teachers build upon students' strengths and knowledge. Rather than presenting skills in a pre-ordained sequence, teachers introduce skills and strategies responsively as they observe students' needs. Teachers have discovered the effectiveness of short, relevant strategy lessons, referred to in this book as mini-lessons (Calkins, 1986; Atwell, 1987).

For example, I noticed my students were having difficulty making inferences. When we were reading *Shiloh* (Naylor, 1991), I asked them to delve beyond thinking, "I hate Judd Travers" to find what clues Naylor provides that reveal Judd's malicious personality. Learning to "read between the lines" is a strategy that helps students build a deeper understanding of the books they read. This type of responsive mini-lesson encourages students to become more conscious of effective reading strategies and supports students as they construct meaning.

Literature circles encourage extensive and intensive reading.

Like many other accomplishments, reading improves with practice. Children need to read widely, which Harste, Short and Burke (1988) refer to as *extensive* reading. Encounters with quality books and memorable characters lengthen the lines during library checkout time. For example, during a literature study of mysteries, I noticed reluctant readers signing out books from a box of mysteries I had gathered; even avid readers appeared freshly inspired. By the end of the mystery unit, our class of 24 students had read 196 mysteries—far exceeding the original goal of reading three books each. Research substantiates teachers' intuitive sense of the positive relationship between silent, sustained reading and reading achievement (Anderson, Hiebert, Scott & Wilkerson, 1985).

Traditionally, teachers have provided school time for independent reading, most often identified by acronyms such as SSR or DEAR. However, "just-reading" (Peterson & Eeds, 1990) is not enough. Literature circles offer opportunities for *intensive* reading in which students savor language, delve into the author's craft, and collaboratively construct meaning (Leal, 1993).

Literature circles invite natural discussions that lead to student inquiry and critical thinking.

Peterson and Eeds (1990) describe dialogue, talking with others about a book you have read, as the best pedagogical tool for text interpretation.

Dialogue recognizes that knowledge is something students actively construct.

> Listening to lectures is a solitary activity. Dialogue is a process of co-producing meaning. Dialogue partners need one another's patience, ideas, and encouragement. The give-and-take nature of the system depends on other participants to take up an idea, expand it, and add to it. (p. 21)

Dialogue also encourages inquiry (Sheppard, 1990). Children frequently are curious about vocabulary and will enter into lively discussions about the meaning of words. As students read, questions arise about important themes. They may resolve questions by revisiting the text or turning to informational material to clarify meaning. For example, when Patti Kamber's class first read *The Night of the Twisters* (Ruckman, 1984), the book sparked questions about tornadoes, which led them to research natural disasters. Teams shared their discoveries during literature circles using informational books. They then re-read *The Night of the Twisters* with a new understanding and set of questions.

Literature circles encourage exploration when we allow *children* to ask questions and "give students a chance to romp with an open-ended question" (Goodlad, 1984). This quote captures the sense of playfulness that is evident as readers toss around ideas. Such natural dialogue resembles the conversations that often take place at our kitchen tables, faculty lounges, or adult book club gatherings.

Literature circles support diverse response to texts.

Students need to respond to literature in a variety of ways (Strickland, 1987). Reader response theory (Rosenblatt, 1978) identifies two stances for responding to literature: efferent and aesthetic. Louise Rosenblatt cautions that "[t]extbooks' and teachers' questions too often hurry the students away from the lived-through experience" (1991, p. 447). Traditionally, reading instruction leaned heavily toward the efferent stance, focusing readers on the acquisition of skills and information. For example, when we ask students to answer questions about the plot and sequence of events in a story, we're setting a purpose for efferent reading. An aesthetic stance, on the other hand, begins with the reader's personal involvement with the text.

Readers who take an aesthetic stance make connections to their own lives and react emotionally. For example, after reading the first chapters of *The Book of Three* (Alexander, 1964), Rachel reacted, "If Taran were a real person, I wouldn't like him or want him for a friend; he only thinks about himself." Her statement spurred immediate reactions from other members in her group. Kristen chimed in, "I know. Taran made me so mad; he's such a baby."

Being aware of the distinction between efferent and aesthetic responses to literature is the first step toward finding a healthy balance in your reading program (Sebesta, 1987). Literature circles can incorporate both stances. After reading, students may summarize the section or book they read either orally or in writing. Teachers can encourage more aesthetic responses by asking children to write a personal reaction, respond artistically, or select a passage to share.

Literature circles foster interaction and collaboration.

Mem Fox asserts, "I'm certain that learning to read and learning to love reading owe a great deal (much more than we ever dreamed) to the *nature of the human relationships* that occur around and through books" (1993, p. 136). Vygotsky's work (1978) also supports the social and collaborative nature of learning. Through literature circles, students bring to their discussions the questions closest to their hearts. They can learn to explore their own reactions and value others' opinions. The teacher's role is to provide the environment in which such discussions can flourish, and artfully extend students' responses.

Recognizing that reading and writing are social acts challenges us to reevaluate the social contexts of our classrooms. Too often competition and individualism in schools preclude student inter-actions (Short, 1990). Literature circles, however, encourage co-operation and respect for diverse interpretations. Students learn classmates' strengths and children become valuable resources for each other. For instance, in my classroom Brett is the authority on Roald Dahl, Shaundra loves any type of fantasy, and Mark is the expert on the Revolutionary War.

Literature circles provide choice and encourage responsibility.

In the past decade, student-centered learning has received wide-spread attention. Teachers who include choice in their language arts programs report improved student involvement and improved attitudes (Atwell, 1987; Calkins, 1993; Swift, 1993). Literature circles can promote choice in several ways: students choose their own books, decide on the number of pages to read, select a group facilitator, and determine their questions, responses, and extension projects.

As an example, let's examine book selection. Teachers can support student choice and encourage independence. First, they must carefully select book titles that accommodate a wide range of reading abilities. They can also help students learn ways to choose books through guidance and demonstrations (modeling). But ultimately, teachers must trust students to select books that meet their own needs and interests.

When our literature circles revolved around Roald Dahl's novels, my less-proficient readers read *Fantastic Mr. Fox* (1970) with support from their Chapter I teacher. Some readers were more comfortable selecting *James and the Giant Peach* (1961), while others delighted in more challenging books such as *Matilda* (1988), *The BFG* (1982), and *Boy* (1984). Brian Cambourne (1988) em-phasizes that student responsibility goes hand in hand with choice. Students are expected to come to literature circles prepared for discussions. They assume responsibility because they feel a sense of ownership. When asked why students enjoy literature circles, one fifth grader said, "We feel so grown up. *We* choose the books, *we* pick the pages, and *we* decide the questions to discuss."

In the school setting, we often limit students' freedom to choose. Choice can be the wild card that makes students embrace tasks with greater enthusiasm. It is a powerful motivational tool and a first step toward developing independence.

Literature circles expose children to literature from multiple perspectives.

Literature circles are enriched by the plethora of quality multicultural literature available that brings us closer to the lives and experiences of others. Our students need to see their lives reflected in the books they read. As Violet Harris (1993) states,

> If literature is a mirror that reflects human life, then all children who read or are read to need to see themselves reflected as part of humanity. If they are not, or if their reflections are distorted and ridiculous, there is the danger that they will absorb negative messages about themselves and people like them. Those who see only themselves or are exposed to errors and misrepresentations are miseducated into a false sense of superiority, and the harm is doubly done. (p. 43)

It's critical when selecting books for literature circles that teachers take Violet Harris's words to heart.

Literature intertwines personal stories with historical and social events to portray the human dimensions of an issue. For example, *Everett Anderson's Goodbye* (Clifton, 1983) and *Toughboy and Sister* (Hill, 1990) capture the pain and confusion young children feel when confronted with the death of a family member. In *Pink and Say* (1994), Patricia Polacco reaches back into her family history to bring forward the story of two young men during the Civil War. The characters in these stories wrestle with universal issues that we all confront.

In the annotated bibliography at the end of this book, we've attempted to incorporate a wide range of perspectives for literature circle choices. Multicultural literature should not be a separate subject but should be woven into the fabric of our classrooms.

Literature circles nurture reflection and self-evaluation.

As more teachers move toward literature-based reading programs, they have become concerned about the need for assessment tools that match what we know about how children develop as readers. Teachers can assess reading comprehension informally during daily reading activities (Cambourne & Turbill, 1990; Paradis, Chatton, Boswell, Smith & Yovich, 1991). Authentic assessment may include reading and writing portfolios, anecdotal notes, and running records of children's oral reading. Students must also become part of the assessment process through reflection, self-evaluation, and goal-setting. (For more information on assessment during literature circles, see Chapters 12 and 13.)

Literature Circles and Teaching Reading

Literature circles are not entirely a new idea. You may already have an independent literature-based reading program in place. You may also have used discussion groups in the past. Whatever your grade level, you have probably developed a program in which you teach reading comprehension and strategies. Literature circles provide an avenue for weaving together all three.

How do literature circles differ from traditional reading programs? Literature circles are not teacher-centered; they do not follow a prescriptive format whereby teachers ask comprehension questions. You won't see workbooks or ability groups. Literature circle discussions are neither scripted nor predictable. They often look more like small town hall meetings, where members may express an idea, refute a popular view, or pose a question that contributes to a deeper understanding.

Three major differences exist between traditional practices and literature circles: (1) the focus of the discussion, (2) the student's role, and (3) the teacher's role.

Focus of Discussion

Traditional literature study emphasizes text analysis and correct interpretation. Teachers frequently ask questions such as, "Describe the main characters in *Bridge to Terabithia*." Literature circle discussions, on the other hand, begin with readers' responses, which Louise Rosenblatt (1978) calls "evocation." During literature circle discussions about *Bridge to Terabithia* (Paterson, 1972), for example, students might talk about friendship, experiences with imaginary worlds, or death. A great deal depends upon the students' experiences. In *Talking About Books*, Karen Smith (1990) notes, "Close reading of a text centers not only on the text, but on the reader as well" (p. 17).

The goal of literature circles is not to dissect and explain the book so that everyone comes to a common understanding. Rather, meaning making depends upon the experiences and contributions each reader brings to a discussion. Reading should stir up human feelings, prompting responses that are sometimes deeply and personally felt. No one explains this more clearly than Mem Fox:

> We need to be seen laughing over books, being unable to put books down, sobbing over sob stories, gasping over horror stories, and sighing over love stories—anything, in fact, that helps our students realize that there is some reward, that there are *many* rewards, to be had from the act of reading. (1993, p. 63)

Reading should also invite sharing. We hope to hear students at recess debating which Patricia Wrede dragon books they prefer, or see them cluster together in the halls evaluating Marty's decisions in *Shiloh* (Naylor, 1991). Such responses often circle back to spark more reading. As Sam Sebesta notes in Chapter 13, literature circles should not only increase comprehension, but also lead to deeper reading.

Student's Role

Reader response theory validates the student's role during literature study. A group of readers, with their unique life experiences and diverse knowledge of the world, may respond differently to the same text. Students have important responsibilities during literature circles; it is not an "anything goes" atmosphere. They must read and come prepared to participate in discussions. Teachers can guide students to turn to the text and their own experiences in order to support their reactions, but students' voices are at the heart of literature circles.

Teacher's Role

During literature circles, teachers act as facilitators and models for student self-reflection, inquiry, and critical thinking. In subsequent chapters, you'll read how teachers encourage independence, even with young students, by stepping back and taking a less dominant role than in the past. Although many of us used to rely upon a teacher's guide to lead reading discussions, we are coming to realize how this may suppress critical inquiry and individual response. Authorities (Anderson, Hiebert, Scott, & Wilkinson, 1985) question the value of reading programs that focus on literal questions with "right" answers. The result of such an emphasis in reading instruction has been that students' voices are lost as they come to believe that "truth only comes from others" (Petersen & Eeds, 1990).

Conclusion

In the next fourteen chapters you'll read stories about teachers who are building their reading programs around literature circles. These classroom stories serve only as invitations; there is no one right way that is being advocated. Selecting wonderful books that encourage response in relevant, purposeful ways will nudge children closer to charting their own literary histories with lovely language, compelling events, and memorable characters. Be it Dorothy or Jo from the old "classics," or Brian Robeson and Gilly Hopkins from the new, we hope every child's reading corner spills over with books that become "treasures in the attic."

References

Alcott, Louisa May. (1868). *Little Women*. Boston: Roberts Brothers.

Alexander, Lloyd. (1964). *Book of Three*. New York: Holt, Rinehart & Winston.

Anderson, Richard C., Hiebert, Elfrieda H., Scott, Judith A. & Wilkinson, Ian A. G. (1985). *Becoming a Nation of Readers: The Report of the Commission on Reading*. Washington D.C.: The National Institute of Education.

Atwell, Nancie. (1987). *In the Middle: Writing, Reading, and Learning with Adolescents.* Portsmouth, NH: Heinemann.

Au, Kathryn. (1993). *Literacy Instruction in Multicultural Settings.* San Diego: Harcourt Brace Jovanovich.

Baum, L. Frank. *The Wizard of Oz* (1900, 1982). New York: Holt, Rinehart & Winston.

Bettleheim, Bruno & Zelan, K. (1981). Why children don't like to read. *Atlantic Monthly*, November, 25–31.

Calkins, Lucy. (1993). (2nd Edition). *The Art of Teaching Writing.* Portsmouth, NH: Heinemann.

Calkins, Lucy. (1986). *The Art of Teaching Writing.* Portsmouth, NH: Heinemann.

Cambourne, Brian & Turbill, Jan. (1990). Assessment in Whole Language Classrooms: Theory into Practice. *Elementary School Journal, 90*, 337–350.

Cambourne, Brian. (1988). *The Whole Story: Natural Learning and the Acquisition of Literacy in the Classroom.* New York: Ashton Scholastic.

Clifton, Lucille. (1983). *Everett Anderson's Goodbye.* Illustrated by Ann Grifalconi. New York: Holt.

Cullinan, Bernice. (Ed.). (1987). *Children's Literature in the Reading Program.* Newark, DL: International Reading Association.

Dahl, Roald. (1988). *Matilda.* New York: Viking Kestrel.

Dahl, Roald. (1984). *Boy.* New York: Penguin.

Dahl, Roald. (1982). *The BFG.* New York: Avon.

Dahl, Roald. (1970). *Fantastic Mr. Fox.* New York: Knopf.

Dahl, Roald. (1961). *James and the Giant Peach.* New York: Knopf.

Fox, Mem. (1993). *Radical Reflections: Passionate Opinions on Teaching, Learning, and Living.* San Diego: Harcourt Brace.

Goodlad, John. (1984). *A Place Called School.* New York: McGraw-Hill.

Harris, Violet. (1993). *Teaching Multicultural Literature in Grades K-8.* Norwood, MA: Christopher-Gordon.

Harste, Jerome C., Short, Kathy G. & Burke, Carolyn. (1988). *Creating Classrooms for Authors: The Reading-Writing Connection.* Portsmouth, NH: Heinemann.

Hill, Kirkpatrick. (1990). *Toughboy and Sister.* New York: Puffin.

Leal, Dorothy. (1993). The power of literacy peer-group discussions: How children collaboratively negotiate meaning. *The Reading Teacher, 47* (2), 114–120.

Naylor, Phyllis Reynolds. (1991). *Shiloh.* New York: Dell Publishing.

Norton, Donna. (1991). (3rd Edition). *Through the Eyes of a Child: An Introduction to Children's Literature.* New York: Macmillan.

Paradis, Edward, Chatton, Barbara, Boswell, Ann, Smith, Marilyn & Yovich, Sharon. (1991). Accountability: Assessing comprehension during literature discussion. *The Reading Teacher, 45* (1), 8–17.

Paterson, Katherine. (1972). *Bridge to Terabithia*. New York: Avon.

Peterson, Ralph & Eeds, Maryann. (1990). *Grand Conversations: Literature Groups in Action*. New York: Scholastic.

Polacco, Patricia. (1994). *Pink and Say*. New York: Philomel.

Rosenblatt, Louise. (1991). Literature S.O.S.! *Language Arts, 68* (6), 444–448.

Rosenblatt, Louise. (1978). *The Reader, the Text, the Poem: The Transactional Theory of the Literary Work*. Carbondale, IL: Southern Illinois University Press.

Routman, Regie. (1991). *Invitations: Changing as Teachers and Learners K-12*. Portsmouth, NH: Heinemann.

Ruckman, Ivy. (1984). *Night of the Twisters*. New York: HarperCollins.

Sebesta, Sam Leaton. (1987). Enriching the arts and humanities through children's books. In Bernice Cullinan (Ed.) *Children's Literature in the Reading Program*. Newark, DL: International Reading Association, 77–88.

Sheppard, Linda Bowers. (1990). Our class knows *Frog and Toad*: An early childhood literature-based classroom. In Kathy Gnagey Short and Katheryn Mitchell Pierce (Eds.). *Talking About Books: Creating Literate Communities*. Portsmouth, NH: Heinemann, 71–81.

Short, Kathy Gnagey. (1990). Creating a community of learners. In Kathy Gnagey Short & Kathryn Mitchell Pierce. (Eds.) *Talking About Books: Creating Literate Communities*. Portsmouth, NH: Heinemann, 33–52.

Smith, Karen. (1990). Entertaining a text: a reciprocal process. In Kathy Gnagey Short & Katheryn Mitchell Pierce. (Eds.). *Talking About books: Creating Literate Communities*. Portsmouth, NH: Heinemann, 17–31.

Strickland, Dorothy. (1987). Literature: Key elements in the language and reading program. In Bernice Cullinan (Ed.) *Children's Literature in the Reading Program*. Newark, DL: International Reading Association, 68–76.

Swift, Kathleen. (1993). Try reading workshop in your classroom. *The Reading Teacher, 46* (5), 366–371.

Vygotsky, Lev S. (1978). *Mind in Society: The Development of Higher Psychological Processes*. Cambridge, MA: Harvard University Press.

Weaver, Constance. (1988). *Reading Process and Practice: From Socio-Psycholinguistics to Whole Language*, Portsmouth, NH: Heinemann.

Chapter 2

A Delightful Journey:
Literature Circles in First Grade

Christy Clausen

It's Monday morning and time to prepare my first grade classroom for today's literature discussion. I call my first group to the meeting area to talk about *Cookie's Week* (Ward, 1988) which these five children read over the weekend. We sit together in a circle and begin talking about the story. The children are eager to share their thoughts and opinions about the book. Nicole shares how cats and dogs often get into mischief. Kanen adds how he knows of other animals that make messes like Cookie. Arielle explains how her cat, Tucker, is just like Cookie, because they both fell into an aquarium and spilled water everywhere. Ashley speaks up and questions, "Who would want to clean up after Cookie?" The members immediately voice their opinions and the conversation continues as we explore Cookie's character traits and her mischievous mannerisms.

Who would have guessed such a simple text and story could generate exciting dialogue? Five years ago I wouldn't have thought that first graders could discuss literature with much depth. Yet, as I ventured into this intriguing area of literacy, my opinions have changed more and more each year regarding children's thought processes, their involvement with books, their appreciation of literature, and the varied ways they respond. Young children can discuss the main idea in a story, specific events, and some literary elements. Most important, they can relate events within the story to their own lives and share personal feelings and reactions. These are my primary goals as I work with beginning readers.

Planning the Journey: Literature
Circle Goals for Beginning Readers

My program with first grade students didn't just happen overnight. Even after several years of trial and error, I still wrestle with various issues. Literature circles are only one part of my total language arts program. In the fall, I place more emphasis on shared reading, news, poetry, and language activities, as you can see in Figure 2-1. By spring, literature circles have become more of a focus as students become more competent readers (Figure 2-2).

Daily Reading Program
(First Grade)

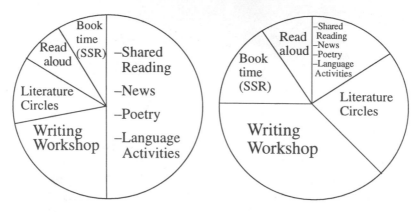

Figure 2-1 Fall   **Figure 2-2** Spring

I first needed to think through my rationale and philosophy about literacy learning before starting out with literature circles. Brian Cambourne's work on specific conditions for learning particularly influenced my thinking and helped set a direction for instruction. His book, *The Whole Story: Natural Learning and the Acquisition of Literacy in the Classroom* (1988), opened my eyes to the value of demonstrating learning strategies, engaging children in active learning, providing choice and responsibility, and eliciting meaningful responses.

Based on what I was reading, I asked myself the following questions:

- What do I want my students to gain from this experience?
- How will reading skills and concepts be taught using this approach?
- Why should I use literature circles with first graders?
- How can I expect young children to read and talk about literature in-depth when they can't even read (or are just starting)?

As I developed answers to each of the questions, I learned a great deal about myself as a teacher.

Goals for Literature Circles

While there are many reasons to use literature circles in a classroom, I have two primary goals. First, I seek to create enthusiasm for reading and a love of literature. I want my students to leave first grade feeling excited, confident, and motivated to become lifelong readers. The children choose books they want to read. Reading is modeled as adults read aloud to them at home and at school. They practice reading books until their confidence is high. The more successful they are, the more they want to read a book over and over again.

My second reason for using literature circles is to emphasize that reading is all about making meaning. The children share their personal experiences and ideas about literature. My role as a teacher is to encourage reflective discussions. Children's comprehension deepens the more children talk about the books they read.

Getting Started: The Five-Day Schedule

A predictable, manageable structure (Figure 2-3) is important to me and to the success of the program. Since my first graders are just learning how to read, it is crucial that I develop a clearly defined program. In the next few pages, I'll describe my five-day plan.

Weekly Schedule	
Friday:	Introduce book choices
Weekend:	Read books at home
Monday:	Discussion groups
Tuesday:	Discussion groups
Wednesday:	Journal writing
Thursday:	Literature response activities and sharing

Figure 2-3 Weekly Literature Circle Schedule

Friday: Introducing and Selecting Books

Fridays mark the beginning of my literature circle cycle. I introduce four book choices. For instance, one week I selected *Leo the Late Bloomer* (Kraus, 1971), *Whose Mouse Are You?* (Kraus, 1970), *Cookie's Week* (Ward, 1988), and *More Spaghetti I Say* (Gelman, 1987). Sometimes I choose books according to a particular theme or author study, but an engaging story is the most important factor. I show each cover, the children predict what they think the story will be about, and I give a brief introduction to the book. Often I read the entire book to my students whenever they urge me to continue with the story. Then I pass around the four book choices and allow the children to peruse them. We always review some important ways to choose a book:

1. Check to see if the book seems interesting to you. Look at the pictures and events.
2. Select a page or two and try to read it. If you have difficulty reading several words on one page, it may be too challenging for you.
3. Choose a book that YOU like, not just because a friend chooses it.

Making Choices and Forming Groups: After the children browse through the books, they write down their first and second choices, and place the completed sign-up ballot in the "Literature Circle Sign Up" can. During recess, I form the literature circle groups. Although I try to give each child his or her first choice, that is not always possible with the limited number of books available; therefore, I assure those who don't get their first choice this time will the next time. After forming the groups, I place each book in a gallon-size freezer bag along with blank "Post-it" notes.

Literature Circle Ballot

Name_____Date_____

1.) First Choice_____

_____

2.) Second Choice_____

_____

Parental Involvement: After reading *Grand Conversations: Literature Circles in Action* (Peterson & Eeds, 1990), I decided to involve parents in the program. The enjoyment and repeated readings at home provide additional support for beginning readers. Since students have talked about the books at home, they come to school eager to share ideas and reactions to the book. The parents' role in the program is primarily to listen and to help their children read the book over the weekend. They encourage conversation while the children read aloud. In addition, the parents help children choose pages to mark with "Post-it" notes. When they return to school on Monday, they are prepared and eager to share.

Occasionally, I have a child who doesn't receive the necessary reading support from home. In this case, I always find time during the school day to read the book with the child one-on-one (usually Monday morning before discussion groups or Friday afternoon before the books are sent home). If I'm unable to find time, I arrange for an older student to listen to the child read and discuss the book at school.

Training the parents to support literature circles is crucial to their involvement and the success of the program. At the year's start, I inform the parents about my literature program during our Curriculum Night. During that time, I ask for their support and assistance in reading and discussing the books their children will be bringing home on Fridays. I give each parent a letter of information (see page 24) explaining what to do when the bookbags come home, ways to help promote discussion, questions to ask their children when reading a story, and how to select pages to share in class. In addition, I send home a reminder letter just before we begin literature circles. Throughout the school year, I continue to inform parents about the literature circle program through our classroom newsletter.

Family involvement is a significant aspect of the literature circle program. I often receive positive feedback from the parents such as, "These book bags are wonderful!" and "What a great program!" As a teacher, I really enjoy the active participation, the assistance, and the dialogue with parents.

Monday and Tuesday: Discussion Days

Mondays and Tuesdays are literature circle discussion days. Since the children bring their bookbags back on Monday, I start the discussion groups that day, and finish by Tuesday. With four groups, I've found it manageable to meet with two groups on Monday and two groups on Tuesday. In recent years, I've received assistance from our reading specialist. She helps reduce my workload and the time I spend with literature circles on the discussion days by meeting with one group as I meet with another. While we meet with discussion groups, the rest of the students work on independent reading choices. For example, they may read Big Books, read with a partner or adult volunteer, read a book of their choice, read from their Poetry Notebooks, or read from charts or boxes of laminated poems.

The discussions begin as the children gather on the rug in a circle with their bookbags nearby. I usually pose a question to generate talk, such as "What did you think of this book?" The conversation builds from there as I participate, pose questions, and listen to the children's responses, ideas, and reactions to the story. I've discovered that first graders have a burning desire to share their favorite parts. If I try to control the flow of the discussion, they often remind me by saying, "Mrs. Clausen, can we share our favorite parts now?" Emergent readers seem to need time to make "I like" statements as a stage in their literacy development. Our discussions usually last 10–15 minutes. With young students, I feel my role is to be an active leader, modeling the types of responses that generate thoughtful insights and that move beyond "I like" statements to making emotional connections to books.

The discussion groups are the most fascinating and challenging aspect of my literature circle program. As Short and Pierce (1990) state, "Much of the talk in literature circles is exploratory, and the participants don't always know where it will lead. Some directions end up being more generative than others. But the dead ends as well as the clear paths are part of the process of exploring literature" (p. 208). Over the years, I've learned that discussions vary, depending on the children's involvement, areas of interest, prior knowledge and experience, and personal investment in the story. (See Chapter 4 for more information about promoting in-depth response with emergent readers.) Three patterns have emerged as I listen and observe first graders in discussion groups.

Discussions most often involve emotions and ideas related to personal experiences.   After reading *The Leaving Morning* (Johnson, 1992), Marlene stated that "It was sad, because they had to leave cousins and everything!" Arielle added, "I think moving is special and I moved once. It feels like camping. But it was sad too, because I missed my friends." The group continued to talk about leaving special places and friends.

Discussions can involve relationships among characters.   For example, one day while discussing *William's Doll* (Zolotow, 1972), Kevin observed that "William's grandmother is the only one who understands him and knows what he really wants." Sparked by Kevin's response, the group began discussing the relationship between the boy and his grandmother.

Discussions can address emotions and the author's craft.   Last spring, while discussing *Now One Foot, Now the Other* (de Paola, 1981), several children expressed strong feelings. Kanen said, "It was touching." When asked to elaborate, he explained that he liked the relationship between Bobby and Bob. He liked the fact that the grandson now told stories to his grandfather. When I asked how the story made them feel, the rest of the children began to share their emotions. Alanna chimed in by saying, "It was happy, then sad, then happy." She explained how the story had a happy beginning, but then it turned sad when the grandfather had the stroke. However, it got happy again when the boy was able to teach the grandfather all the things they used to do together. Audrey agreed, and told us how her mom cried when they read the story together over the weekend. The conversation moved in the direction of the author's craft, so I asked the children what they thought of the writer. Several children voiced their opinions and mentioned other stories he had written.

Wednesday: Journal Writing

On Wednesdays, the children write in their response journals. Writing allows them to reflect on and internalize the meaning they've gathered from the story. I want my students to see that what we say and feel can be written down, and that writing is another way to share our thoughts and ideas with others.

Children need good models and examples of reflective writing, so I begin each journal writing day with a mini-lesson on *how* and *what* to write. During this lesson, I model how I get my ideas, what I decide to write, and how I make connections with the story. I do this by "thinking aloud." After I read my entry, I ask for volunteers to explain what they're going to write about that day. As a few children begin to share, more hands fly up as children volunteer their ideas. Their responses provide additional models. Talking is a helpful form of rehearsal for these young children. Children soon turn to their journals and begin to write. Here are some journal entries about *Leo the Late Bloomer* (Kraus, 1971) and *William's Doll* (Zolotow, 1972) that show both retelling and personal reactions:

> William really wanted a doll. His dad kept bringing other stuff. He brought him a basketball and a train. But he still wanted a doll. One day his grandma visited. William showed her how he could use the basketball. He showed her the train. He said to his grandma, "I want a doll." So she got him a doll.—Kevin

> The part when he bloomed made me happy. It reminds me of when I couldn't read, and I was trying. Now I can read and write.—Eric

> I wonder how William felt when his father didn't give him a doll. But I know how William felt when he got a doll.—Beau

I use spiral binding when I make the journal so that it's easier for children to turn pages. The journal includes spaces for each weekly entry and usually lasts all year. Each page includes room for the title of the book, the date, an entry space for writing, and a "comments to the writer" section on the back.

Each Wednesday I share a different prompt or journal starter (see Figure 2-4). My purpose for providing prompts is to guide children as they begin to write personal responses. Some children rely on the starters as a scaffold. Others choose to retell the story in their own words, react to an exciting part in the story, share personal experiences, write about a character, or describe their favorite part. While journal prompts may serve as a useful tool, I'm careful to ensure they don't become a prescribed format.

Journal Prompts

I think . . .
I feel . . .
I wonder . . .
I wish . . .
If I were . . .
That reminds me of . . .
I noticed . . .

Figure 2-4 Journal Prompts

Responding to the children's written entries is crucial. I read their journals during my lunch period (25–30 minutes) so the children can read my written responses that afternoon or the next morning. I enjoy seeing their eyes light up when they read my notes. There's something magical about seeing a child delight over the reading-writing connection through dialogue journals. As I write back to the children, I try to keep my responses genuine. For example, I often write about my own feelings, such as my reaction to Audrey's response to *My Mom Travels a Lot* (Bauer, 1985).

> If I were the little girl I would be happy and sad. I felt like the girl because my mom went on a church thing and she was away for three days and I was sad. If I was the little girl I would know how she feels. Mrs. Clausen, do you know how I felt? Yes, No, Maybe. I love my mom a lot Mrs. Clausen.
> —Audrey
>
> I do know how you feel. My mom just came back from being on a trip. She was gone for two weeks! I missed her so much!
> —Mrs. Clausen

At other times, I ask questions to encourage more thoughtful reactions or simply reflect their thoughts and feelings. Initially, I relied on a list of suggestions for responses to journals; however, I've found that the best exchanges are ones that are natural and responsive.

Thursday: Literature Response

Thursdays are reserved for creating and sharing literature response activities. The children's responses reflect the meaning they constructed from the books. Some examples of response activities include the following:

- read another book by the same author
- rewrite the story from a different point of view
- paint a mural depicting feelings about the story
- dramatize the events
- write a letter to the author to share reactions
- talk about the story with a friend

Because I believe children should be engaged in projects that are meaningful, I carefully demonstrate a new way to respond each Thursday. My goal is to model a variety of responses so that children can expand their repertoire.

I try to encourage students to respond genuinely and to make connections to the literature. For example, after Ashley finished discussing *Cookie's Week* (Ward, 1988), she went to her seat and pulled out her writing materials. As the whole class moved from literature circles to writing workshop, I noticed Ashley deeply absorbed in her writing. I noticed she'd written her own version called "Cookie's New Baby Kitten." Ashley reacted naturally and made a personal connection to the book.

Another day, a group of readers decided to write letters to the authors of their literature circle books, so I gave a mini-lesson on letter writing. Some letters were more detailed than others, yet all were sincere and meaningful to the children. Here are some samples:

Dear Syd Hoff,

> I want to know how your pictures got so good. Was it practice? Also, how did you think of the animals in your stories?   Love, Kanen

Dear Angela Johnson,

> I think your book (*The Leaving Morning*) had some feelings in it because I don't think he really wanted to move away. Do you? I hope you write back to me.   Your friend, Kevin

Dear Crosby Bonsall,

> I think you're a good writer. When I grow up I want to be a writer like you. I'm seven years old. I hope you can write me back. In my school we have some of your books. At my class we have a checkout thing and I checked one of your books out. It is called *The Day I Had to Play With My Sister*.   Love, Audrey

A few weeks later, we received responses from some of the authors in the mail. The children were thrilled and began on their own to write letters in response to the books they read.

Stepping Stones: Literature Circle Teaching Strategies

The predictable five-day structure helps tremendously with management, organization, and planning. As I continue on my journey with literature circles, I see five particular "stepping stones" or teaching strategies that enhance literature circles.

Use of Prediction: Prediction is a strategy that good readers use automatically. Children need opportunities to predict outcomes before they read. They need to learn to check and confirm their predictions. Since predicting is so important to the reading process and comprehension building, I model this strategy when the children sign up for books each Friday. We look at the covers, the titles, and the pictures and then make predictions about the book. When I read aloud or read Big Books, I also model the types of questions students can ask themselves as they read in order to clarify meaning.

Repeated Readings: I emphasize rereading texts so that children can build fluency. I share with parents the importance of reading books more than once. In the beginning of the year, particularly, this is easy because the books are often short and contain a simple text. As the year progresses and books get longer, I've found it's still worthwhile to ask children to reread parts or sections of material.

On Monday and Tuesday mornings, when the children gather on the rug, I ask them to first reread the story or sections they're going to share. This helps refresh their memories and provides another opportunity for repeating the reading experience. In addition, I often ask the children to read with a partner just before they write in their journals or begin a literature response activity. When I ask them to reread, they immediately open their books and begin reading with joy! The hum of voices fills the room and I realize the value of allowing children time to build fluency and savor the book.

Choice: Over the years, I've tried to incorporate more student choice in book selection, journal writing, and response projects. I've seen children demonstrate more ownership and enthusiasm for literature circles when they are allowed options. Every Friday, when I show the book selections, they always smile, clap, and cheer. I often hear "oohs" and verbal responses such as "This is going to be hard to choose!" When I pass out their book choices, they run to see what books their classmates have chosen. I've also found that the children's written and project responses are more meaningful, detailed, and unique when I provide options.

Ownership: Along with choice, I try to promote as much ownership as possible. I ask the children for advice when discussion groups don't flow smoothly. I invite the children to help me brainstorm ways to solve problems that arise in the literature circles.

I also encourage children to assess their own reading experience and participation in the literature circle program. As a result, I notice growth in children's abilities to express their strengths, needs, and goals.

I recall one afternoon near the end of the year when I told my students we needed to end literature circles because I had run out of multiple copies of books. Immediately the children frowned, were silent for a moment, and then questioned me. One child said, "Why can't we just get more books?" I explained how we'd used all we had. Then another child blurted out, "We could do literature circles by the author like we did that one other time!" Someone else chimed in, "Or we could use those books!" (pointing to the student-authored books published throughout the year). Courtney then added, "We could each bring a book from home, like each of us bring a different Clifford book!" As our conversation continued, I realized their ownership in this program. They wanted the literature circle experience to continue, and so I incorporated their suggestions in our final literature circle set. After all, we were partners in our classroom. I respected their opinions; they respected mine. I've seen the power of choice and ownership in learning.

Range of Books: It is important to consider carefully the selection of material for first graders. Since I always have a wide range of reading abilities, I offer books with a range of readability levels. With less able readers, I often assign a partner, an older student, or I set aside time to assist the child. Audio tapes are another way to provide scaffolding for struggling readers.

Looking Back:
Reflections on Literature Circles in First Grade

I recall one spring day after lunch when a small group of children grabbed their literature circle books and gathered together on the rug. They organized themselves into a circle and Kevin shouted out, "Hey, it's literature circles!" The others chanted, "Yeah!" On their own, they asked each other questions and shared favorite parts of the story. What a joy to see spontaneous literature circles initiated by children!

As I reflect on my journey with literature circles, I am delighted at what young children can accomplish. I still struggle with my role as the teacher, asking myself questions such as "Is it necessary for beginning readers and writers to use journal prompts? How do I encourage natural response without taking over?" As I search for answers to those questions, I know that young children can and do connect literature to their own lives. I'm confident they have taken steady steps on their path toward becoming lifelong readers.

References

Bauer, Caroline Feller. (1985). *My Mom Travels a Lot*. Illustrated by Nancy Winslow Parker. New York: Puffin.

Cambourne, Brian. (1988). *The Whole Story: Natural Learning and the Acquisition of Literacy in the Classroom*. New York: Ashton Scholastic.

de Paola, Tomie. (1981). *Now One Foot, Now the Other*. New York: G.P. Putnam's Sons.

Gelman, Rita. (1987). *More Spaghetti I Say*. Illustrated by Jack Kent. New York: Scholastic.

Johnson, Angela. (1992). *The Leaving Morning*. Illustrated by David Soman. New York: Orchard.

Kraus, Robert. (1971). *Leo the Late Bloomer*. Illustrated by Jose Aruego. New York: Windmill.

Kraus, Robert. (1970). *Whose Mouse Are You?* Illustrated by Jose Aruego. New York: Macmillan.

Peterson, Ralph & Eeds, Maryann. (1990). *Grand Conversations: Literature Circles in Action*. New York: Scholastic.

Short, Kathy Gnagey & Pierce, Kathryn Mitchell. (1990). *Talking About Books: Creating Literate Communities*. Portsmouth, NH: Heinemann.

Ward, Cindy. (1988). *Cookie's Week*. New York: Scholastic.

Zolotow, Charlotte. (1972). *William's Doll*. Illustrated by William Pene du Bois. New York: Scholastic.

Literature Circles: Parental Involvement

On Friday of each week, each child will bring home a book he or she has chosen. Let your child read the book to you or read the book aloud together. The book your child brings home will usually be short, yet engaging material, often with a repetitive pattern.

Steps on How to Use the Literature Circle Books:

1) Please have your child read (or read with him or her) and talk about the story as you read. Talking about books enhances your child's understanding, which is the underlying reason for reading.

2) Read the story once or twice each night. Good books are meant to be read again and again for enjoyment!

3) Have your child use the "Post-it" notes in the plastic book bag to mark any pages of interest that he or she would like to share and talk about in class. What kinds of things should your child mark? Your child may want to mark places in the book that are funny, interesting, puzzling (things he or she doesn't understand), or passages that relate to his or her life. Your child might want to mark a place where he or she notices the author's style, something about one of the characters, the main idea within the story, certain details, or the illustrations.

4) Send the book back to school on **Monday** of each week with the pages marked with "Post-it" notes. We will talk about the book in literature groups on Mondays and Tuesdays. On the rest of the days we will do a variety of activities pertaining to you child's chosen book.

Types of Questions to Ask Your Child to Promote Talking About the Book:

- What do you think this story is going to be about? How can you tell?

- What do you think is going to happen next?

- How do you think the story is going to end?

- Have you ever felt like the character in this book?

- How are you alike or not like the characters in the story?

- Does this remind you of anything you've done before?

Chapter 3

Learning Together:
Sharing Control with Emergent Readers

Margee Morfitt

As I was writing this chapter, out of curiosity I asked my first and second graders what they thought other people should know about literature circles. As they began to respond, I realized their comments were worth recording. I quickly grabbed paper and pen and wrote as they spoke. Their responses were thoughtful and affirming, especially Suzanne's: "You can really get along with a book better. You learn together. Because of other people, you're collecting ideas. They help you understand the book, and you help them understand the book, and together you understand more."

This first grader had clearly articulated the heart of literature circles. Reading over her response and the responses of other students, I reflected on what had occurred in our classroom during the year that allowed Suzanne and her classmates to gain such a clear understanding about the purpose and value of literature circles.

I began literature circles in my primary classroom a few years ago when I became convinced that literature circles would allow time for reading deeply, and that I could help students become not just skillful, competent readers, but thoughtful, responsive readers as well. I wondered how to guide students in this endeavor without taking the lead so much that the unexpected or unplanned couldn't occur. I was comfortable leading group discussions about stories, knowing what types of questions I wanted to ask, what skills and strategies I wanted to teach, and what I wanted students to take away from a story. By choosing literature circles, however, I was relinquishing my role as group leader. Literature circles would allow children to discuss what *they* saw as important in a story. It was a time for *their* questions and observations. Could we do this? What if they just responded with "I liked the story. It was funny"? I wanted to help my students go beyond "I like" responses without completely controlling the content and direction of the literature circle discussions and response projects.

Trusting Student Choice

Choice is at the heart of literature circles, yet it has been difficult at times. At first, if a child's choice was not appropriate, I determined what I felt was a better fit for the child. As I have watched children in literature circles, I have come to see that children have many reasons for their choices, and that I must respect those reasons. I often learn new things about a child through his or her choice and our subsequent discussions. For instance, a child may choose *The Tenth Good Thing About Barney* (Viorst, 1971) because of a similar experience with losing a pet or *The Art Lesson* (de Paola, 1989) in response to a strong interest in art.

I begin a literature circle set by choosing three to five titles relating to a theme. I look for both fiction and informational books that will have enough substance to inspire thought and a desire to discuss (see Chapters 4 and 9). It's challenging to find quality informational books that are both easy to read and intriguing enough to spark conversations. As we begin, I give book talks and form literature circle groups, as Christy Clausen describes in Chapter 2. Choice is a very positive and motivating factor. One of my first graders made an interesting observation about choice and literature circles: "You work with people you normally wouldn't work with, so it's like you make friends with them and the book."

Developing Independence in Reading

With primary-age children, the actual reading of the story for literature circles can be a challenge. Early in the year, the books chosen for literature circles may be too difficult for children to read independently. I used to worry about this, but I know now that choosing books with sufficient depth to allow for insights and discussion is a more important selection criterion than readability. In order to support emerging readers, I often read the book to a group, or ask a parent to read to a group. I also provide a cassette tape of the story, which allows the children an opportunity to "read," even if I am busy and no parent help is available.

As students become more independent readers, they begin to read their literature circle book with a small group, a partner, or on their own. I suggest independent or partner reading when I know students are ready for it, but usually make it an option. Many first graders and some second graders continue to need support all year. My students are astute at recognizing when they need assistance from a partner, an adult, or a recording. I find that they are often skillful at choosing a compatible partner. Sometimes children read at vastly different speeds, and can't compromise or adjust, while other partners work beautifully together.

While I work to give control of the reading to the students, I ask that students read their literature circle book several times during the week. Repeated readings offer students many chances to revisit the story, gaining new information, insights, and increased confidence with the text.

Encouraging and Extending Journal Response

From the very beginning of the year, students respond in a journal after they finish reading their literature circle book. I ask them to write or draw what they liked, noticed, or wondered about a story. At first, they often copy a favorite sentence or draw a simple picture with few, if any, words.

For example, in October, as we were reading scary stories, Landon drew the main character in *Abiyoyo* (Seeger, 1986) and wrote, "I like the expression on his [Abiyoyo's] face." Mark simply drew the tree from *Ghost-Eye Tree* (Martin & Archambault, 1985). Suzanne wrote of *The Little Old Lady Who Wasn't Afraid of Anything* (Williams, 1986), "I like this part: 'And scare all the crows away!'" Kenny's response to the same book had already moved beyond the "I like" stage. He wrote, "I wonder why the lady said that she wasn't afraid of nothing but she ran away from the pumpkin."

Eliciting Quality Response

Early on, I accept all journal entries but, as the year progresses, I encourage richer response. One way I elicit more complete response is by walking around as students are making their journal entries, asking them to read what they have written and commenting or asking for more information. My verbal questions and written comments often lead to more thoughtful entries.

Responses also improve if students see and hear quality examples. If students only hear "I like this story because . . . ", responses usually remain at that level. I open up new possibilities by modeling journal entries in reaction to stories we have shared together. I may focus on things I notice about a character, how the story touches me, words and phrases I'm curious about, or perhaps questions I have about the story. What is important is that the entry is sincere and thoughtful.

I also see carry-over from our conversations to the students' writing. For instance, we were working on understanding and describing characters during shared reading and small group mini-lessons. We discussed words that would describe characters besides the obvious and easy ones (such as "funny" and "nice"). We brainstormed a list that included words like "foolish," "obedient," "thoughtful," "stubborn," "determined," and "kind." Later, during literature circles, many students incorporated words from our list into their journal entries and, when asked, could explain why those words described the characters.

Prompting Response

When I first read *The Art of Teaching Writing* (1986) by Lucy Calkins, I was struck by the idea of keeping written response authentic. I hesitate to use prescriptive questions, since I want children's response to be genuine. When I do provide questions, I do it only in response to the need of a particular child or a specific book. For instance, a book like *Mrs. Katz and Tush* (Polacco, 1992) is perfect for thinking about characters: "What do the two characters have in common? How does Mrs. Katz remind you of someone you know?" Once students become more confident writers, I may use the questions in the appendix from *Read On: A Conference Approach to Reading* (Hornsby, Sukarna & Parry, 1986, pp. 157–162) to focus on elements of literature. These questions can trigger response that students might not otherwise consider and lead them to reflect more deeply on character, setting, plot, and mood. For example, the questions on mood include: How did you feel while reading the book? Why? What was the funniest part? What was the saddest part? What was the most exciting or strangest thing that happened? What do you remember most about the story?

   The length and quality of response will vary greatly among first and second graders. I accept that differences exist and nudge each child to reflect and question more deeply at his or her own level. My desire is for responses to become thoughtful and genuine, and to reflect a child's growth as a reader, writer, and thinker.

Creating a Climate for Discussion

Each year I spend the first few months setting the groundwork for "grand conversations" (Peterson & Eeds, 1990). During the first literature circle sets, I create a format and a climate that allows me to move out of the role of leader, yet gives my students a comfortable structure. When groups meet for the first time, I stress that every member of a literature circle has something to say, and that we all must be careful listeners and speakers. I begin by talking about how to start discussions, how to share what we have to say, how to add our ideas if they follow someone else's, and how to respond to questions. I tell the group we will be sharing what we like, what we notice, and what we wonder about the stories we read.

It is not easy for six- and seven-year-olds to learn how to share ideas without the teacher calling on someone for answers and without other students interrupting. After the first literature circle meetings, I ask the class to help create some guidelines for successful discussions. Figure 3-1 shows the list our class developed:

Guidelines for Successful Literature Circle Discussions

1. Remember to put your book and journal down and look at the speaker.

2. Listen carefully and make appropriate comments when a group member finishes.

3. Make sure everyone in the group gets a chance to contribute and share.

4. Have fun!

Figure 3-1 Guidelines for Successful Literature Circle Discussions

I continue to help my students develop specific discussion skills and strategies through whole group and small group mini-lessons throughout the year. Although you'll find what works best for you, I've discovered five ways I can support thoughtful discussions with my young readers.

1. Begin by Modeling

With first and second graders, I believe it is important for me to be present during literature circle discussions. Early in the year, I encourage thoughtful responses by sharing questions and answers of my own. I may simply ask students, "Why?" as they talk about who or what they like in a story. I may also ask them to re-think an opinion they have expressed. It is a challenge to do this without taking control of the group, but many primary-age children haven't experienced this type of discussion and need to hear thoughtful participants in conversations. They need to learn how to go beyond surface-level observations and think through ideas. During a discussion of *The True Story of the 3 Little Pigs!* (Scieszka, 1989), I asked the group if they believed the wolf's version of the events. That simple question led them to reexamine what the wolf had said, how he might have said it, and whether he could be trusted. As Kathy Short and Gloria Kauffman discuss in *Creating Classroom for Authors* (Harste, Short & Burke, 1988), I want students to realize that what matters is not that everyone agrees, but that individuals can express ideas and opinions, and support them. When students begin to ask one another, "Why?" I know we're headed in the right direction and I know it's time for me to step back a little more.

2. Participate as a Group Member

Initially students look to me for direction about who should begin the discussion or who should speak next. It is tempting to take on this role, hoping to make the discussion continue smoothly, but I emphasize that, in a small group discussion, people don't need to raise their hands to be called on. We need to look at and listen to one another, then decide when to speak.

Early in the year, I suggest that students begin discussions with their journal entries. This seems to work well, and some groups continue this pattern all year. Other times, groups begin by sharing a favorite part of the book. Some children prefer to begin with a retelling. I also encourage students to mark specific language they like or parts they don't understand as they read.

These methods are just strategies to help children begin independent small group conversations. I have come to believe that students have more ownership when they decide how to begin the discussion. My job is to provide an environment that supports, encourages, and values the exchange of ideas.

3. Ask Questions and Make Observations

After reading Jan Brett's version of *The Mitten* (1989), students expressed interest in the illustrated borders and shared the clues they had found. I asked why the illustrator might have used borders in that way. As they thought about that, Kenny answered very seriously, "Because it'd be helpful to little children." Talking about the borders reminded Daniel that he had seen similar borders used in *The Wild Christmas Reindeer* (Brett, 1990) and he wondered if it was a Jan Brett book. Landon wondered if she'd illustrated *Sam Johnson and the Blue Ribbon Quilt* (Ernst, 1983) because that book has similar borders. Although I sparked the conversation with a question, I did not plan this discussion on the illustrations. The children themselves recognized that borders were important to the story and made it the focus of their conversation as they talked about the illustration styles of other books.

4. Support the Discussion as Necessary

Listening to emergent readers talk about books is often delightful, with the unexpected thrown in, but the flow is not always smooth or focused. Sometimes the conversations don't always go in directions I expect. There are times when I gently re-focus the group, asking questions that will make students look and think again. I try to follow up on their ideas with questions that lead to deeper reflection or an interesting view of the story. I don't hesitate to share my experience as a reader and try to remain a participant rather than the discussion leader.

5. Observe Discussions

It is important for me to learn how to support good discussions. I take notes during literature circles to aid my understanding, recording what I hear children say, as well as noting my own comments. I find this gives me a role to play other than discussion leader. I focus on the interests and insights the students have, instead of my ideas of how the discussion should go. This provides individual assessment opportunities and ideas for future mini-lessons on particular skills and strategies.

Spotlighting Students' Use of Strategies

As the year progresses, I begin to spotlight effective strategies and thoughtful responses during literature circles. When a group discussed "Bees and the Mud" in *Mouse Soup* (Lobel, 1977), Daniel asked, "How did the bees get out of the hive anyway?" Allyson opened her book, turned to the story, and read the part that would answer his question. Daniel looked it over and appeared satisfied that his question had been answered. Other questions followed Daniel's: "Why did the bees follow the mouse?" "How did he trick them?" "How could the bees be so dumb?" The group referred to the book to answer the questions. I then pointed out that some of their questions were "in the book" questions (Raphael, 1982), which they could answer by rereading the text. I also pointed out that other questions were "in the head" questions, which could not be answered just by looking for information in the text. Students could find the answers to these questions only by thinking about what the book said and what they, as readers, thought or felt. Since that discussion, I have seen Allyson, Daniel, and many others turn back to the book to answer questions.

Allowing Students to Lead

I find a great deal happens if only I have the patience to wait and let students take the lead. A group of children discussed *The Little Old Lady Who Was Not Afraid of Anything* (Williams, 1986) and shared favorite parts. As they talked about the objects that followed the little old lady, they debated whether it could really happen. I was tempted to interject my questions, but didn't. Then Emilee pointed out that all the things that followed the little old lady (pants, shirt, pumpkin, hat, gloves) were in the first picture, hanging on the line, or sitting by the doorstep. This was a revelation to me. I have read the book countless times, but never noticed that before. The group became very animated. They excitedly flipped pages back and forth, checking to see if the objects really were the same. They chattered about how the clothing could come alive and follow the little old lady. Suzanne suggested that, if it was midnight, that was the "ghosts' hour" and anything could happen. Kenny disagreed, and thought it was "all in her head" because she was walking alone and was worried. The group didn't come to agreement, but all the students had opinions and reasons for their ideas.

On another occasion, students read mysteries. The group reading *Miss Nelson is Missing* (Allard, 1977) was having a lively conversation, discussing all the clues that pointed to the fact that Miss Nelson was indeed Miss Viola Swamp. Andrew and Jacob, two emergent readers, were sure they had found all the clues. They quickly paged through the book, showing the group what they had noticed. Allyson and Christie pointed out clues on the dressing table in Miss Nelson's bedroom that Andrew and Jacob had missed. Emilee pointed out the box in the closet that said "wig" if you turned the picture upside down. Then Jacob and Andrew pulled out *Miss Nelson has a Field Day* (Allard, 1985) and exclaimed that they had found more clues in it that Miss Nelson and Miss Swamp were the same person. They had picked the book out of our class tub of mystery books, and searched it for evidence to support their ideas. They compared the house Miss Nelson entered in one book to the house entered by Miss Swamp in the other, and concluded that they were the same. These discoveries and exchanges amazed me. Children can and do make discoveries and explore books without a teacher's direct intervention, if we provide opportunities to read widely and to wonder about literature.

I do not claim, however, that these types of discussions, discoveries, and explorations happen by accident. I talk with students about books on a regular basis, as I read aloud to them throughout the day. I ask questions. I wonder aloud. I notice words, phrases, and details. I ask students to do the same. Stories are important to us. We talk about books because we love them, because they fascinate us, and because they touch our hearts. Literature circle discussions are not a departure from what we do as a whole class with books. Small group literature discussions, however, allow more students to express opinions, ask and answer questions, and make observations.

Responding to Literature

After reading and discussing their literature circle books, students choose a response project. The purpose of the project is—in the words of one of my students—"to give people a feel for the book, to make people want to read the book, to show what it's about." I also want to give students a chance to think more about a book, to revisit it, and perhaps gain a better or different understanding. Students prepare their response projects, then present them to the class.

Choosing Response Projects

Several years ago, when I began literature circles in my classroom, I would often decide what the response projects would be, and all students would do the same project. For instance, I would ask each group to do a booktalk about their story. This made it easy to introduce new project ideas, but I began to see that some books cry out to be retold, while others lead naturally to further written response, painting, or drawing.

Children have unique needs and talents. Some have a flair for the dramatic arts, others for the visual arts, and others for writing. Now I give students more freedom to choose projects for themselves. Early in the year I limit the possibilities, suggesting and explaining only a few. As the year goes on, I add to the list of possible projects, often incorporating students' suggestions. I encourage children to try a variety of response projects to explore new talents and ways of making meaning.

Creating Response Projects

I give students more control over response projects by asking them to make a plan. These plans can be oral or written, but students must decide what they will do to present the story and what materials they will need. I offer suggestions and guidance where needed.

Early in the year, I suggest a short list of four possible response projects: retelling, painting, giving book talks, or acting out the story. I provide guidance for all four types of response and how each might work for a given story. The groups meet and choose from the list of possibilities I present. Groups may choose to break into two smaller groups because some want to do a retelling and others want to do a book talk. Each group decides how they will do their project. I move from group to group as they work. I make suggestions and provide support, but try not to impose my vision of a project on them.

Last year, a group that was dramatizing their story received further guidance from a parent volunteer. The group who did a book talk decided together that each person would choose a favorite page to read. I was listening in, and worried that they wouldn't be able to read the pages they chose, since it was quite early in the year. Fortunately, I overcame my desire to step in. The students picked their pages, helped each other practice, and arranged themselves in a logical order for presenting their project to the class. Their presentation was well done and gave a good feel for the book.

The next group of children chose to retell their story. I listened as they worked and offered a few suggestions, but they already had some fine ideas, remembering key words and phrases from *Abiyoyo* (Seeger, 1986), such as "big as a tree," "staggered," and "now the father was a magician." As I listened to them practice, Christie asked, "But how will we be able to remember it exactly the same way?" I asked, "Does it need to be exactly the same?" They decided it didn't, but that they should include certain main points each time. The retelling was quite successful, using the storybook language but not sounding stiff or rehearsed.

The fourth group had a clear idea of what they wanted to paint: the ghost-eye tree. They wanted to create a group painting on a large sheet of butcher paper. I suggested that they draw the tree first so they would know how big it would be, but otherwise I left them alone. The students presented the mural (Figure 3-2), summarized the story, and enthusiastically described how their painting represented an important scene.

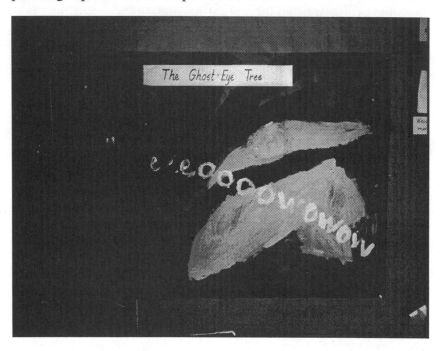

Figure 3-2 Ghost Eyed Tree

Expanding Response

As the year progresses, students generate ideas for responses, often ones that haven't occurred to me. For example, two students asked to draw and write on overhead transparencies to retell the story; this style of retelling became popular with the class.

Other successful projects have included game boards, dioramas, clay figures, puppets, story maps, and a variety of retelling techniques. After reading *Harold and the Purple Crayon* (Johnson, 1955), Allyson and Shannon decided to recreate the story by having one of them draw it on butcher paper (with a purple crayon, of course) while the other read the story. They did practice runs so they could work out timing and signals if the artist needed the reader to slow down. It was a great performance and encouraged many students in the class to read the book for themselves. Projects may take any form, as long as the response leads children back into a book.

Dealing with Reality

I can't say that response projects are always thoughtful or always successful in meeting my goals. First and second graders often have grand plans that they are unable to execute because they are, after all, young children who may lack the experience, skill, or fine motor control required to complete their plan. Puppets may not turn out to be nearly as detailed or beautiful as imagined. Students sometimes want to try a project because it sounds neat or fun, but don't know how it ties in with the book. For instance, Michael wanted to do a game board, but didn't know how to make it represent the book he had read. I talked to him about the story and together we looked at a game board other students had created to represent *The Art Lesson* (de Paola, 1989). Their game board used events from the story as cards that allowed players to move. For instance, one card said: "Tommy draws on the sheets. Go back three spaces." Another said: "Tommy's teacher likes his painting. Go ahead two spaces." By looking at how others had retold a story through a game, Michael was able to think about how he might do this for his book.

Made a game board to retell a story.

Allowing students control over the creation of response projects can be messy, frustrating, and sometimes anxiety-producing. I could step in more often and control the content and direction of projects. Sometimes I'm tempted. If I resist that urge, however, I find students do just fine without me. I give advice. I guide. I suggest. I ask students to reconsider, to think through an idea. I ask how the project relates to a story, how it increases their understanding, and how it will help others understand the book. I point out possible pitfalls. I have even been known to veto an idea on rare occasions. But I am learning that children are capable of incredible things and can learn a great deal through developing and carrying out their own plans.

Learning From Response Projects

As I judge the success of children's response projects, it is important for me to remember that the object is not for students to turn out a perfect product every time. Did students have to look more closely at the story, or reread the text in order to complete their project?

Did the project lead to better understanding? Did the project give the rest of the class a good idea of what the book was about? Did it make someone want to read the book? Did students learn what it takes to plan, complete, and present a project? If I can answer yes to some or all of those questions, I know the experience has been worthwhile.

Presenting Response Projects

Presenting projects usually goes well, but sometimes it falls short of my expectations. After one set of presentations, I felt discouraged. Most were very minimal. I began to think that perhaps I had relinquished too much control to my students or was asking for more than they could give. Instead of stepping in and taking charge, as I wanted to, I asked the class to help me write some guidelines that might make presentations better in the future. Figure 3-3 lists the guidelines they developed:

Guidelines for Response Projects

1. Begin with the title and author of the book.

2. Give a short summary or retelling of the story if it's not part of your presentation.

3. Speak clearly and loudly enough.

4. Give people a reason to read the book.

Figure 3-3 Guidelines for Response Projects

Now, before response project presentations, we review these guidelines to make sure children are ready to present successfully. After they present the project to the class, I comment on what worked well and make suggestions that might help the whole class during the next round of response projects.

Questions That Remain

Despite all the exciting and affirming experiences I've had venturing into literature circles with young children, questions remain. I love what I see and hear happening in my classroom, but I know I haven't come to the end of my journey. I listen to colleagues who work with older children, to Lisa Norwick talking about student-led mini-lessons (Chapter 10), to Anne Klein sharing examples from her students' discussions (Chapter 6), and to Patti Kamber describing her students' self-reflections (Chapter 8), and I wonder if my students can go further than they've gone. Although I recognize developmental constraints, I don't want to underestimate my students. I continue to wrestle with issues of control versus independence: How can I allow young children to stretch and grow, to go beyond what I imagined was possible?

Could I do more to involve children in book choice?

I give students choice within a theme, but I have usually selected that theme myself. I have chosen the themes because they fit with the curriculum or my interests. I also have to deal with the availability of multiple copies of a title and financial constraints. In the past, this meant I had to purchase books before I met my new students and had a chance to discover their wishes or interests. I rationalize the limitations on the choices available during literature circles because students have choice during independent reading, but I still wonder.

Should I remove myself further from discussions?

I believe in the value of my presence and input during discussions. I want to build a strong foundation for my students, so they know what discussions can be. I continuously examine my role in the discussions. If I remove myself more often, how far (and where) can they take the conversation? I have given over a great deal of control, but is it possible to give over more? And should I? What is the best way to do it?

I've found that being present for literature circle discussions provides me with opportunities to encourage a closer look at the story and chances to model effective discussion techniques. I can also gather material for assessment and see areas where my students need more support. I still have questions. Should I remove myself from discussion, or is the support I offer my emergent readers and what I gain in terms of knowledge about students reason enough to stay?

Literature discussion groups do sometimes meet without me. During these times I move from group to group, catching snatches of discussion. I have to be sure I've provided enough experiences to ensure emergent readers will know how to have quality discussions. If I pull out too soon or too completely, students don't get the support and feedback they need. Simply letting children choose the books they want to read and putting them together in groups will not necessarily result in engaging discussions. I'm still learning how much control I can share with my emergent readers.

How can I best guide and nurture genuine response?

With time and experience, I find it easier to let go and trust children, but letting go is sometimes anxiety-producing. I want response to be genuine. I don't want to turn response projects into just another type of book report, completed to satisfy the teacher, without a real purpose for the children. What do I, as an adult, do in response to a good book? Shouldn't children's responses be just as natural and genuine?

I don't expect to answer all my questions right away. Some will be answered as I try new things next year and find ways to give students more choice, control, and responsibility for their own learning. Some questions may be answered as I talk with colleagues. Other issues may take a great deal of time, thought, and study to resolve. New questions may arise. My journey of discovery and growth will continue, as it should.

Returning to Suzanne's quote at the beginning of the chapter, I recognize that it's the journey that's important. "You learn together. Because of other people, you're collecting ideas. They help you understand the book, and you help them understand the book, and together you understand more."

References

Allard, Harry. (1985). *Miss Nelson Has a Field Day.* Illustrated by James Marshall. Boston: Houghton Mifflin.

Allard, Harry. (1977). *Miss Nelson is Missing.* Illustrated by James Marshall. Boston: Houghton Mifflin.

Brett, Jan. (1990). *The Wild Christmas Reindeer.* New York: Scholastic.

Brett, Jan. (1989). *The Mitten.* New York: Scholastic.

de Paola, Tomie. (1989). *The Art Lesson.* New York: Putnam.

Calkins, Lucy. (1986). *The Art of Teaching Writing.* Portsmouth, NH: Heinemann.

Ernst, Lisa Campbell. (1983). *Sam Johnson and the Blue Ribbon Quilt.* New York: Mulberry.

Harste, Jerome, Short, Kathy & Burke, Carolyn. (1988). *Creating Classrooms for Authors: The Reading-Writing Connection.* Portsmouth, NH: Heinemann.

Hornsby, David, Sukarna, Deborah & Parry, Jo-Ann. (1986). *Read On: A Conference Approach to Reading.* Portsmouth, NH: Heinemann.

Johnson, Crocket. (1955). *Harold and the Purple Crayon.* New York: Harper.

Lobel, Arnold. (1977). *Mouse Soup.* New York: Harper & Row.

Martin, Bill Jr. & Archambault, John. (1985). *The Ghost-Eye Tree.* Illustrated by Ted Rand. New York: Henry Holt.

Peterson, Ralph & Eeds, Maryann. (1990). *Grand Conversations: Literature Groups in Action.* New York: Scholastic.

Polacco, Patricia. (1992). *Mrs. Katz and Tush.* New York: Bantam.

Raphael, Taffy. (1982). Teaching children question-answering strategies. *The Reading Teacher, 36* (3), 186–191.

Scieszka, Jon. (1989). *The True Story of the 3 Little Pigs!* Illustrated by Lane Smith. New York: Viking.

Seeger, Pete. (1986). *Abiyoyo.* Illustrated by Michael Hays. New York: Scholastic.

Viorst, Judith. (1971). *The Tenth Good Thing About Barney.* New York: Macmillan.

Williams, Linda. (1986). *The Little Old Lady Who Was Not Afraid of Anything.* New York: Trumpet.

Chapter 4

Nurturing Response with Emergent Readers

Katherine L. Schlick Noe

The first grade teacher sat across the table from me, leaning forward, her finger jabbing for emphasis. "This is why I do literature circles," Margee said. She was talking about Anna, as she told me what had happened that morning. "She's one of those children who benefit so much from literature circles. Anna's not a strong reader. She will consistently go back to books that are familiar and comfortable. She stays with those stories because it hasn't all clicked yet.

"But she can express her deep feelings and understanding when she's allowed to discuss. Then Anna is always able to elaborate. She knows what she means by her responses. If only she could read!"

That morning, during a discussion of *Grandfather's Journey* (Say, 1993), several children talked about how sad the book was. Margee asked them what the author did to make them feel sad. "What words does he use?" she asked.

She read aloud the line, ". . . when I cannot still the longing in my heart" and asked them what that meant. Several students offered literal paraphrases, such as "It's like you can't stand it anymore."

Anna was quiet, thinking. Then she said, "It's like when you're really, *really* thirsty and you just *have* to have a glass of milk!"

Guiding children toward metaphorical response to literature may seem a challenge when new readers are struggling with the very act of reading. However, many children come to a personal understanding of stories all on their own. These readers show the ability early on to relate stories to other books they have read, connect events to their own lives, talk freely about lessons they have learned from a book and, in other ways, indicate that they are making meaning from what they read. Can these differences in response be explained completely by maturation, ability, and development—or can teachers nurture emergent readers to move to higher levels of response more quickly?

This chapter takes a closer look at both Christy Clausen's (Chapter 2) and Margee Morfitt's (Chapter 3) first-grade classrooms to find an answer to this question. You will see how those teachers set the stage for children's growing independent relationship with books and select books that nurture and prompt children's meaningful response. In the first part, I will explore issues specific to emergent readers. Then, I will examine seven questions that teachers commonly ask about literature circles in primary classrooms.

How Readers Differ in Literacy Development

Let's first take a look around a literature circle. Amanda holds her book confidently, eager to begin. She has read her book at home over the weekend, and has her "Post-it" notes ready, marking the places she wants to discuss. When it's her turn to share a passage, she imitates the voice of Bob, the grandfather in Tomie de Paola's touching story, *Now One Foot, Now the Other* (1981). She is a fluent, confident reader who clearly knows what makes her book a good one. Although her classmate Barry also enjoyed the book, he struggled to read it over the weekend. His grandmother read it to him first, then he read it with his older sister several more times before he found something he wanted to mark with a "Post-it" note. Now in the literature circle, Barry sits back as the others ask questions about the grandfather.

Every child brings unique experiences, abilities, and interests to literature. Amanda and Barry typify the wide variation in new readers' development. Literature circles can prepare beginning readers at all stages of development to participate in and benefit from literature. Teachers who want to nurture young readers to go beyond "I like" in their responses, to help them make deeper connections with literature, may want to consider three interactive factors that influence children's growing literary understanding: individual development and literary experience, instruction, and text selection.

The Role of Individual Development
and Literary Experience

The success of literature circles in first grade depends less on whether children read independently (or at all) than on whether they have some idea that stories are exciting and meant to be discussed. Young readers' experience with the world and with reading plays a large role in their preparation for literature circles. If children come to the classroom with established book knowledge—they know how to handle a book, laugh about a book, and talk about a book—literature circles can progress further and more quickly than if students have limited literary experience.

Margee often observes sophisticated responses from her more-advanced readers, but not always. Sometimes she is surprised by children who don't read well on their own, but who exhibit great listening comprehension. Often these students come up with richer insights about books than others at higher independent reading levels. Anna's analogy at the beginning of this chapter is one such example.

For the most part, Margee and Christy find that children who have been read to at home and who have been engaged in conversations about books often find it easier to express their ideas during literature discussions. Even with a strong literary background, however, some children are not yet ready to delve beneath the surface of books. No matter how much instruction the teacher offers, they do not seem to get further than "I like."

The Role of Instruction

Instruction plays a crucial role for children with limited literary experience. Christy has faith that if she continues to provide a model of thinking and responding more deeply to books, she will build a foundation that those children, when ready, will use for understanding and responding to literature.

Instruction must go hand in hand with the teacher's understanding of each child's developing literacy. Literature circles help bridge the wide variation in reading styles and abilities that emergent readers bring with them to the classroom. The power of literature circles at this level centers on creating a community of readers, since all children can respond to and enjoy books with supportive instruction. The teacher's role is to nurture children's growing ability to think deeply about books.

Teachers can model various levels of response to books. Margee shows her students that talking about books includes focusing on the surface ("I like this part because it was funny") as well as examining what characters do or how the author words a certain phrase. By taking part in the conversation, she provides the model of a fluent reader who continually asks questions as she reads. For example, when Margee showed her students her own journal entry about the mood evoked in *Through Grandpa's Eyes* (MacLachlan, 1980), she noticed that many students followed her example. Her modeling of response to various literary elements prompted her students to branch out into a wider range of response.

There is no one point at which the process of reading clicks all at once for a child. Sometimes, it's simply a matter of the child's growing literacy development meeting the right book with the right kind of teacher support that turns on the light for the child. Both Christy and Margee watch for this seemingly serendipitous event.

The Role of Text Selection

The quality of books selected for first grade literature circles has a tremendous influence on children's reading development. Early in the year, Christy chooses predictable and repetitive texts that magnetically draw children in even before they realize they are learning to read (Figure 4-1). Some good examples are *Cookie's Week* (Ward, 1988) and *Whose Mouse Are You?* (Kraus, 1970). As the children progress through the year, she carefully reviews books for her literature circles in light of her children's developing needs, watching for signs that students are ready to move to meatier books.

Sample Books for Beginning Literature Circles

Rosie's Walk (1986) and *Good Night, Owl!* (1972)—Pat Hutchins
Cookie's Week (1988)—Cindy Ward
Dear Zoo (1983)—Rod Campbell
The Chick and the Duckling (1979)—Mirra Ginsburg
Things I Like (1989)—Anthony Browne
Whose Mouse Are You? (1970)—Robert Kraus
Come Out and Play Little Mouse (1987)—Robert Kraus
Where Are You Going, Little Mouse? (1986)—Robert Kraus
Not Me, Said the Monkey (1987)—Colin West
Pumpkin, Pumpkin (1986)—Jeanne Titherington
Sheep in a Jeep (1986)—Nancy Shaw

Figure 4-1 Sample Books for Beginning Literature Circles

Christy and Margee have discovered that without high-quality literature, it's difficult to sustain an engaging conversation about a book. Genuine discussions arise most often when books are read that contain memorable language, realistic plots, and characters to whom children can relate. Margee knows this well. The few times she tried stories about which she felt lukewarm, she was disappointed with the depth of discussion. Her students were not drawn into the stories because there was not much there to talk about.

The depth at which young readers will respond depends to a great degree on which literary elements are emphasized within a story. If the story highlights character, children may comment on and ask questions about characters. If it features plot or setting, children may respond most easily to one of those elements. Probably because characters and plot are featured in books for beginning readers, first graders most easily talk about those elements. It is more difficult to discuss the minimal settings found in many books for emergent readers. Discussions *can* dip beyond the surface level if a book has a strong, apparent theme, such as learning from others, growing up, overcoming loss, or developing friendships. Often with such books, Christy finds that her students are adept at identifying themes—even ones she herself has missed!

Questions Teachers Ask

Primary teachers have many concerns and questions about nurturing response during literature circles. Let's consider seven common questions teachers often ask.

Can I do literature circles when my students are not yet fluent readers?

Children do not need to be fluent readers to benefit from literature circles. They do, however, need to understand the purposes of reading and the roles books can play in learning about themselves and the world around them. For example, Jack struggled with learning to read, but showed remarkable sophistication in his responses to books Margee read to him. He was unable to read even simple pattern stories on his own, had a weak sight vocabulary, and could not grasp phonics. But Jack asked perceptive questions about stories and shared thoughtful responses. When Margee read the story to him or provided a tape of the book, he came back with all kinds of observations. Many students like Jack can participate in wonderful literary discussions before they can read the book with complete accuracy.

In Chapters 2 and 3, Christy and Margee describe how they use literature circles as one component of a total reading program. They offer many suggestions for helping beginners in the learning-to-read stage. Figure 4-2 lists four strategies to help children learn to read independently while they are beginning to participate in literature circles.

Strategies to Promote Independent Reading

- Select predictable, repetitive, rhyming books for early literature circles.
- Provide literature circle books on tape.
- Enlist parents and other family members to read the literature circle books to and with their child.
- Encourage repeated readings of the book.

Figure 4-2 Strategies to Promote Independent Reading

When should I start literature circles?

In her first-grade class, Christy starts literature circles in November, after her students have developed cohesion and trust as a group. After several months of school, students are comfortably settled into the classroom routines and are immersed in shared book experiences, writing, storytelling, daily oral language, and a host of other literacy building blocks. As she described in Chapter 2, Christy begins literature circles with predictable, rhyming books that both extend and support the children's growing independence with word identification and story knowledge. The literature circles introduce students to the language of talking about books, help them share and listen, and teach them about literary elements such as character, setting, and plot.

As the year progresses, Christy gradually introduces less-predictable books with more clearly defined plots, characters, and themes. Once children are able to discuss and respond to books, they can delve more deeply into aesthetic response, explore authors' craft, and develop a beginning grasp of themes. During these later literature circles, children begin to elaborate in their discussions and journal writing.

What books should I use?

Books that prompt rich discussion may differ from the books teachers choose to "teach reading." For example, in November Christy introduced *Cookie's Week* (Ward, 1988), a predictable book about a mischievous cat whose week is filled with misadventure. Although the children found the book very funny, their discussion remained concrete and fairly superficial. Several journal responses mirrored their conversations:

> "I like *Cookie's Week* because Cookie is always in trouble."

> "I like Cookie's week book because I like the book. I like this page because the cat fell on the toilet and it is funny."

For Christy's students, *Cookie's Week* served an important function early in the year as a foundation for learning about literature circles. However, she soon incorporated more substantial books to help her students deepen their levels of response. She searches for books that "delight as well as instruct, inviting the reader to visit again and again" (Peterson, 1991, p. 136).

Tomie de Paola's poignant stories of children's loving relationships with grandparents, *Nana Upstairs, Nana Downstairs* (1973) and *Now One Foot, Now the Other* (1981), consistently spark a personal response in young readers, perhaps because so many can identify with the characters. Following a lively discussion of *Now One Foot, Now the Other*, Christy watched a group head back to their desks to begin journal responses. Before most children had written their names and the date, Eric was well into his entry. She observed that he wrote quickly, flipping over page after page. Curious, she moved closer. He had filled nine pages of his journal in a very short time. The following journal entry illustrates Eric's very personal connection with this book.

> I think it was nice when Grandpa went out with Bobby. I remember me and my Grandpa went out with me to a mall and gave me a Godzilla movie. I liked it. It was funny. I liked to see Gigan, Ghidrah, Godzilla and Angerus jump around. In some parts Godzilla and Angerus talk. Me and my Grandpa enjoy watching them. My Grandpa was just like Bobby's Grandpa. He even got sick. But one thing bad he died. He died a few days ago. I was very, very, very, very sad. I cried every day. I could not stop. It was sad. Even my mom, sister and dad cried. Me and dad were saddest. Because it was my dad's dad. But now my Grandpa is with my Grandma. They're probably having lots of fun up in heaven now. I wish I was there with them. But it won't happen for a long time. But it will happen. I wonder what he's doing now. Did anyone in your family die? I'm just wondering. Maybe? Yes? No? Well, anyway I like the story. By the way even if a person does die still feel happy because if you love someone you will love them for ever.

The criteria for selecting books with depth appropriate for first grade literature circles are similar to those used for older readers (see Chapter 10). Christy chooses books for literature circles based on several criteria (Cianciolo, 1987). (See Figure 4-3).

Criteria for Selecting Quality Books for Primary Literature Circles

- The story should be well crafted, with clearly articulated literary elements of character, plot, setting, and meaningful theme.

- The content of the book should both reflect and extend children's understanding of their own world and the lives of others. The book should have sufficient depth to provide something to talk about.

- Text and illustrations should form a unified framework. The format must be appealing and readable. The illustrations should enrich and reflect the content.

- The story should both reflect the way people talk and offer memorable language.

- Characters should reflect the range of diversity found in the real world, providing an authentic and unbiased glimpse of lives that may be similar to or different from the lives of readers.

Figure 4-3 Criteria for Selecting Quality Books for Primary Literature Circles

Several books mentioned early in this chapter provide an excellent beginning point for literature circles when children are just beginning to talk about and respond to books. However, as children become more fluent readers, it's important to incorporate more complex books in order to elicit deeper responses (Kiefer, 1993). The books in Figure 4-4 meet the criteria described above for selecting quality literature and have proved successful for literature circles with beginning readers.

Picture Books with Depth for Emergent Independent Readers

Fly Away Home (1991) and *The Wall* (1990)—Eve Bunting
Everett Anderson's Goodbye (1983)—Lucille Clifton
Everett Anderson's Nine Month Long (1978)—Lucille Clifton
The Josefina Story Quilt (1986)—Eleanor Coerr
Nana Upstairs, Nana Downstairs (1973)—Tomie de Paola
Now One Foot, Now the Other (1981)—Tomie de Paola
Koala Lou (1988)—Mem Fox
Wilfrid Gordon McDonald Partridge (1985)—Mem Fox
Friends (1982)—Helme Heine
At the Crossroads (1991)—Rachel Isadora
The Leaving Morning (1992)—Angela Johnson
When I Am Old with You (1990)—Angela Johnson
The Quilt Story (1985)—Tony Johnston
Mama, Do You Love Me? (1991)—Barbara Joosse
Peter's Chair (1967)—Ezra Jack Keats
My Grandma Leonie (1987)—Bijou le Tord
Mama One, Mama Two (1982)—Patricia MacLachlan
Through Grandpa's Eyes (1980)—Patricia MacLachlan
Working Cotton (1992)—Sherley Anne Williams
A Chair for My Mother (1982)—Vera B. Williams
My Grandson Lew (1974) and *William's Doll* (1972)—Charlotte Zolotow

---

Figure 4-4 Picture Books with Depth for Emergent Independent Readers

How do I get started?

Begin by choosing books with depth that you really like to read aloud. The best conversations seem to come when the teachers and the children are excited about the books. Involving children in conversations about read-alouds is also important. When teachers demonstrate an interest in children's opinions and encourage their thinking and questions about read-aloud books, young readers will clearly get the message that their opinions are valued.

Let go and allow children to say what they want to say about books. This is often difficult for teachers, but stepping back from the role of director to that of guide is crucial. At the same time, teachers need to model some good examples of things to talk about in literature circles and strategies for using the books to support response. Because children do pick up on teacher modeling, they can use those examples in genuine ways. In Chapter 3, Margee provides specific guidelines for helping children take more control and responsibility for the success of literature circles.

Think deeply about a book before bringing it to a literature circle. Christy asks herself such questions as, "What does it say to me? How does it make me feel? What am I interested in talking about with other readers?" When she joins a discussion group, she shares her responses in order to bring out natural, genuine conversations from children. That is not to say that she expects children to have the same reaction to a book that she does. But she knows that if she can glean a meaningful idea from a book, then, in her conversation, she can ask questions of the children and guide them in a direction if needed. She can model responses that truly come from her heart.

How can I tell that my students are engaging in meaningful response?

Christy and Margee use the following indicators as signs that a child is making deeper connections to literature:

Asking questions of each other. In Christy's class, literature circle discussions often begin with children sharing the important parts they have marked. She vividly remembers her surprise the day Beau leaned over to Eric and asked, "Why was that part important to you?" Her experience had led her to expect first graders to struggle with asking each other questions. Children often just want to share their own responses and may have a hard time listening to and focusing on others. This time, with no prompting from Christy, the boys conversed back and forth, discussing the author and how she wrote the book.

Supporting a viewpoint with evidence from the text. As one of Margee's groups examined "the scary page" from *The Ghost-Eye Tree* (Martin & Archambault, 1985), Richard exclaimed, "Look! There are eyes in the tree!" Alexander suggested it could be an owl, but Margee asked if an owl would make the kind of shriek described on the page. Several children agreed with Richard, who thought the eyes belonged to a cat—a cat from the beginning of the book. They began looking for places in the book where the cat appeared, to verify that the eyes glowing from the tree were the cat's. They found the cat at the beginning and in Mr. Cowlander's shed and decided that, indeed, the eyes did belong to the cat. However, Alexander came the next day ready to present new evidence. He showed how the cat was following the kids and was there to lap up the milk, but pointed out that you could see the outline of an owl in the tree if you looked carefully. Even though all the other children had agreed that it probably was the cat, Alexander pursued evidence from the book to convince them that he was right.

Talking about authors' works. After reading *Now One Foot, Now the Other* (de Paola, 1981), Christy asked one group what they thought of the author. They responded with wide eyes and the exclamation "Great!" Audrey volunteered that her mom cried when she listened to it and felt this was the best book Tomie de Paola had written. She explained how much she also liked another of his books, *The Clown of God* (1978). As the children continued to talk about authorship, Alanna added that *Now One Foot, Now the Other* reminded her of *Knots on a Counting Rope* (Martin & Archambault, 1987) because of the similar relationship between a boy and his grandfather.

Relating an incident from the story to the child's own life. After the literature circle discussion, Nicole wrote in her journal about her own grandfather. She explained that he is old and is having trouble walking and hearing: "I felt sad because my mom was crying last night because Grandpa wasn't doing very well. My eyes watered. I did this because he can barely take a walk and hear."

Another child found a very personal connection with Leo, the young tiger who struggled to be like everyone else in *Leo the Late Bloomer* (Kraus, 1971). He wrote, "The part when he bloomed made me happy. It reminds me of when I couldn't read, and I was trying. Now I can read and write."

Incorporating language from the story. Darren said about Leo, "I feel sorry for Leo because he was a late bloomer *and then in his own good time he bloomed.*" Christy watches for times when children use language from the story in their journal responses, an indication that they are taking as their own the vocabulary they read in books.

Connecting a character or event in one story with similar features in other works. Warren noticed that all of the witches in *The Frog Prince Continued* (Scieszka, 1991) came from other stories. He quickly identified the fairy tales the witches came from. The reason he liked the book, in fact, was that the author and illustrator used the witches from other stories, a feature that he found very interesting.

Revisiting and rethinking incidents. Kenny wrote in his journal that he really liked the page in *Jim and the Beanstalk* (Briggs, 1970) where the giant wrote the thank-you note. But he wondered why the illustrator "spelled some of those words wrong." He counted how many words the giant had misspelled. That led his group to talk about how the giant didn't know a whole lot, and that maybe he hadn't been to school. They talked in depth about the giant, drawing inferences and making connections.

How can I elicit more in-depth written response?

No matter how much they connect with a book, readers at all levels may have difficulty responding in writing if faced with a blank page. In addition, writing is a challenge for these young students who have not yet mastered all the conventions and who struggle with the physical act of writing. Early in the year, Christy and Margee model personal responses in order to show children how a reader probes the meaning within a story. The following journal prompts (also described in Chapter 2) can lead young readers to express those deeper connections they've found in a book and provide the initial scaffolding for these emergent writers:

> I wonder . . .
> I noticed . . .
> I felt (or feel) . . . because . . .
> I think . . .
> That reminds me of . . .
> I wish . . .
> If I were . . . , I would . . .

Christy and Margee model each of these prompts to demonstrate the kinds of thinking they elicit. They encourage students to try out these journal starters, but they also expect children gradually to begin to use their own. As students become more fluent writers, the teachers invite more open-ended responses.

How can I elicit meaningful conversations?

Children who struggle with writing often have good ideas and will share reactions or follow up on other children's questions. Their journal responses may remain at the "I like" stage, but given a chance to respond orally to others' ideas, they can think more clearly, and delve more deeply into a story. Since first graders often struggle with writing, it's important to provide emergent readers with both oral and written ways to respond to literature.

Begin with open-ended questions. The first thing Christy asks when she gathers a group for discussion is, "What did you think of this story?" She has found that broad, open-ended questions are the best way to get children talking. Her approach lets students know that this is their discussion and that she doesn't have a specific agenda of questions that they must respond to each week. Her students know there is an inviting conversation about to begin.

Christy purposely asks open-ended questions to promote risk taking. If she finds that a discussion begins to lag, she will have children turn to the "Post-it" notes that they have used to mark pages in their books. She will say, "Why don't you share what you've marked and tell us why you've marked that page." She finds this prompt useful when discussions fade.

Follow up on good comments or questions to challenge students' thinking. Margee listens carefully for comments or questions that demonstrate a child's deeper understanding of or engagement with a book. She takes the opportunity to elicit more information or to prolong a discussion that seems to be gathering steam. She has found that first graders are often in such a hurry to share their ideas that the group may roll right over a perceptive comment. She models careful listening to children's questions and responses, then follows up by exploring possible answers or extending the comment. Her intent is to ask leading questions to prompt children to think a bit more.

One group who read *The True Story of the 3 Little Pigs!* (Scieszka, 1989) accepted without question that the wolf was not really a bad character; they were convinced that he was innocent of any wrongdoing. Margee turned to the last page of the book and read the wolf's last line: "But can you loan me a cup of sugar?" She asked the children how they thought he might have said that, and then she read it again with varying intonation. She saw glimmers of recognition in the children's faces as they realized that maybe he really was a "bad guy," and maybe he had been trying to convince readers otherwise. Margee sees her role in the group as a facilitator who can point out discrepancies and help children take another look, rather than accepting things at face value.

Draw out reluctant participants. Christy also watches for the child who sits quietly, not participating. She often turns to a shy student and asks, "What are your thoughts?" or "How do you feel?" Such prompts help the children feel that they are being welcomed into the conversation, and gives Christy a chance to find out what they are thinking about the story.

Summary

First graders can respond to good literature from the heart, just as older readers do. Teachers who want to support beginning readers' personal connections with literature need to consider how students differ in their early literacy experiences, and provide instruction to foster children's connections with books. In addition, selecting books with depth will support young readers in their growing ability to read, talk about, and write about good literature.

References

Briggs, Raymond. (1970). *Jim and the Beanstalk*. New York: Coward-McCann.

Browne, Anthony. (1989). *Things I Like*. New York: Knopf.

Bunting, Eve. (1991). *Fly Away Home*. Illustrated by Ronald Himler. New York: Clarion.

Bunting, Eve. (1990). *The Wall*. Illustrated by Ronald Himler. New York: Clarion.

Campbell, Rod. (1983). *Dear Zoo*. New York: Four Winds Press.

Cianciolo, Patricia. (1987). Developing the beginning reading process with picture books. Paper presented at meeting of the "Five Year Olds in School" conference, East Lansing, Michigan.

Clifton, Lucille. (1983). *Everett Anderson's Goodbye*. Illustrated by Ann Grifalconi. New York: Holt.

Clifton, Lucille. (1978). *Everett Anderson's Nine Month Long*. Illustrated by Ann Grifalconi. New York: Holt.

Coerr, Eleanor. (1986). *The Josefina Story Quilt*. Illustrated by Bruce Degen. New York: Harper & Row.

de Paola, Tomie. (1981). *Now One Foot, Now the Other*. New York: Putnam's.

de Paola, Tomie. (1978). *The Clown of God*. New York: Harcourt Brace Jovanovich.

de Paola, Tomie. (1973). *Nana Upstairs, Nana Downstairs*. New York: Penguin.

Fox, Mem. (1988). *Koala Lou*. Illustrated by Julie Vivas. New York: Harcourt Brace Jovanovich.

Fox, Mem. (1985). *Wilfrid Gordon McDonald Partridge*. Illustrated by Julie Vivas. New York: Kane/Miller.

Ginsburg, Mirra. (1979). *The Chick and the Duckling*. Illustrated by Jose Aruego and Ariane Dewey. New York: Macmillan.

Heine, Helme. (1982). *Friends*. New York: Atheneum.

Hutchins, Pat. (1986). *Rosie's Walk*. New York: Macmillan.

Hutchins, Pat. (1972). *Good Night, Owl!* New York: Macmillan.

Isadora, Rachel. (1991). *At the Crossroads*. New York: Scholastic.

Johnson, Angela. (1992). *The Leaving Morning*. Illustrated by David Soman. New York: Orchard.

Johnson, Angela. (1990). *When I Am Old with You*. Illustrated by David Soman. New York: Orchard.

Johnston, Tony. (1985). *The Quilt Story*. Illustrated by Tomie de Paola. New York: Putnam's.

Joosse, Barbara. (1991). *Mama, Do You Love Me?* Illustrated by Barbara Lavallee. San Francisco: Chronicle.

Keats, Ezra Jack. (1967). *Peter's Chair*. New York: Harper.

Kiefer, Barbara. (1993). Envisioning experience: The potential of picture books. In Sam Sebesta and Ken Donelson (Eds.), *Inspiring Literacy: Literature for Children and Young Adults*. New Brunswick, NJ: Transaction Publishers, 67–79.

Kraus, Robert. (1987). *Come Out and Play, Little Mouse.* Illustrated by Jose Aruego and Ariane Dewey. New York: Greenwillow.

Kraus, Robert. (1986). *Where Are You Going, Little Mouse?* Illustrated by Jose Aruego and Ariane Dewey. New York: Greenwillow.

Kraus, Robert. (1971). *Leo the Late Bloomer.* New York: Windmill.

Kraus, Robert. (1970). *Whose Mouse Are You?* Illustrated by Jose Aruego. New York: Macmillan.

le Tord, Bijou. (1987). *My Grandma Leonie.* New York: Bradbury Press.

MacLachlan, Patricia. (1982). *Mama One, Mama Two.* Illustrated by Ruth Lercher Bornstein. New York: Harper & Row.

MacLachlan, Patricia. (1980). *Through Grandpa's Eyes.* Illustrated by Deborah Ray. New York: HarperCollins.

Martin, Bill Jr. & Archambault, John. (1987). *Knots on a Counting Rope.* Illustrated by Ted Rand. New York: Scholastic.

Martin, Bill Jr. & Archambault, John. (1985). *The Ghost-Eye Tree.* Illustrated by Ted Rand. New York: Holt.

Peterson, Barbara. (1991). Selecting books for beginning readers. In Diane DeFord, Carol Lyons, & Gay Su Pinnell (Eds.), *Bridges to Literacy: Learning from Reading Recovery.* Portsmouth, NH: Heinemann, 119–147.

Say, Allen (1993). *Grandfather's Journey.* Boston: Houghton Mifflin.

Scieszka, Jon. (1991). *The Frog Prince Continued.* New York: Viking Penguin.

Scieszka, Jon. (1989). *The True Story of the 3 Little Pigs!* Illustrated by Lane Smith. New York: Viking.

Shaw, Nancy. (1986). *Sheep in a Jeep.* Illustrated by Margot Apple. Boston: Houghton Mifflin.

Titherington, Jeanne. (1986). *Pumpkin, Pumpkin.* New York: Greenwillow.

Ward, Cindy. (1988). *Cookie's Week.* New York: Scholastic.

West, Colin. (1987). *Not Me, Said the Monkey.* New York: J.B. Lippincott.

Williams, Sherley Anne. (1992). *Working Cotton.* Illustrated by Carole Byard. San Diego, CA: Harcourt.

Williams, Vera B. (1982). *A Chair for My Mother.* New York: Greenwillow.

Zolotow, Charlotte. (1974). *My Grandson Lew.* Illustrated by William Pene du Bois. New York: Harper & Row.

Zolotow, Charlotte. (1972). *William's Doll.* Illustrated by William Pene du Bois. New York: Scholastic.

Chapter 5

Finding a Balance:
Literature Circles and "Teaching Reading"

Penny Redman

A cluster of fourth graders settle down on the carpet at the south end of the room. At the other end of the room, two dozen fifth and sixth graders do the same as my team teaching partner and I ready our mini-lessons for the day. Reading workshop is about to begin. Our multi-age classroom is large but never seems quite big enough for these growing bodies and all of our projects. Now that it is spring, the students know the basic routine and await today's lesson. The structure of reading workshop is printed on a chart at the side of the room. We refer to it daily or whenever we want to adjust our schedule for a particular project.

Reading workshop is not the only time during the day when we teach reading. Reading is an integral part of almost every moment of every day. Literature circles are only a part of how students in my classroom become strategic readers. In this chapter, I'll describe how literature circles fit into my reading program.

Daily Schedule

Reading workshop is the framework into which I fit my lessons, literature circles, and other reading activities. Our schedule provides a comfortable structure to ensure that there is time for mini-lessons, independent reading, literature circle discussions, journal responses, and other reading activities. I needed a schedule when I first began exploring literature circles. It helped me make the transition from basals to whole class novels to literature circles. My students seem to appreciate some predictability in their day. They look forward to reading a chosen book or talking with their peers about what just happened in their novel. Alicia, a fourth grader, enjoys her literature circle meeting because "you can share opin-

Weekly Schedule

	8:30-8:55	8:35-9:05	9:05-10:15	10:15-10:30	10:30-12:05	12:05-12:30	12:30-1:00	1:00-1:45	1:45-2:00	2:00-2:40	2:40-3:00
Attendance, flag salute, etc.	P.E.	Theme/ S.S./ Sci.	Recess	Spelling a Reading Workshop	Lunch	Recess	Writing Workshop	Recess	Math.	Story
	Music						Writing Workshop		Math.	
	Math.						Library		Computer Lab	
	Music						Writing Workshop		Math	
	P.E.						Writing Workshop		Math	

Figure 5-1 Weekly Schedule

ions and ask other people if you don't get something in the story." She knows that there is a time set aside during the day to do this.

The art of teaching is finding what works for you and your classroom. Some of my colleagues ask me for "the *right* way to do literature circles." I have yet to structure my reading workshop in precisely the same way from one year to the next. I adjust as I learn more and as the groups' dynamics and students' needs change.

Time is always a concern for teachers. I am never in total control of my schedule. By the time I work around music, P.E., and library—not to mention recesses and lunch—it is a challenge to find an uninterrupted reading time slot daily. Sound familiar? You'll see in the time schedule in Figure 5-1 how I've made time for reading this year.

Reading Workshop Structure

Having carved out a daily time for reading, I design a structure for each reading workshop. (See Figure 5-2.)

Monday, Tuesday, Thursday, Friday	Wednesday
10:50–11:05 Mini-lesson	Booktalks
11:05–11:10 Status-of-the-class	Book presentations
11:10–11:40 Literature study	Vocabulary activities
11:40–11:45 Debriefing	Current events
11:45–12:05 Independent reading	Special projects

Figure 5-2 Reading Workshop Structure

There are many other aspects of reading that don't seem to fit into those four days, so one day each week we depart from this format. We read the local newspaper and discuss current events. I booktalk several books from our classroom or school library to encourage students' independent reading. Students also present what we call book presentations on these books. Other possibilities for this day are special projects or activities using vocabulary from our literature circle novels or a content area.

Mini-lessons are short, usually teacher-directed lessons focused on one of three categories: (1) literature selection and the author's craft, (2) procedures, or (3) specific reading skills and strategies. *Status-of-the-class* (Atwell, 1987) is the time when students tell what they plan to do during the literature study time. *Literature study* includes both literature circles and a variety of other reading and writing activities. *Debriefing* is a time for oral evaluation and assessment by the literature circle group and the whole class. *Independent reading* provides a quiet time for everyone to read and an opportunity for me to confer with students. I'll present more about the specific aspects of the schedule throughout this chapter. As with all schedules, we adjust and change when we need more time to gain control over a new skill or when a discussion seems too good to stop.

Mini-Lessons

I sometimes wonder if my "mini" lessons are really so mini! My goal is to limit this block of time to no more than 10 minutes, but often 15 is more realistic. Why *mini*? I want my students to love and enjoy literature. The best way I can see for that to happen is to give them as much time as possible for reading and interacting with literature. My students spend less time discussing skills or strategies and more time using them in a meaningful context. This is a big departure from my early years of teaching, when I spent considerable time introducing a basal story, vocabulary, and various publisher-selected skills. This allowed little time for my students to read and reflect on what they had read. I now keep my lessons short and allow students more time to read, discuss, and respond. How do I teach children all they need to know about reading in such a short time? I can't. The mini-lesson is not the only time to engage children in the magic and the strategies of reading. Throughout the reading workshop time and throughout the day, I assist students in making connections between reading and writing.

Procedural Mini-Lessons

In the fall, as we become more comfortable with classroom routines and expectations, procedural mini-lessons are the most common. While some of these may seem mundane, I've found that when I work these out with students early in the year, everyone is clear about procedures and expectations and the rest of the year flows much more smoothly. These lessons include the subjects listed in Figure 5-3.

Procedural Mini-Lessons

- How to move to the literature circle
- How to choose a book
- What to do when you encounter a passage you don't understand
- When to write journal entries
- What to write in journals
- What is needed to prepare for a literature circle
- What skills are needed to have a conversation
- What are options during literature study time

Figure 5-3 Procedural Mini-Lessons

Skill and Strategy Lessons

As the year progresses, my mini-lessons focus on specific reading skills and strategies. In my district, I am expected to teach specific strategies. Skill and strategy lessons are not restricted to district guidelines; my goal is to focus on any strategies that lead to more proficient reading. Through observation and assessment of students, I often find that students have some strategies well in hand and need no further direct instruction; others need additional practice and assistance. Figure 5-4 lists some examples of strategy lessons.

Reading Strategy Mini-Lessons

- Summarizing
- Supporting an opinion with details from the text
- Distinguishing between fact and opinion
- Determining the author's point of view or purpose
- Inferring a character's motives, feelings, or traits

Figure 5-4 Reading Strategy Mini-Lessons

Mini-Lessons on Authors' Craft

Let me illustrate a specific mini-lesson on one aspect of authors' craft. One of the objectives for fourth, fifth, and sixth graders in my school district is to identify similes. I had noticed similes in several books students were reading, so this seemed the ideal time to highlight this literary device. I selected Jane Yolen's *Owl Moon* (1987) from the bookshelf and started reading aloud. Many had heard this story before but once again delighted in the beautiful illustrations and language. When I had read "a train whistle blew, long and low, like a sad, sad song," I paused. "What do you think she really means? Why do you think she worded it that way?"

I paused at several other similes. At the end of the story, we discussed similes and created a chart listing their critical attributes. We talked briefly about why writers use similes. In the picture book *Nettie's Trip South* (Turner, 1987), we read of trees that were described as being "like old men with tattered gray coats." We looked at three or four examples from other books and compared them to our chart of the attributes of similes. I consulted *Using Picture Storybooks to Teach Literary Devices* (Hall, 1990) and *Beyond Words: Picture Books for Older Readers and Writers* (Benedict & Carlisle, 1992) as sources of picture books with examples of similes.

Throughout the week, students discovered similes and metaphors in their literature circle books and in their individual reading. Charissa found "like a rock in a stream" in *Maniac Magee* (Spinelli, 1990) and Drew noticed "as if he were not a boy, but a pincushion" in *Chocolate Fever* (Smith, 1972). As the class listened to *Stone Fox* (Gardiner, 1980), students heard the character's face described as "hard as stone." Eyes lit up and several students blurted out, "That's why they call him Stone Fox!" We recorded similes on tagboard strips and taped them to the wall above the chalkboard. During literature circle discussions, students shared similes they noticed in their novels and the groups talked about the authors' choice of language. A few children even incorporated similes into their own writing. My main objective was to have students identify similes in stories and appreciate the authors' use of figurative language. The mini-lesson raised the students' awareness of similes and extended this awareness throughout the year.

Mini lessons I also find valuable in helping students to examine the authors' craft are listed in Figure 5-5.

Mini-Lessons on Authors' Craft

- Literary devices
- Different types of openings and leads
- Development of suspense
- Character development
- Plot development
- Description of setting
- Creation of mood

Figure 5-5 Mini-Lessons on Authors' Craft

Mini-Lessons Based on Students' Needs

I've begun to realize that mini-lessons are most effective when I tailor them to my students' needs and interests. I recognized this recently when I attended a national conference for teachers. I had already been to several sessions and garnered the ideas and inspiration I was craving. My next choice was a session on portfolios. I waited, anticipating some new ideas for student portfolios or research I could use to support what I was doing. The speaker rose and began to read his paper on using portfolios with graduate students. His presentation did not meet my needs and my mind wandered. I was struck by the implications for my classroom. Students are expected to listen, respond, and often follow up on the ideas presented. In the past, I used to rely on a predetermined list of lessons based on a curriculum guide. Now I look at their work, listen to their questions, observe them in action, and take my cues for mini-lessons from their demonstrated needs.

Tim wrote volumes in his literature journal. He was justifiably proud of all that he had to say; however, mechanics were a stumbling block. Tim was not alone. Brady also felt punctuation and capitalization were unnecessary for a burgeoning fourth grade writer. I had difficulty understanding what Courtney and Christine had to say in their journals. The main purpose of the entry in a spiral-bound notebook is to carry on a dialogue between the teacher and a student about literature. However, some mechanical difficulties hindered the communication. In looking at the journals, I decided that my students needed to reread, revise, and edit their journal entries if they were to convey their impressions and make their points clear to outside readers.

I needed to make a decision. Would the whole class benefit from a mini-lesson on editing, or should I take aside a small group that particularly needed this focus? I decided to focus on editing with the whole class. With the permission of the writers, I made transparencies of exemplary journal entries. As a class, we listed what writers do to help us understand what they have to say. We recorded the skills we'd learned so far in and out of school to help us. They mentioned conventions such as putting a capital letter at the beginning of a sentence and using ending punctuation. More ideas came with prompting. For some students, neat handwriting was an issue; for others, spelling was their obstacle.

Students mentioned that it was helpful in their journals to do more than just retell the plot. It was more interesting when they added their own reactions and opinions. I suggested reading their journal entry aloud to themselves or having someone read it to them to make sure it sounded clear. I asked students to rework one of their journal entries. Many were excited about the idea of exchanging journals and reading each others' entries. Later I looked at the revised entry for evidence of the skills we had listed. Some students still needed some individual assistance and guidance, but the quality of the journal entries had improved noticeably. I found that I needed to repeat this lesson periodically.

The longer I work with students in literature circles, the more faith I develop in their ability to raise questions about their own learning, as well as in my ability to identify and address their needs.

Literature Study Choices

Status-of-the-class is a strategy I gleaned from Nancie Atwell's book, *In the Middle* (1987). I first began using it with students in writing workshop; it seems equally useful for reading. The form has my students' names down the left side of the paper and a column for each day of the week where I record student choices during literature study (Figure 5-6). Often students plan to do two things in the time given (e.g., write a journal entry and then read) and I record both choices on the form. It takes less than three minutes to note what students plan to do. In our classroom, the status form helps us monitor student choices.

Status of the Class   week of 5/2 - 5/6

Name	M.	T.	W	Th.	F
Lindsay	W	LG		R	RJ
Andrew B.	J	R		L.G.	
Brady	J	P		R	LG
Micah	BP	LG		J	J
Marcial	LG	J		J+B	R
Diana	LG	R		R	JR
Chelsea	J	R		L.G.	P
Courtney	J	R		R	LG
Drew	R	R+J		LG	J
Alicia	R	LG		R	W
Phil	J			LG	R
Mitsu	LG	R		R	R
Steve	R	J		R	LG
Andrew M	R	R		J	LG
Karen	LG	R		R+W	R
Tim	R	LG		R	J
Leslie	R	J		LG	R
Christine	LG	R		R	W
Devon	J+W	R		J	LG
Lael	J	LG		R	R
Chris	R	B		J	LG
Brian	R	J		LG	R
Brett	LG	R		R	J
Chrissa	J	LG		R	R
Collin	R	J		LG	W

— KEY :
— LG = Literature group
— R = Read
— J = Journal
— W = Writing
— B = Browse
— BP = Book presentation ☑ = absent
    A = Assignment

Figure 5-6 Status of the class

Since literature study time includes literature circles, as well as other reading and writing activities, students' choices include those shown in Figure 5-7.

Literature Study Choices
• Meet in a literature circle
• Write in journal
• Work on a piece from writing folder
• Read (literature circle book or other book)
• Work on individual book presentation
• Browse for a new book to read
• Complete a special assignment

Figure 5-7 Literature Study Choices

Providing choices gives students a great deal of ownership, but the freedom can also be a challenge for some. Teachers are often concerned about monitoring student choices. I've found the status form and list of choices helps me nudge students in productive directions.

Let me give you an example. In February, two literature circle groups were reading *My Side of the Mountain* (George, 1959) and *Hatchet* (Paulsen, 1987) as part of our unit on strong main characters. When I called their names for a status check, students in those two groups simply answered "literature circle." Other students answered that they planned to read or write in their journals and I noted their choices on the status form. I reminded several children of specific activities they needed to finish. For example, John had met with his literature circle one day and read for two others. I was uncertain whether he had completed his required journal entries for the week. I asked John if they were done. "Oh yes," he said sheepishly, "I do need to work on that." The status-of-the-class helps students focus and plan their time.

Following the status-of-the-class, literature circles groups gather at their meeting spot and the rest of the class begins their chosen activities.

Literature Circle Discussions

Students settle around a table or pull chairs into a circle. When I had a "one teacher" classroom, one group met at a time. In our team teaching situation, we always have two groups meeting. At the beginning of the year, the teachers take an active role but, as the year progresses, the students take charge of the group discussions. Later in year, it's possible to have more circles meeting simultaneously while we move about the room and observe. Students take more responsibility for keeping a conversation going when we are not always there to make it happen.

Students use a literature circle evaluation form and record the book title, group names, and the degree of preparation and participation. (See Chapter 12 for ideas on assessing participation during literature circles.) The discussion leader is responsible for keeping the discussion going and filling out the check sheet. Some groups seem to flow from the very first day, while others need to learn the social skills involved in having a conversation.

Diana, Brian, Chelsea, and Sang Yup gathered around the round table. Each brought a pencil, journal, and a copy of *Hatchet* (Paulsen, 1987). We had been reading novels with strong main characters. These students listed *Hatchet* as one of their choices when we presented books to the class. Each member was required to come to the literature circle with a passage to share and one or two questions written in their journal. Often students shared journal entries or illustrations of particularly memorable parts of the book. In the center of the table were "Post-it" notes and the literature circle check sheets. Chelsea was the leader and she looked around to see whether everyone had the necessary materials. Each group had a calendar marked with the pages they needed to read each day. Prior to their meeting, students marked the passages they wanted to share. Brian asked the group to turn to pages 20–21 and read several paragraphs that described the main character's frantic call over an airplane microphone following the pilot's heart attack.

> He let go of the mike. His voice was starting to rattle and he felt as if he might start screaming at any second. He took a deep breath. "If there is anybody listening who can help me fly a plane, please answer."
>
> Again he released the mike but heard nothing but the hissing of noise in the headset. After half an hour of listening and repeating the cry for help he tore the headset off in frustration and threw it to the floor. It all seemed so helpless. Even if he did get somebody, what could anybody do? Tell him to be careful?
>
> All so hopeless.
>
> (Paulsen, 1987, pp. 20–21)

Brian explained that he chose that part because it is particularly exciting. Sang Yup said that he liked that part, too. The group discussed the main character's dilemma and what they thought he should do. The group continued to discuss, share passages, and ask questions.

Sometimes during a literature circle discussion, children share their journal entry about a book: questions, illustrations of a favorite part, a poem about the main character, or some other choice. When necessary, I prompt the leader to ask the opinion of someone who has not spoken or to urge members to find a place in the story that supports their idea or opinion. Mostly, however, I take anecdotal notes about how the discussion is going. I use the notes during our debriefing. As the groups conclude, they check their calendars to see how far they plan to read prior to their next meeting and adjust their plans if necessary.

What is the rest of the class doing while these groups are meeting? Those not involved in a literature discussion group participate in other aspects of literature study. For instance, while Chelsea and her group began to talk, I saw that Steve was reading. Drew and Andrew were busy working on a diorama for a book presentation on *Tales of a Fourth Grade Nothing* (Blume, 1972). Salim had just finished his independent novel and wanted suggestions for a new book. We looked through the shelves and discussed the types of books he enjoyed. Together we came up with several possibilities. Karen was wondering what to write about in her journal. We pulled out the list of journal suggestions from her reading folder (see page 73). She decided to summarize and react to the section she had just read. Sitting next to Karen, Matt wrote his opinion of the main character in his literature circle book, *Julie of the Wolves* (1972).

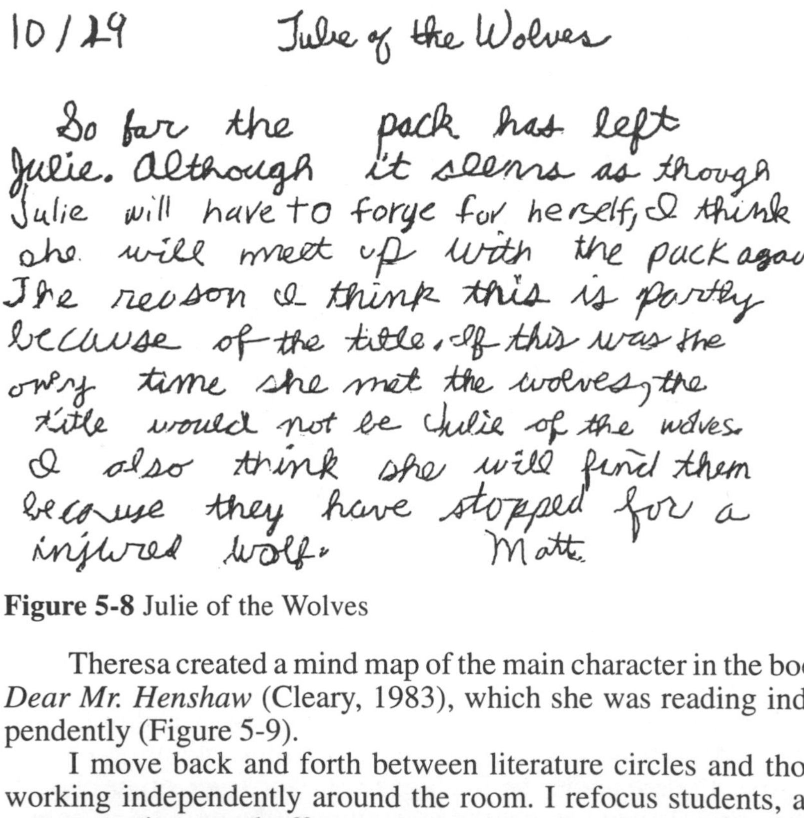

10/29   Julie of the Wolves

So far the pack has left Julie. Although it seems as though Julie will have to forge for herself, I think she will meet up with the pack again. The reason I think this is partly because of the title. If this was the only time she met the wolves, the title would not be Julie of the wolves. I also think she will find them because they have stopped for a injured wolf.   Matt.

Figure 5-8 Julie of the Wolves

Theresa created a mind map of the main character in the book *Dear Mr. Henshaw* (Cleary, 1983), which she was reading independently (Figure 5-9).

I move back and forth between literature circles and those working independently around the room. I refocus students, answer questions, and offer encouragement. In our class, students are not always on task, so we continue to teach, model, and clarify our expectations.

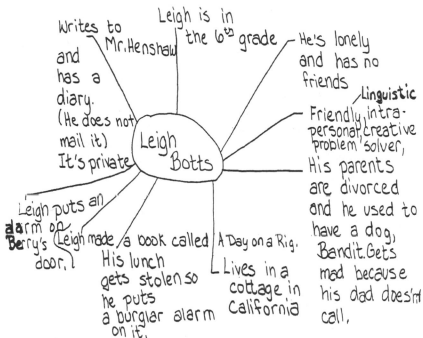

Figure 5-9

Debriefing

At the end of each literature study time, we spend five minutes debriefing. During this time, students assess how things went and receive feedback. We discuss what went well and what could have gone better. During one of our debriefings, I talked about the group that had discussed *My Side of the Mountain* (George, 1959). I noted how members cited examples from the text to back their opinions, related events in the story to other stories they had read, and shared how they would have acted in similar circumstances. Students commented that they listened to what others in the group had to say, agreed or disagreed politely, and looked at the speaker. All these things contributed to a good discussion.

During the debriefing time, students who meet in literature circles discuss how their groups functioned. Students who are not involved in a literature circle explain how they used their time productively. Together we celebrate successes and address problems when they arise.

Occasionally, I ask a student to videotape or audiotape a specific literature circle discussion or even the entire class during literature study time. These tapes provide a useful tool for debriefing. We learn a great deal by stepping back to look at physical posture and listening behaviors, interactions, and the type of questions students ask. We emphasize the positive comments and behaviors and work toward repeating them.

Independent Reading and Conferences

We conclude our reading workshop time with independent reading. For fifteen to twenty minutes, students read in their literature circle novel or a book of their own choosing. They scatter throughout the room and locate a comfortable spot to read. Some children head for cozy corners and sit on the carpeted floor, while others prefer to remain at their desks. The cleanup team for the day has the privilege of using the floor cushions. Students quickly settle in and silent reading begins. I check my class list to see which students I haven't met with recently.

For instance, one day I began with Devon. He was leaning against the wall reading. As I sat next to him, he began to read aloud. This was part of our routine. I listened for a while, jotting down notes on the Independent Reading Strategies form (see page 68). After a page or two, Devon and I talked about the book. We discussed what had led up to the particular events he was reading about, what he thought of the book, and what he predicted would happen next. As we concluded, we discussed the reading strategies he used that were effective.

Sometimes I talk with students about ways to become better readers. Some days I get totally involved with one student; other days I spend a few minutes with one child and then move on to another. I keep my notes and observations in a three-ring binder with a section for each student. I check off the names of students with whom I have read and talked. My goal is to read and talk with each student at least once each month.

Management Issues

As students move back to their desks after independent reading, several place their reading folders on my desk. Students keep a reading folder in which they tuck their spiral notebook and a handout on procedures for writing journal entries. The folders also include a reading log (see page 177) and Suggested Journal Responses (page 73).

At the beginning of the year, we randomly divide the class into four groups (yellow, green, red, and blue) with matching folders. During lunch on Mondays, I read journals from all six red folders. On Tuesdays I read from the blue folders, and so on. Reading only one fourth of the journals at a time has proven manageable. On Fridays I only read specific journals in which I have asked a student to clarify, elaborate, or rework an entry. The spiral notebook serves both as a literature response journal and a personal dialogue between the student and the teacher. Each week students are required to write at least two literature response entries.

[handwritten margin note: keep records for each student in a sectioned 3 ring binder]

Literature Circle Extensions

At the end of each literature circle set, students prepare a way to share their novel with the rest of the class. They begin with a summary of their book. Groups choose a favorite or exciting part to read aloud to the class. Students then select from a variety of visual responses, such as puppet shows, skits, and drawings for the overhead projector. (See Chapters 10 and 11 on response to literature.)

Once projects have been presented, we take a breather before beginning the literature circle cycle once again. During this two- to three-week break, we may prepare a class play, perform choral reading, form expert groups on topics of interest, or enjoy a poetry study. Students generally participate in about four literature circles during the year.

Conclusions

As I read other chapters in this book, I see that there is much more I could be doing. I scan the annotated bibliography for new titles. I'd like to try some of Patti Kamber's suggestions in Chapter 8 for establishing a respectful climate for discussions. Lisa Norwick and Barry Hoonan (Chapter 10 and 11) inspire me to encourage a wider range of student response. I've also begun to involve my students in making decisions, something I could never have imagined doing when I first began teaching in 1966.

As you will note from reading this book, there are many variations in literature circles. The structure will differ depending on the ages of the students, their prior experiences with literature circles, and availability of books. Your decisions will be affected by your openness to change, teaching experience, knowledge of children's literature, and comfort with student-centered learning. It's a matter of finding a balance.

References

Atwell, Nancie. (1987). *In the Middle: Writing, Reading, and Learning with Adolescents*. Portsmouth, NH: Heinemann.

Benedict, Susan & Carlisle, Lenore. (Eds). (1992) *Beyond Words: Picture Books for Older Readers and Writers*. Portsmouth, NH: Heinemann.

Blume, Judy. (1972). *Tales of a Fourth Grade Nothing*. New York: Yearling.

Cleary, Beverly. (1983). *Dear Mr. Henshaw*. New York: Dell.

Gardiner, John Reynolds. (1980). *Stone Fox*. Illustrated by Marcia Sewell. New York: HarperCollins.

George, Jean Craighead. (1959). *My Side of the Mountain.* New York: Dutton.

George, Jean Craighead. (1972). *Julie of the Wolves.* New York: HarperCollins.

Hall, Susan. (1990). *Using Picture Storybooks to Teach Literary Devices.* Phoenix, AZ: Oryx Press.

Paulsen, Gary. (1987). *Hatchet.* New York: Viking.

Smith, Robert Kimmel. (1972). *Chocolate Fever.* New York: Yearling.

Spinelli, Jerry. (1990). *Maniac Magee.* New York: HarperCollins.

Turner, Ann. (1987). *Nettie's Trip South.* Illustrated by Ronald Himler. New York: Macmillan.

Yolen, Jane. (1987). *Owl Moon.* Illustrated by John Schoenherr. New York: Philomel.

INDEPENDENT READING STRATEGIES

Name_____ **Date**_____

Title_____ **Author**_____

Does the book seem to be at an appropriate level?

STRATEGIES TO REINFORCE:

____ Self-corrects when a miscue is made that affects meaning
____ Retains the meaning in a text when a miscue is made (i.e. read "Mom" for "mother" or "house" for "home")
____ Remembers new words when encountered later in text
____ Enjoys reading (attentive and focused)
____ Observes punctuation in oral reading
____ Attempts to sound out unfamiliar words
____ Can summarize what has been read with some detail
____ Is able to make predictions
____ Can draw some conclusions

STRATEGIES TO ELIMINATE:

____ Focuses on "sounding out" so much that meaning and flow are lost
____ Stops reading when word is unknown and waits to be told the word
____ Continues reading when meaning is unclear

COMMENTS:

STATUS OF THE CLASS
Date_____

Name	Monday	Tuesday	Wednesday	Thursday	Friday

Key

LG = Literature Group
R = Read
J = Journal
W = Writing
B = Browse
BP = Book Presentation
A = Assisgnment
    Absent

Chapter 6

Sparking a Love for Reading:
Literature Circles with Intermediate Students

Anne Klein

I love books. I spend hours reading and talking about books. My students are now recommending books to me and calling each other on the phone to talk about books. Literature circles helped spark this love of reading.

For the past three years I've used literature circles with fourth and fifth graders in my multi-age classroom. As I listen to my students discuss the current topic of homelessness within their small literature groups, I'm impressed at the breadth and depth of their conversations. Eight different novels are being discussed simultaneously in the room. One group wonders why the author uses the scene with a magical elf village in *Afternoon of the Elves* (Lisle, 1989) to draw the two main characters together. Another grapples with why Felice Holman includes several short chapters about a subway driver in *Slake's Limbo* (1974). Two groups focus on the meaning of the title, while two others talk about what it would be like to survive on their own. In the group reading *When the Road Ends* (Thesman, 1992), the children discuss the relationship between two of the characters. Their discussions flow from questions of wonder to opinions with conviction as they discuss many aspects of their books independently.

How did they arrive at this point? I believe the key is the classroom environment. I will describe the structure and progression I use to introduce literature circles. We begin by reading a novel together, then move into literature circles using multiple texts.

Getting Ready

I had always used trade books in my classrooms as supplemental reading and considered reading aloud an integral part of the total reading program. I became fascinated, however, with the idea of allowing children to select their own books and wondered whether students would actually read and discuss the books on their own. I read books such as *Creating Classrooms for Authors: The Reading-Writing Connection* (Harste, Short & Burke, 1988), *Reading Process and Practice: From Socio-Psycholinguistics to Whole Language* (Weaver, 1988), and *Grand Conversations: Literature Circles in Action* (Peterson & Eeds, 1990) and visited several classrooms to see literature circles in action.

While each class looked and sounded a bit different, I noticed some underlying similarities. Reading was valued and considered important, and expectations were clear to the students. They chose what they read, were highly engaged with books, and participated in animated discussions. Using what I learned and observed, I planned how I would set up literature circles in our classroom.

Beginning the Year

Selecting just the right book to launch literature circles is critical for establishing a positive atmosphere and attitude. (See Chapter 9 for more information on selecting novels.) It's important for me to use a book I love, as well as one that is new to the students. I selected *Night of the Twisters* (Ruckman, 1984) as a whole class read. This dramatic story tells of two friends who are babysitting when a tornado hit their town. The characters and setting are well developed, and the novel is rich with descriptive passages, effective dialogue, and plenty of suspense.

Getting Started

I explained that we would read and discuss *Night of the Twisters* together in order to have a common frame of reference as we explored a variety of ways to respond to literature. I booktalked the novel and introduced the use of small "Post-it" notes or a bookmark for keeping track of interesting or unusual words, passages, or questions for the group (see page 82). For example, Jared was unsure of the meaning of "cogitates" and "pining" in the novel and listed the words on his bookmark. Other students preferred to use "Post-it" notes on the page where these words or passages were located.

I read the first chapter of *The Night of the Twisters* aloud to the class. The students had a choice of listening to the story or reading along in their own copy. At the end of the first chapter, I asked students to respond in their journals. This first session took about 45 minutes.

On the second day, my students and I shared our journal entries and noted the variety of reactions. Highlighting the diversity of response encouraged risk taking during this initial stage of reading and writing. After the discussion, the class began to read the next chapter of the book silently.

Occasionally I selected a question or activity related specifically to each section of the book we had finished. Other days students could choose from a list of Suggested Journal Responses (Figure 6-1) and Possible Response Questions (see page 83).

Suggested Journal Responses

Summary/Reaction—Describe your reactions or thoughts about what you read.

Diary Entry—Pretend you are the character. What happened to you and how did you feel? What did you think?

Letter to a Friend/Author/Character—Write a letter reflecting your thoughts, questions, and feelings about the book.

Interview—Interview a character from your book and respond as if you are the character.

Illustrate a Key Scene/Character   Using the text, illustrate a descriptive passage.

Venn Diagram—Show how two characters/settings/plots/ books are alike and different.

Pop-Up—Make a pop-up of a significant scene, including a written description of the scene and/or your reaction.

Timeline—Keep a timeline of key events. Show whether they are positive or negative.

Character Web/Mind Map—Using the text, find four to six qualities that describe your character and list specific passages for support.

Pamphlet—Create a pamphlet about the characters or significant scenes from the book.

Sketch-to-Stretch (Harste, Short & Burke, 1988, pages 353–357)—Create a visual representation expressing your reactions to and understanding of the conflicts or characters in the book. Focus on what stays with you from the book.

Write a Poem—Describe your character, setting, problem, plot, or theme, using a form of poetry.

Response Questions—Answer one or two of the questions from the Possible Response Questions list.

Figure 6-1 Suggested Journal Responses

I found that early conversations about journal entries helped students increase the range and depth of their responses. The class tried a variety of response activities for the first chapters of *The Night of the Twisters* (Ruckman, 1984). For example, the first day students wrote about a "red letter" and "black letter" day in their lives. After the next reading, they described what they liked about their best friend. They next created a Venn Diagram showing the similarities and differences between Danny in *Night of the Twisters* and Howard in *The Kid in the Red Jacket* (Park, 1987), which I was reading aloud. At the peak of the action, student wrote what they would do, where they would go, and what they would need if a tornado was reported in their area.

Nurturing Discussions

In Chapter Five, the tornado is heading straight for the boys. Students were focused on the story and naturally made predictions. They wanted to know what was going to happen to the boys. The tension was perfect for a lively discussion.

Four or five volunteers brought their journals, books, and their bookmarks or "Post-it" notes to the front of the room. I explained that their discussion might seem awkward at first, since everyone would be watching and listening, but encouraged them to talk about the story. At the beginning, the students were very self-conscious. Within a few minutes, however, a heated exchange began about what was happening to the main characters. I stopped the conversation and asked the students if they could tell when the discussion started sounding natural. The class noticed that when the group turned to specific passages in the book to prove their points, they became animated and forgot about their audience. Conversations were also more effective when they looked directly at the person speaking and responded to what that person said. They noticed that when there was a lull in the conversation, it was helpful to go back to their journal or the book. We continue listening to the group and talked about what we saw happening. I'm convinced that taking time for such initial reflections helps students grow as participants in literature circles. Discussions such as these continued throughout the year.

Some years I use a second whole class novel before starting small group literature circles, depending on the dynamics of my class and book availability. Other years I plunge right into literature circle sets. Some of our literature circles focus on genres (biographies, mystery, and historical fiction), authors (Gary Paulsen and Judy Blume) or themes/topics (perseverance, courage, and homelessness). My sets vary, depending on the interests of the students and the fact that I have students more than one year.

Homelessness: A Sample Literature Circle

Early in the year, students expressed an interest in the issue of homelessness. They had read and heard about families in our community that didn't have homes and wondered whether there was something they could do to help. Several students brought in clothing and books to send to the families. They continued to mention their concern throughout the year as they read about people's needs in the newspaper and heard about them on television.

I read several children's novels on my own that related to homelessness and used Ray Kettel's annotated list of books on homelessness in the May 1992 issue of *Book Links*. As I read, I wondered how my students and their families would react to the sensitive topics (mental illness, alcoholism, and abuse) that were bound to arise. Despite my apprehension, I decided to follow the students' interest and my belief in the importance of this theme. My parent letter outlined my rationale and the books we planned to use. I asked students and their families to watch for articles, television specials, and newscasts on homelessness. Many brought in summaries of shows and clippings from the newspaper, which we displayed on a special bulletin board.

Introducing the Topic

Before introducing the books, we created two charts that we referred to throughout our study. On the first chart, students listed knowledge statements, such as, "All homeless people live in cardboard boxes" and "There are organizations that can help homeless people." Some of these statements were misconceptions, some were opinions, and some were valid facts. On the second chart, we listed our questions about the topic.

I read aloud Eve Bunting's picture book, *Fly Away Home* (1991), as a way to examine the issue of homeless children. After reading, we all illustrated what the book meant to us. Their sketches served as a springboard for discussion. The students commented on how friendly and supportive the two homeless families were in the story. They wondered what it would be like to live in an airport, always trying to blend in with the surroundings and not draw attention to themselves. They discussed the artist's use of the color blue. Almost everyone brought up the boy's inner struggle as he wished for the bird to go free. They all hoped the boy and his father would find a home of their own (Figure 6-2).

Introducing Books and Selecting Groups

I selected eight books with a variety of reading levels, diverse cultures, and both male and female protagonists (see Figure 6-3). (Other titles on this topic are listed in the annotated bibliography

Figure 6-2

under the themes of Perseverance and Courage and Dealing with Issues of Poverty.)

Novels for Literature Circles on Homelessness

Cave Under the City (1986)—Harry Mazer
Maniac Magee (1990)—Jerry Spinelli
Monkey Island (1991)—Paula Fox
Slake's Limbo (1974)—Felice Holman
When the Road Ends (1992)—Jean Thesman
Afternoon of the Elves (1989)—Janet Taylor Lisle
Toughboy and Sister (1990)—Kirkpatrick Hill
The Loner (1963)—Ester Wier

Figure 6-3 Novels for Literature Circles on Homelessness

I gave short book-talks and occasionally read a passage from the novels we would be using for literature circles. I stated whether a book was an "easy read" or "a bit of a stretch."

I explained that a few of the children in the novels *were* homeless, while others *were like* homeless children because they had uncertainty in their lives. These characters weren't sure where they would be living or getting their next meal, and often found themselves responsible for many day-to-day decisions. If a novel dealt with mental illness, alcoholism, or abuse, I also mentioned that in the booktalk so students who might be bothered by the content could select another title.

As I introduced books, I wrote the titles on the board and displayed each book along the chalk tray. The students looked through the books, asked questions, and then selected their first, second, and third choices. I reminded students to select a book they really wanted to read, rather than one their friend chose. The factors I considered when composing the groups were gender and grade level balances, as well as group dynamics.

Observing Literature Circles

Each group met and decided the format they would use for reading. Some choose to read independently, others read aloud as a whole group, and a few read with partners. Their methods varied from day to day.

I find that conversations are most dynamic when students have read a large section of their book or they are at an exciting part. We set aside one day a week for literature circle discussions; however, some groups chose to meet more than once a week. When students came to a confusing passage, they often wanted to read together and discuss the book. These natural discussions deepened meaning and enhanced understanding. Students became more excited about what was happening in the story and made predictions about what they thought would occur next.

Twice a week, students responded in their journals in a variety of ways. They often used the list of questions attached to their journals (see Possible Response Questions, page 83). Some students illustrated particularly descriptive passages. For example, Kelly illustrated the vivid scene in *Monkey Island* (Fox, 1991) in which a group of people destroyed the shelters of the homeless (Figure 6-4).

Others wrote a variety of poems about their characters, what they were like and what they were going through. Many students simply wrote what they thought of the story, characters, and plot. Several times a week I collected their reading journals, wrote comments, and asked questions in order to extend their thinking about the story.

Each week, the students read four days, completed two journal entries, and met once to talk about the book. At the end of the literature circle set on homelessness, students completed the Discussion Summary form (see page 185 in Chapter 12), in which they gave group members feedback.

As I read their journals, I assessed and recorded types of student responses. Their responses revealed whether students were struggling with the novel and when they moved to deeper levels of understanding. The assessment forms I've found most helpful are described in Chapter 12.

Students created response projects to share their books with the class. As a group, they selected the format that best represented

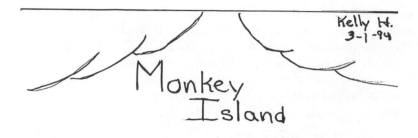

Figure 6-4

their book. They used the list of suggested ways to share books described in Chapter 10. Students used a form to plan what they would do and which section of the book their project would highlight, and how the project reflects an important part of the novel (see page 192). I gave the plan a quick check before they began work.

Three groups prepared dioramas of key scenes from their novels. The group reading *Afternoon of the Elves* (Lisle, 1989) created a Readers Theater script of the final three chapters of their book. The setting of Spinelli's novel, *Maniac Magee* (1990), was portrayed through a three-dimensional map, highlighting what happened at each location. Readers of *The Loner* (Wier, 1963) crafted a mural, and another group acted out three favorite scenes from *Monkey Island* (Fox, 1991). The group reading *Cave Under the City* (Mazer, 1986) prepared a Big Book of key events.

Once projects were complete, I collected planning sheets and took anecdotal notes directly on the Extension Planning and Evaluation form during presentations. We viewed a videotape of their presentations and students completed the Literature Circles Self-Evaluation form on page 186 in Chapter 12.

Expanding Literature Circles

Students began to realize that there are many people who have houses, but don't have homes. There are also children who don't have a home, but who have parents and a support system that gives them a sense of security. My student teacher read several selections from *Home: A Collaboration of Thirty Distinguished Authors and Illustrators of Children's Books to Aid the Homeless* (Rosen, 1992). The class published writings of what home meant to them or of places that made them feel safe and secure. Matthew's poem (Figure 6-5) was one of many responses.

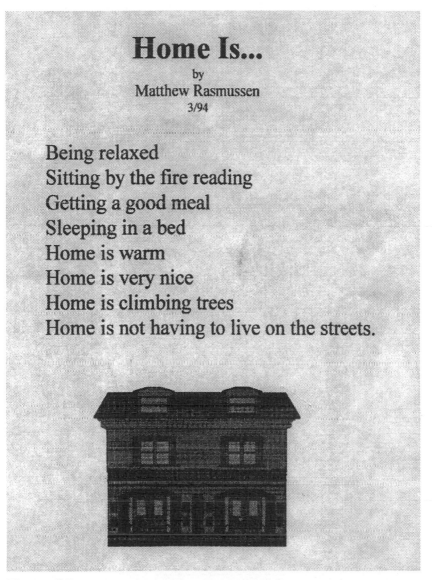

Home Is...
by
Matthew Rasmussen
3/94

Being relaxed
Sitting by the fire reading
Getting a good meal
Sleeping in a bed
Home is warm
Home is very nice
Home is climbing trees
Home is not having to live on the streets.

Figure 6-5

During this unit, *Chive* (Barre, 1993) was our class read-aloud. In this book, Chive's family is forced to sell their farm and move to the city, where they eventually become homeless. This moving story is told in two "voices" (eleven-year-old Chive and his friend Terry) and evolves over a four-year period. To help students keep track of the sequence, I prepared a large timeline across the front of the room. After each chapter, a student wrote a brief summary of what had happened. As we listened and created the timeline, the story unfolded before us. Students came to love and respect Chive, feeling almost as though they had lost a friend when the book ended. As a class, we wrote to Shelly Barre expressing our love of the characters and story, and asked questions about her process in writing the book. To our delight, she responded with a four-page letter.

The students also watched several taped television specials about homeless people and the services available to them. After each video, everyone wrote in their journal about what they had learned. We discussed new information and what surprised us. While watching these shows, students became more aware of the large numbers of homeless children in our community.

I read facts about homelessness aloud from two informational books. *The Homeless* (Jenkes, 1994), written for adults, describes the complex problems of the homeless and increased my understanding of this issue. During free moments when we were waiting to go to lunch, be dismissed, or go to an assembly, I also read excerpts from *No Place To Be: Voices of Homeless Children* (Berck, 1992). These moving first-person accounts of life on the streets or in shelters helped build a more realistic picture of what it means to be homeless.

Final Thoughts

I've found that students in my class love books and are always anxious to begin another round of literature circles. I continue to read and exchange ideas with colleagues about how to meet the wide range of students' needs and deepen the quality of their responses. My students appreciate having a choice in the books they read, the opportunity to read good books, and time to talk with classmates about their literary experience. Literature circles are a powerful way to spark a love of reading and deepen children's understanding of the world around them.

References

Barre, Shelley. (1993). *Chive*. (1993). New York: Simon & Schuster.

Berck, Judith. (1992). *No Place to Be: Voices of Homeless Children*. Boston: Houghton Mifflin.

Bunting, Eve. (1991). *Fly Away Home*. Illustrated by Ronald Himler. New York: Clarion.

Fox, Paula. (1991). *Monkey Island*. New York: Greenwillow.

Harste, Jerome C., Short, Kathy G. & Burke, Carolyn. (1988). *Creating Classrooms for Authors: The Reading-Writing Connection.* Portsmouth, NH: Heinemann.

Hill, Kirkpatrick. (1990). *Toughboy and Sister*. New York: Puffin.

Holman, Felice. (1974). *Slake's Limbo*. New York: Scholastic.

Jenkes, Christopher. (1994). *The Homeless*. Cambridge, MA: Harvard University Press.

Kettel, Ray. (1992). Children and the homeless. *BookLinks*, *1* (5), 51–55.

Lisle, Janet Taylor. (1989). *Afternoon of the Elves*. New York: Orchard.

Mazer, Harry. (1986). *Cave Under the City*. New York: Harper & Row.

Park, Barbara. (1987). *The Kid in the Red Jacket*. New York: Knopf.

Peterson, Ralph & Eeds, Maryann. (1990). *Grand Conversations: Literature Circles in Action*. New York: Scholastic.

Rosen, Michael J. (Ed.). (1992). *Home: A Collaboration of Thirty Distinguished Authors and Illustrators of Children's Books to Aid the Homeless*. New York: HarperCollins.

Ruckman, Ivy. (1984). *Night of the Twisters*. New York: HarperCollins.

Spinelli, Jerry. (1990). *Maniac Magee*. New York: HarperCollins.

Thesman, Jean. (1992). *When the Road Ends*. New York: Avon.

Weaver, Constance. (1988). *Reading Process and Practice: From Socio-Psycholinguistics to Whole Language*. Portsmouth, NH: Heinemann.

Wier, Ester. (1963). *The Loner*. New York: Scholastic.

BOOKMARK	BOOKMARK
Name:_____	Name:___Jared_____
Title:_____	Title:_Night of the Twisters_
Author:_____	Author:_Ivy Ruckman_
List favorite or important pages, quotes, scenes, or interesting or unknown words.	List favorite or important pages, quotes, scenes, or interesting or unknown words.
	cogitates p. 8
	pining p. 8
	mrs Smiley p 33 (legs)
	sucking sound p.49 what caused it?
	bathroom scene p.54
	cyclone p. 91

Figure 6-6

POSSIBLE RESPONSE QUESTIONS

1. AUTHOR

Why do you think the author wrote this book?
What is the author trying to tell us?
What did the author have to know in order to write this book?
What would you ask the author if he/she were here? Why?
What did the author do to "hook" the reader?

2. CHARACTERS

Who are the main characters? Describe them.
Would you like any of the characters? Why or why not?
Do some characters seem more "alive" and believable than others? Which? Why?
How do the characters change in the story? What makes or helps them change?
Are any characters like others you have "met" in other books? Which ones? Why?

3. PLOT

What happened in the story? What was the sequence of events?
Were you able to predict the ending? How? Why or why not?
Which part was MOST important in the story? Why?
What other ways might the story have ended?
What is the main thing the author is saying?
Is there a main point or theme to the story? What? How do you know?

4. SETTING

Where and when does the story take place? How do you know?
Which part of the story best describes the setting? Why? How?
Do you know a place like the one in the book? Where is it? Describe it.
How does the author create the atmosphere for the setting?

5. MOOD

How did you feel while reading the book? Why did you feel that way?
What was your favorite part? Why? What was your least favorite part? Why?
How did the author make you feel the way you did?
Does the mood of the story change? How? Where in the story?

6. STYLE

How does the author keep you interested in the story?
What pictures does the author leave in your mind? Describe them.
What special words or lovely language does the author use? Keep track of them.
Is there anything else that makes this author's perspective or style unique? What?

Chapter 7

Going with the Flow:
Getting Back on Course
When Literature Circles Flounder

Kary Brown

> Over time, I have slowly learned that the answers are not in
> the books. The books and the experts can cause us to reflect
> and give us new ideas, but they cannot be used as prescrip-
> tions. The most highly acclaimed book and the most
> knowledgeable expert are, at best, useful resources. We teach-
> ers have to find our own answers and tailor our lessons to
> our particular group of children and ourselves. This is no
> easy task. (Routman, 1991, p. 21)

Will my students ever achieve "grand conversations" (Peterson
& Eeds, 1990) about good books? I kept asking myself this question as I began implementing literature circles with my fifth graders. As I tried new aspects, I would refer to professional resources
for wisdom and guidance. Most of the books I consulted described
an ideal class doing the perfect lesson. The structure flowed
smoothly from beginning to end. I began to think it couldn't just
be *my* classes that struggled with meaningful responses and discussions. As I read, several questions kept swirling through my
mind. Do all teachers find success with literature circles right from
the start? Do other teachers go through a frustrating transitional
phase before encountering success? What struggles might teachers experience as they first try literature circles? I found that the
professional resources did not address the hurdles teachers might
encounter in becoming a successful facilitator of literature circles.

Although I eventually experienced great successes with literature circles, it was not easy. After several successful years with
literature circles, I encountered a new class full of unique personalities and discovered that the tried and true methods no longer
worked. Having developed a view of how children grow as readers, I was able to adapt and make changes, keeping my philosophy

intact. Just as learning to read is a complicated process, so is becoming an effective teacher and facilitator of reading. We shouldn't apologize for the many stages we go through as we adapt and implement new ideas. I've found this quote from *Invitations* (Routman, 1991) particularly reaffirming:

> I think we need to be honest about exactly how difficult the transition is. So many teachers read about how whole language classrooms are supposed to look and function, and then worry that they're not measuring up. They wonder what's wrong with them because they are still struggling and full of self-doubts. Let me say it loudly and clearly. I don't know any teachers who are not struggling, and I don't know any teachers who have it "all together." (p. 22)

In this chapter, I will share the transitions I made as I developed and modified my literature circle program over a period of four years.

Getting My Feet Wet

My first year of teaching consisted of what I now refer to as "basalizing" literature. As an undergraduate, I was taught how to use literature in the classroom by developing a unit of study in which the children would respond in a prescribed manner. I was in control of the learning. I began by prereading the book I had selected for my class to read. I then developed a reading schedule, a set of questions, and a vocabulary list. As I led whole class discussions, I noticed that only a small percentage of students truly participated. Looking back, I see how restrictive and teacher-controlled my reading program really was. The students were not allowed any choice in what they read. They rarely shared what they were personally learning or feeling about the story. Every child searched for the answers that I believed to be important.

I do not regret the processes I used during the first year. Being a new teacher, I felt more comfortable being "in charge." As I gained confidence and experience, and broadened my understanding of how children learn to read, I knew I needed to move forward toward a more child-centered reading program.

Jumping In

During the next year, I grabbed hold of any information I could find about the reading process and jumped right into literature circles. That was my first mistake. I was so excited and eager to have my students experience literature circles that I forgot to build a framework. I envisioned how literature circles should look, and we jumped into journal responses and literature group discussions.

I soon became frustrated at the lack of depth in students' conversations and responses. The class was frustrated, too, as we attempted to wade our way through. From these experiences, I learned the importance of modeling, demonstrating, and guiding students. Merely asking them to engage in a conversation about a book did not ensure a successful discussion.

I discovered several necessary ingredients for "grand conversations." I had to paddle back upstream and model such simple skills as how to sit in a group, how to listen actively, and how to constructively confirm, question, and disagree with one another. I needed to model how to write effective journal responses, how to create questions and comments for the group, and how to choose appropriate extension projects. These important basic skills provide the foundation for effective literature circles.

Calm Waters

After three years of making gradual changes, I realized that the struggles, determination, and patience had paid off. It was February and our fifth-grade class had just completed a unit on biographies. The students chose books about artists, authors, scientists, explorers, and political leaders. For each category, I gathered five to eight books that represented diverse cultures as well as a wide range of readability levels.

It is virtually impossible to paint an accurate picture of these literature circle discussions. I saw the excitement and interest in the children's eyes as they discovered similarities and differences among the lives of these people from the past. For example, the students who were studying artists were intrigued at the difficult childhood many of the artists had experienced. I heard genuine questions and thoughtful responses. Their interest was evident in their body language as they moved close together and listened intently. The students were engaged in literature circles just as I had envisioned.

Literature circles continued to flow smoothly through the rest of the year, but none compared to the biography unit. I wish I could have bottled the magic I saw and heard in the groups as they shared and discussed their reading. How could we repeat this experience? In order to learn from these discoveries, I identified six factors that played a role in the success of literature circles (See figure 7-1).

With growing enthusiasm and confidence about using literature circles, I began to plan for the following year. I videotaped discussions as models for the next year. I jotted down notes describing aspects that I wanted to remember. I was certain that the following year would be even more successful because of my fortified experiences and new-found confidence. I thought I had reached smooth waters.

Factors that Influence Literature Circle Success

- group dynamics
- modeling
- degree of choice and ownership
- book selection
- student motivation and interest
- previous experience with literature circles

Figure 7-1 Factors that Influence Literature Circle Success

Treading Water

I began as I had other years, following a sequence like those described in previous chapters. I believed we had embarked on another successful year. As we began our discussions of *Bridge to Terabithia* (Paterson, 1972), I guided the students through the processes of preparing for and participating in literature circles. While my expectations and structure had been successful in the past, this year was different. The class floundered when I began to wean the children away from my continual guidance into more self-directed learning. As we struggled together, I had to adapt my literature program.

After agonizing over our unsuccessful attempts at literature circles, I changed the structure by rescheduling the groups. In the past, two groups met simultaneously during our reading time. I moved back and forth between groups making notes and praising effective group strategies. Other times, I remained with one group through a session, alternating groups weekly. Realizing that these students were not yet independent, I had only one group meet at a time. Sometimes this meant the groups did not meet as frequently as before, but the quality of discussions began to improve because I was there to provide support.

I decided to have the entire class read the same novel. This simpler format provided a helpful scaffold as students learned guidelines for participating in literature circles. Focusing on a common book allowed us to discuss obstacles as well as discoveries. Later in the year I hoped to offer children more options about the books they read, beginning with two choices and eventually providing more. Choice is a strong motivator for children once they have internalized how literature circles work.

I also adjusted the way in which I gave assignments. In past years, I gave students a menu of required work that listed the number of responses, project choices, and deadlines. Students were responsible for completing assignments and being prepared for their literature discussions. In past years, students welcomed this responsibility and were capable of managing their time. This year, however, the menu seemed to stall students. They became overwhelmed by having all the requirements in front of them at once; they didn't know where to start or how to proceed. Taken aback, I decided to give them single, short-term goals and due dates to help them focus on the task at hand and complete their work. Although the changes were minor, the atmosphere in the class immediately felt more relaxed and focused.

Students need choice but not too much at once. Need some structure

Developing quality discussions can be the most valuable and rewarding, as well as the most difficult, aspect of literature circles. As in previous years, we discussed events in the story and students' reactions. We generated responses together and pointed out how to move beyond retelling to interpretations and personal reactions.

With our first literature circle novel, I provided specific prompts as we read a whole class book in common. We then generated a list of possible journal response questions from which the children could choose. In previous years, I could soon wean the students from dependence on me for prompts. This year, however, many students continued to need this support throughout the year. I learned that what works one year to promote higher-level discussions may not work the next year. This class seemed to need continual guidance in order to produce quality responses.

You need to custom design a program to fit the class.

I modeled appropriate listening and conversation skills by asking a small group of students to demonstrate the skills we had been learning in front of the whole class. Then, for several months I participated in their small groups, modeling and providing guidance. Usually, I attempted to move out of the literature circles to encourage children to become more independent. This year, however, the students were not able to maintain discussions on their own.

When I stepped out to the periphery of the group, and encouraged them to conduct discussions on their own, the students merely read their written responses and didn't react to one another. They seldom risked asking questions if they disagreed with or were unsure of ideas that were being shared. Frequently their conversations came to a standstill and they would turn to me as they tried to keep the conversation going. I raised questions to help them resolve their impasse and offered them assistance. Still, the silence lingered.

some groups will have problems

Instead of remaining on the fringes of the groups, I stepped back in. I realized that I needed to participate as a group member until they could carry on independently. With the reassurance of my presence and gentle prompts, students seemed willing to share their viewpoints and ask questions of one another. I was more of a key player in their discussions than I would have liked, but this group needed extra support.

helping students delve deeper with good questions

Later in the year, when students' skills and their knowledge about participating in literature circles had grown, I could sit on the edges of groups and write anecdotal notes. As students became more confident, my presence in the group actually hindered the discussions. They were ready to sail without me.

Swimming with the Current

As the year progressed, I discovered that the dynamics of this class were very different from those of any other year. They did not seem to bring with them a strong love of reading or show much enthusiasm for the choices I provided. It was also a very active and animated class and tended to be chatty and unfocused. My initial reaction was to fight this behavior and try to get them to take things more seriously. I continually vied for their attention and tried everything I could to get them involved.

Eventually, I decided to stop fighting them and join them. I focused on their humor, silliness, and dramatic flair, and began to approach reading from a more creative perspective. I discovered that drama, music, and art were the tools these students used to express themselves most effectively. I realized I had relied too heavily on the written word as the sole means of response. (In Chapters 10 and 11, Lisa Norwick and Barry Hoonan describe similar realizations and provide suggestions for response through the arts.) I decided to provide options for artistic responses. They responded in ways I had not yet tried; the creativity and depth surprised me. The new response format seemed to naturally carry over to discussion groups and livened up their conversations. I found success when I learned to adapt my teaching to the strengths, rather than the weaknesses, of the group.

After the students read *The Fighting Ground* (Avi, 1984), I began to see how the arts could inspire response. In small groups, students painted one character's view of war on a sheet of large white paper. We discussed how an image could represent feelings and create a mental picture. They described their interpretation of the artist's choices and shared their insights.

Figure 7-2

Student's Artistic Response

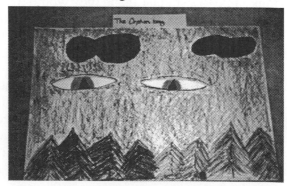

Figure 7-2 shows one group's representation of the feelings of the young boy whose parents were killed in *The Fighting Ground*. As Jamie and Nikoya explained it, "Our picture has eyes in the sky because he was scared and he didn't know what to do. We also put the eyes in because he didn't know what to think about who was the enemy anymore. He was also lonely." In the ensuing discussion, other students added that eyes could also represent the only sense the boy could use to understand the tragedy. Since he was French, he couldn't understand either the German soldiers or Jonathan. Matt added that the little boy may have been too afraid to speak. Other kids also remarked that he may have seen his parents being killed. We decided that perhaps the dark clouds in the picture represented the death of his parents.

Literature circles were once again close to what I envisioned. The students had developed into productive participants. They understood expectations and could follow through on their tasks, assignments, and projects independently. They had learned to solve problems with group members and combine ideas to deepen their understanding of a story. The class spilled over with excitement and enthusiasm for reading, making all our struggles, adaptations, and determination worthwhile.

Why did it take so long? Many factors played a role. Looking back, I've identified five key components that you may find helpful as you adapt literature circles in your classroom. (See Figure 7-3.) Within each of the five components, the progression moves from an emphasis on teacher support encouraging student independence. For example, you may want to begin literature circles by having students meet once a week and meeting with one group each day. As you become more comfortable, you may decide to have two days each week set aside for discussion days. In Chapter 10, Lisa Norwick describes the next step, which is to ask students to determine their own meeting schedule for the week.

Smooth Sailing

During the last literature circle set of the year, the children chose one of five books of multicultural experiences: *In the Year of the Boar and Jackie Robinson* (Lord, 1984), *Words by Heart* (Sebestyen, 1968), *Letters from Rifka* (Hesse, 1992), *Sing Down the Moon* (O'Dell, 1970), or *Number the Stars* (Lowry, 1989). The discussions were lively and stimulating. Students used evidence from the books to support their reactions. They willingly turned to one another, asking questions and clarifying information, and empathizing with the hardships each story presented.

One particular instance in May seemed to epitomize how far this group had come since fall. Dusty, who was reading *Words by Heart,* asked me, "Did Papa die? I don't know if he died." I asked

---

Progression of Adaptations for Literature Circles

Reconfiguring Schedules

- Each literature group meets once a week, one group a day
- Each group meets two specific days of the week
- Each group meets as needed during the week, with one weekly meeting required

Restructuring Book Selection

- Use picture books to introduce literature circles
- Use a whole class novel at the beginning of the year or when introducing literature circles
- Students choose from two or three related books
- Students choose from a larger selection of books

Modifying Assignments

- Give daily deadlines and short-term goals
- Develop a menu of choices to be completed weekly
- Develop a contract of required work; kids pace themselves

Adapting Discussions

- Teacher leads the literature circle discussion
- Develop a system of "tickets to talk" so everyone gets equal sharing time
- Teacher participates as a member of the group
- Teacher sits outside the group and observes
- Students lead literature circle discussions
- Tape record or videotape so students can self-reflect

Guiding Journal Responses

- Use "Post-it" notes or bookmarks to note passages to share
- Model responses to the class or use past student samples
- Offer a few choices for response
- Develop a menu of choices
- Incorporate response through the visual and performing arts

---

Figure 7-3 Adaptations for Literature Circles

if Dusty had discussed this with his group. Since he hadn't, he proceeded to ask group members if they knew the answer. The children began to really wonder and question their understanding, because this information was not explicitly stated in the novel. The group eagerly gathered in the corner of the room and started tossing out evidence from the story, intently flipping pages, searching for the answer in the book. The students continued to be concerned about whether Papa had died or whether he had just been badly hurt. At last they found the answer. Their bodies slumped, the tone of their voices changed, and their faces showed their shock as they discovered that Papa had died. The discussion revealed their utter sadness and disgust at the unfair treatment Papa and his family suffered just because they were black. The students found the outright prejudice that the book described appalling.

At the end of the unit, the group chose Michael Jackson's song, "Black or White," to represent the theme of the book. They described how they had chosen the song because it conveyed the message that people's skin color should not matter and that everyone should be treated equally. The whole class then wrote journal responses describing their reaction to the song. These were indeed "grand conversations"! Although the instruction meandered in directions different from other years, literature circles were on course.

As I prepare for yet another year and another group of unique children, I wonder what course we will take as we set sail on our adventures into literature circles. How will I nurture meaningful discussions next year? What new struggles and challenges will I face? What new lessons will I learn? Rather than following a predetermined course, I'll use students' strengths and interests as a compass. I've learned to "read the wind" and teach more responsively.

References

Avi. (1984). *The Fighting Ground.* New York: J. B. Lippincott.

Hesse, Karen. (1992). *Letters from Rifka.* New York: Holt.

Lord, Bette Bao. (1984). *In the Year of the Boar and Jackie Robinson.* New York: Harper & Row.

Lowry, Lois. (1989). *Number the Stars.* New York: Dell.

O'Dell, Scott. (1970). *Sing Down the Moon.* Boston: Houghton Mifflin.

Paterson, Katherine. (1972). *Bridge to Terabithia.* New York: Avon.

Peterson, Ralph & Eeds, Maryann. (1990). *Grand Conversations: Literature Groups in Action.* New York, NY: Scholastic.

Routman, Regie. (1991). *Invitations: Changing as Teachers and Learners K-12.* Portsmouth, NH: Heinemann.

Sebestyen, Ouida. (1968). *Words by Heart.* Boston: Little, Brown.

Editor's Note: In the past year, we have shared various drafts of this book with many teachers. Carolyn Callaghan is a middle school teacher currently substituting in several districts and has shared our interest in literature circles. Her experience substituting in a classroom that purported to be "doing literature curcles" serves as a warning to all of us not to take for granted that all teachers share the same vision of literature circles in action.

Literature Circles: Good Intentions

Carolyn Callaghan

The lesson plans read: "1:30-2:05—Literature Circles. Ms. Jones will come in to lead students. You only need to help monitor student behavior."

My day as the substitute in this fifth grade class has gone smoothly, according to lesson plans, and I look forward to observing the next phase of our day. As an English major, I anticipate students reading novels of their choice in groups, discussing plot, writing styles, characterization.

I do not anticipate Ms Jones.

She enters the classroom out of breath, flustered.

"Sorry I'm late," she mumbles ominously. Her facial expression defies me to question her three minute tardy entrance. Her teacher face in place, she turns to the class, whose faces are rapidly draining of interest.

"I'm looking for quiet tables . . . thank you, Megan, I like the way you stopped talking . . . thank you, Brandon, I like the way you make eye contact . . . Jacob, sit down . . . I'm waiting for everyone to get quiet . . . Katie, will you pass out the books . . . Jacob, I asked you to sit . . . "

Ms. Jones' pursed lips are as tight as her purple dress. She is prepared to stand there indefinitely. This is a battle she never loses; eventually the class quiets and even Jacob takes a seat.

"Before we begin, who can help us review the expected behavior in Literature Circles?"

Hands wave wildly. Ms. Jones calls on selected students. As Megan, Jacob, Rebecca and others respond, the rules for Literature Circle Reading sound more like dictatorial edicts. Every group reads the same book. Every group consists of four students. Every group has already chosen its reading location, and no group may change. Everyone must follow along in the book while every group member takes a turn reading. (A teacher will be checking to see that any given student, at any given time, can point to the group's exact place in the book.) Everyone will read no more than half a page at a time; the group's facilitator will begin the day's reading, and reading rotation is always to the facilitator's left. Every group is to read chapters five and six.

"Who did Literature Circles with Mrs. Smith last year?" demands Ms. Jones.

Again hands fly. She chooses four students who are graduates of the same indoctrination techniques she taught a year ago. They come forward and demonstrate Literature Circle Discussion Technique. One student is the group facilitator, and is given a laminated, color-coded card with general, all-purpose questions. The facilitator reads Question Number One to the group; the person to his/her left must respond to the question. Eye contact within the group is maintained at all times.

"Who is your favorite character thus far, and why?" reads Brandon.

Rebecca, well-trained, quickly responds. "Jemmy, because he's brave."

"Very good, Rebecca." approves Ms. Jones. "Next?"

"I like Jemmy, too," copies Jacob.

Ms. Jones' teacher face frowns. Everyone senses that Jacob has made a near-fatal mistake.

"Jacob, you can agree with Rebecca, but you must come up with your own reason."

"But I like Jemmy for the same reason," laments Jacob, eyes downcast, hopes of getting off quickly and easily disintigrating.

"Jacob, maintain eye contact. Your must have your own reason. You can't simply agree with the previous student. We'll come back to you. Megan?"

The rest of the group, learning from Jacob's mistake, quickly come up with original (if not sincere) responses. Ms. Jones faces Jacob, who is now wishing that he had never volunteered for this suicide mission. Time passes.

"Well, Jacob we can't wait any longer. Facilitators, it is your job to keep the discussion moving. Keep an eye on the clock; don't let anyone take too much time thinking about his answer."

I gasp, inaudibly thank goodness, at this last dictum. Don't let students spend too much time thinking about their answer?

Evidently I have not misunderstood, because Ms. Jones has given the order to disperse and read. Everyone has a paperback copy of Clyde Robert Bulla's *A Lion to Guard Us*. I move about the room listening to various groups, hoping that once students are involved in their reading, literature can be resuscitated.

But the damage is done. Students are more concerned with reading EXACTLY half the page than with what is printed on the page. Poor Rebecca becomes absorbed in the dialogue and reads aloud an entire page; she is chastised by her group members as they ponder a way to undo the damage—"You read more than half a page! It was Brandon's turn!"

I watch Ms. Jones flit from group to group. I see her point to Nate's open book; he is not reading aloud, but has been following along, according to the rules, and is therefore able to show Ms. Jones the group's precise location. She nods, satisfied, and moves on.

The group I am observing finishes reading and begins to argue about who approaches Ms. Jones for the laminated color-coded question card. I whisper, perhaps because I too fear Ms. Jones' disapproval, that it is the facilitator's job. Amanda approaches Ms. Jones; she is praised for being the correct student to ask for the card. Amanda returns to the group and rattles off the first all-purpose question. Each member dutifully responds.

We are saved by the recess bell and the sense of relief is palpable. Books are stacked hurriedly in the center of each group. It is the facilitator's task to return books to the shelf. The color-coded laminated cards are returned to Ms. Jones; she frowns as Molly extends her card.

"Molly, this card is bent. Class, you must be more careful with these cards. These are my property. They take a lot of time to make. Your certainly don't want me getting into your desks and bending your papers. You need to respect my property."

Molly is both surprised and aghast that she had committed the sin of bending; I suspect the damage is a result of absent minded fidgeting rather than a flagrant act of vandalism. However, glancing at Jacob, I wonder if he is mentally storing this information for future use.

Dismissed, students scramble for the door, grabbing jackets, four-square balls and jump ropes as they disperse. Literature circles are over for the day, and, for the day, forgotten. These students are survivors of out-dated text books, over-crowded classrooms, blended families and MTV. They will also survive Ms. Jones. But their love of reading must surely be scarred.

Reference

Bulla,Clyde Robert. 1981 *A Lion to Guard Us*.New York: Harper Illustrated by Michele Chessare

Chapter 8

Invisible Scaffolding:
Fostering Reflection

Patricia Kamber

Before my first experience with literature circles, I had snapshot images in my mind of how I wanted the circles to look. My fifth-grade classroom would be a humming place of collaboration; there would be small groups of students spread about the room, comfortably engaged in stimulating, intense conversations about great books. By the end of each conversation, all students would end up understanding themselves and the world a little bit better. However, reality clashed with those images when we held our first literature circles. The only humming I heard was from Erica as she twirled her long brown hair absent-mindedly around her pencil. Evan and Megan's "intense conversation" focused on who was farthest ahead in the book and who was the best reader. Sean and Ian certainly looked comfortable in the reading corner, although I knew that lying on their backs, toe to toe, would probably not lead to a "stimulating discussion." What was happening here?

As we debriefed after that first session, I asked the students to discuss the experience. Most liked the idea of talking in small groups but felt it was too chaotic. Some complained that they just didn't know what to do. Surprisingly, they all wanted to try the circles again. I shared with them that the literature circles did not exactly match my visions either. I had been confident they would enjoy the book and knew they would benefit from a discussion, but I too felt the experience was overwhelming. I realized during that conversation that, although the children wanted and needed to voice their ideas, most did not know how to work together effectively in a student-led group. When I used words like "deep," "empathetic," and "reflective" during the debriefing, their glazed eyes told me they had no idea what I was talking about. Their impatient voices asked, "What do you mean by empathetic?" "What is deep?" "Who cares! Why are we even doing this?"

Now, six years later, literature circles are a successful, invaluable component of the curriculum in our fifth-grade classroom. In this chapter, I will try to articulate the invisible scaffolding that underlies successful literature circles, bringing reality closer to my ideals.

Examining Genuine Conversations

My most heartfelt goals as a teacher have always been to encourage ideas and risk-taking. I truly want the students to enjoy the learning process. What I didn't know six years ago was that one should never assume *anything*. I knew that, before I dug myself in any deeper, I would have to take the time to analyze what happens in the literature discussions that really sparkle.

We are all touched by books in unique ways. The experiences we've had in our lives, our emotions, and what we know about the world all influence our responses to literature. Through our responses, we grow and make connections to each other. This line from Anne Morrow Lindberg's book, *Gift From the Sea* (1955), captures my feelings about our need to collaboratively make sense of what we read: "In varying settings and under different forms, I discovered that we all are grappling with essentially the same questions, and were hungry to discuss and argue and hammer out possible answers" (p. 7).

Using one of my adult literature groups as a model, I consciously began to observe the dynamics that make the depth of sharing in a group seem both natural and personal. We sit in a circle facing each other. We look at each other when we speak. We try to let one person speak at a time, but sometimes the excitement overtakes politeness. Often feelings are reflected back. If one person is pensively quiet, we gently nudge her into the conversation. At the start of each discussion, we recall significant events, and this seems to help us focus. We share pieces of the book in order to better understand the story and relate the bits to our own lives, thereby widening our perspectives. Some of us mark favorite parts to share; others note setting or character descriptions to be revisited with the group. Some bring notebooks filled with quotes and passages, written in response to the literature we read.

We learned the skills that enable us to have high-quality conversations. It is not an innate ability. Most of us learned through trial and error, and from the good examples and high expectations of adult role models. As we mature, we find that many professions require effective communication skills. We learn the art of empathetic listening, how to logically expand an idea, and how to show respect and encourage others. As adults, genuine conversation has become effortless and natural. Our group communication skills, honed from years of experience, provide us with the motivation and framework to analyze literature and understand other perspectives.

Most children do not have many opportunities to talk with each other in small groups in school. As John Goodlad (1984) states, "Most of the time, teachers tell or explain . . . Students rarely turn things around by asking the questions. Nor do teachers often give students a chance to romp with an open-ended question" (p. 109). Goodlad found very little classroom time was spent on discussion. "Not even 1% required some kind of open response involving reasoning or perhaps an opinion from students. Usually, when a student was called on to respond, it was to give an informational answer to the teacher's question" (p. 22).

In our room, when opportunities did arise, discussions were focused on solving problems I had designed. Even those experiences were often frustrating for both myself and the students, usually due to negative group dynamics. Most students had not learned how to work effectively in small student-directed groups. I decided I needed to teach the art of dialogue by slowing down, modeling, and never assuming anything.

Building Relationships and Establishing Trust

In September, most of our activities are focused on fostering a sense of community and creating a classroom that is conducive to learning. The following are six activities I use early in the year to help deepen our understanding of each other, and to develop personal self-worth that later will enhance the quality of our literature circles.

Summer Reflections

I begin in August by sending a letter to each student introducing myself. I ask each student to bring five items, with a short written reflection for each, that best represent how they spent their summer. Items might be photos or souvenirs of a trip, a good book they may have read, a dried flower from a hike, or even their bike helmet if biking is a favorite activity. I ask each student to share his or her items the first week of school. Photos and descriptions of items are then placed in their portfolios.

Autobiographies/Personal Memoirs

After reading aloud *Boy* (Dahl, 1984), *Trina Schart Hyman: Self-Portrait* (Hyman, 1981) and *Zlata's Diary: A Child's Life in Sarajevo* (Filipovic, 1994), I ask the students to develop their own written memoirs. These memoirs are made available for all the students to read and are later placed in their portfolios.

Peer Interviews

Students work in pairs to interview each other. The interview questions are generated as a class activity and include questions about hobbies, interests, family, ambitions, likes and dislikes, and pets. Each student writes one to two pages about the person they interviewed. I take a photograph of each student in the class to be placed with the interview. All the pages are collected and published in a class book called "Our Classroom Community" that we read and share with parents.

Compliment Box

When students experience or notice an act of kindness, they jot it down on a piece of paper and put it in the Compliment Box. At the end of the day, I read the notes aloud. These treasured notes are then saved in each student's portfolio.

Self-Portraits

Students are asked to draw a detailed picture of themselves. Around the portrait, students write words that describe themselves physically and personally. These are displayed on a bulletin board titled "Getting to Know You" and later become the cover of the students' portfolios.

Class Constitution

At the beginning of the year, we also spend time developing a clear sense of each individual's needs and learning styles within the large group context. Using attitude and learning surveys, students reflect on what helps and hinders their learning. Students work individually and in small groups to list the rights that they feel are important, elaborating on their rationale. These lists are then presented to the whole class. As a class, we synthesize the small group lists into a whole class list of ten rights. This becomes our class constitution. The following is this year's edition.

> We, the Fifth Graders of Room Eight, have established the following rights for the purpose of creating a learning environment that is a positive place to be and challenges us to reach our highest potentials.
>
> 1. The right to be imaginative and original.
> 2. The right to work in peace and quiet when necessary.
> 3. The right to express ourselves and be heard.
> 4. The right not to be copied.
> 5. The right to have a recess.
> 6. The right to privacy.
> 7. The right to remain silent.
> 8. The right to bear materials.
> 9. The right to be safe.
> 10. The right to learn.

Setting the Stage for Literature Circles

We begin to prepare for literature circles by discussing the purposes of reading and how we can become successful readers. This year, the children came up with the list in Figure 8-1.

Needs to Become Successful Readers

We need to feel we are important to the group.

We need to feel we belong.

When we feel capable, we will take more risks.

We need to listen to each other.

We need a lot of time to read.

We need a lot of time to talk about what we read.

Figure 8-1 Needs to Become Successful Readers

Elizabeth made personal connections about reading when she wrote wistfully:

> Reading is important to me because I get to learn things I've never even for one minute thought about before. I can learn about the past, the present, and future. Sometimes I read things I never, never realized, like how terrible the past was at times. I was shocked when I read *War Comes to Willy Freeman.* Sometimes I feel less lonely like when I read *Are You There God, It's Me Margaret?* She was scared about moving. Margaret had to leave her friends and home and now so am I and this scares me. A lot. I have practically lived on Bainbridge Island all my life. It's all I remember. It has all my good memories. And now I'm leaving it.

We also invite parents and community members into our classroom to share with us how they use reading, writing, math, and science in their lives. The interviews provide powerful opportunities for the students to attach a real purpose to the concepts and skills learned at school. The students then publish this information in an expanded version of our classroom community book.

Next, I ask the students to booktalk their favorite books. We discuss the poetry and magic created by words. We admire and are inspired by challenging life stories. Students empathize with protagonists and react verbally to nasty antagonists. In these conversations, students become aware that others have also experienced similar joys, sorrow, fears, and laughter from books. Together we make a class list of the attributes of a good book. (See Figure 8-2.)

Attributes of a Good Book

- The beginning should be interesting and get the reader's attention.
- The characters should do things in an interesting way.
- The characters should have at least one big problem and have a hard time solving the problem.
- The characters should be so well described that you can imagine them like someone you know well or don't want to know well.
- The story is so good, you wish it would never end and it makes you read very slowly at the end.
- There should be several parts that make your heart go faster or slower.

Figure 8-2 Attributes of a Good Book

The children then compile their ideas about why they would like to talk about books (See Figure 8-3).

Reasons to Talk About Books

- to voice our ideas
- to learn about other people's ideas
- to sort out our ideas and toss them around and see how they turn out
- to understand ourselves and each other better
- to understand the world better

Figure 8-3 Reasons to Talk About Books

Together the students and I study current reading research. We read articles about how comprehension is enhanced when all the language processes are used: reading, writing, speaking, and listening. Students are intrigued by research that states that discussion reinforces long-term memory and improves higher-order thinking skills. They learn that readers who articulate their understandings and learnings to others have a greater chance of recalling that information at a later date. We make a joint commitment to make reading real literature an integral part of our classroom.

Beginning Literature Circles

We begin our first sets of literature circles by using familiar picture books. Based on Regie Routman's definition in *Invitations*

(1991), I define literature circles as a place where every student has an opportunity to speak and be heard when students discuss a book they have all read. Circles are meant to be lively and stimulating. The students are responsible for the direction of the conversation in the literature circles. Each student comes prepared with a written or artistic response to use as a springboard for conversation. They decide what to discuss; I act as a guide and fellow reader. I want them to have a choice about their reading because, by following their interests, they are more apt to become passionate, lifelong readers. I will now briefly outline our structure for literature circles since other chapters have covered this topic in detail.

Once we've finished the literature circles with picture books, I select multiple copies of several books on a single theme, topic, or genre. These books cover several reading "levels" and include areas of student interest. Literature circles are developed around themes such as survival, personal growth, or friendship. Other literature circles revolve around genres such as historical fiction, science fiction, or fantasy. Literature circle discussions also enrich our content area studies of flight, inventions, the brain, great scientists, and the environment. Informational materials, such as textbooks, newspapers, and CD-ROM programs, supplement students' understanding about various time periods. The interplay between novels and reference materials gives students a deeper and more lasting understanding of history. Eventually, I hope to collect multiple copies of high-quality content area books so that students will have a common frame of reference.

I introduce each book by giving short book talks or reading an exciting or interesting passage. Students then sign up for their first three choices. I organize groups according to book choice and behaviors. Once all the students have their novels, the group meets and chooses a facilitator. The group then decides which pages to read for the following day's discussion. After reading the section, students respond in their journals in preparation for the next day's literature circles.

We continue in this manner until the book is completed, which usually takes two to four weeks. We then start a two-week cycle of self-selected individual reading, during which students independently read a novel of their choice. During this period, I hold individual conferences with students about their literature circle participation, response journals, and projects.

Encouraging Positive Group Dynamics

To develop positive group dynamics, we discuss the learning process in general. I have the children list activities that feel natural to them. They usually come up with activities such as walking, bike riding, and swimming. We talk about how they learned to do those things. They discovered that for each activity there is an awkward, difficult phase. With effort and practice, however, the skill becomes so natural that they no longer even think about it. We connect this activity to our plans for literature circles. We discuss how they may have to go through a difficult, unnatural phase as they learn the group skills necessary for natural conversations. The four skills we focus on are:

- facilitating a group discussion
- empathetic and reflective listening
- clarifying for greater understanding
- debriefing and self-reflection

I provide a basic definition of each term in class. As the children practice each skill, they enhance the definitions by using their own words and meanings. The following are the students' definitions and my descriptions of the skills they practice.

Facilitating: The art of leading a discussion and ensuring that all members have an equal opportunity to voice ideas.

At the beginning of literature circles, I ask one group to practice while the other students observe. I participate as if I were a student facilitator, modeling effective speaking and listening. Afterward, I ask the observers for comments about positive and negative behaviors. We talk about the effect of these behaviors. Then we replay the same conversation with the students role-playing the skill. With the third round, I role-play a student with negative and distracting behaviors, so the other members and the facilitator can practice refocusing that student. For the rest of the year, students take turns as facilitators during literature circle discussions. These group leaders place a card with the reminders listed in Figure 8-4 on their desk.

The Facilitator:

- ensures that all members participate and have an equal opportunity to voice their thoughts.
- maintains his/her own enthusiasm and keeps up a lively pace.
- ensures that the group stays on track.

Figure 8-4 Role of Facilitator

Empathetic and Reflective Listening: The process of entering fully, through your imagination, into another person's feelings, to put yourself into the other person's shoes. The act of listening to another person is a good way to show that you value that person.

You not only hear the other person's ideas, but you also hear the emotions behind them. To communicate your understanding of another person's meaning.

We role-play positive and negative verbal language and eye contact, discussing which behaviors encourage us to continue, and which block constructive talk. We discuss how people feel when they are "put down." We list negative statements: "That's dumb, why would you think THAT?" "Ms. Kamber, Jason is only on page . . . he's so slow." "Do I have to be in a group with Sarah? She just sits there." We then contrast these with more positive statements. We discuss stock phrases, such as "good idea" or "excellent," which become hollow when overused. We brainstorm ways to disagree effectively, and then practice the suggested techniques. The more students listen to and encourage each other, the more likely they are to feel valued and accepted. The following are examples of empathetic response:

> "I can see why you are upset. Gangs scare me too."

> "You're happy because we're reading a book about a girl who is not a wimp. I kind of like it too."

> "You're bored because you already know this, but I never heard of it before. What exactly does it mean, 'heavier than air'?"   .

> "I understand. You think it was just as bad for Sam to steal his father's gun as it was for the Tories to steal the Rebels' food."

> "Your explanation is that if you apply more energy to the thrust, you will increase the speed of the plane, as long as the other variables don't change."

Clarifying: *Asking questions to understand each other and the world better.*

We avoid asking questions that interrogate another member's knowledge. Interrogation implies inequity between group members and builds walls that block free-flowing conversation and risk-taking. Our main focus is to understand each other and the book at a deeper level. This is best achieved by talk that goes beyond recall and involves the highest levels of analytical thinking. Genuine needs and the desire to understand are reflected in the samples that follow:

> "Your great-grandparents lived there? What was China like then? Do you know what it is like now?"

> "Does anyone know what 'socialist' means?"

> "What do you mean by his 'dad had to put up with a lot of mockery'? What is mockery?"

Debriefing/Self-Reflection: *To share observations about the literature circle experience. To consider what has been done well, and to make decisions about what needs to be improved. To think over possible strategies and to set goals.*

Debriefing is an extremely valuable element of literature circles in our classroom. Debriefing provides the opportunities for students to take responsibility for their learning. As students review their literature circles, they analyze what they learned and which strategies worked best. Immediately after our literature discussions, I ask students to write a response. Later, those comments can be shared with the whole class, in small groups, or individually.

During the debriefing, students discuss the highlights, the challenges, and the strategies that would improve the next set of literature circles. The students become quite skilled at recognizing their individual and group needs and at working to effect change. They learn that reflection is a valuable tool for improving learning. For example, early in the year, many of the students' debriefing comments focused on behavioral issues about someone other than themselves; someone was not paying attention, another was too controlling, still another was not participating at all. As a class, we brainstormed solutions to these problems. They decided it would be helpful if I would sit outside of the groups and tally the number of responses given by each member during the literature circle. I also took anecdotal notes on the types of responses I heard. Later, I shared the results privately with each member, setting up individual contracts with those who needed the most significant change. The changes in behaviors were dramatic; awareness and follow-through had been the key. Later in the year, students' needs became increasingly more introspective, and focused more on personal skills than on group behaviors:

> I think I will try and read a little more slowly because I noticed Justen somehow learned more about the characters than I did. When I asked him how he knew that, he showed me a page with a description of Will that I didn't notice before.—Erica

> I struggled a lot again today encouraging Sharon to contribute. She looked like she really wanted to say something and her notes were prepared. I really wanted to know what she thought about Cimorene, because she might have another perspective. But no luck.—Peter

During our whole class debriefing, Peter had appropriately refrained from voicing his feelings because he didn't want to embarrass Sharon. Later he signed up for a private debriefing conference with me. With obvious sincerity, he asked, "How can I get her to stop being shy?" His question led to a thought-provoking whole class mini-lesson about learning styles, developmental stages, and how to give positive support. Peter continued to gently encourage Sharon during the next two circles, with limited success. However, several literature circles later, Sharon began to take risks and express herself more freely. During a whole class debriefing, she raised her hand and, with a huge smile, said, "Today *we* had a great discussion!" Peter and I exchanged smiles.

Participating verbally was also a challenge for Michael. Time after time, he wrote about his desire to express his thoughts in the literature circle, and his frustration that he rarely did. He always listened carefully during our whole class debriefings when we discussed effective communication strategies and continued to write goals about participation on his debriefing forms. Several months later, a more confident Michael wrote:

> Today I contributed to the group! I decided I would answer whatever anyone asked before I even got to the group. I remembered that they were not going to test me. I looked them in the eyes and was friendly. It all turned out great! I had a lot to say.

When students are asked to reflect on their skills, they become more aware of them, as evidenced in Mallory 's reflection:

> I've gotten a lot better at talking since the beginning of the year, because now I don't lay low in the group and wait until somebody else says something similar to what I wanted to say. Instead, I say what I want to say, and sometimes it can be a little too much. I know it's too much because they start looking around and flipping their pencils.

In literature circles, students often ask questions that invite a peer to consider an alternative perspective. As students express different interpretations, they must often go back to the book and reread it at a deeper level, or share background experiences to support their beliefs, as noted by Cameron and Dan during the debriefing after reading *Roll of Thunder, Hear My Cry* (Taylor, 1976).

> I said things today that other people thought differently about, which made them talk about their reasons, which made the whole talk soar! Like when I said T. J. was nice and John disagreed, we looked up places to prove it. Another important idea today was when Dan said, "I think Cassie doesn't even know why she was treated so unfair. What do you think?" I hadn't even thought about this at all, but I did then.

> When I read that the kids dug a ditch so the bus would crash I thought that was very bad, but then Anna-Lisa

showed me three different pages of times the bus driver had picked on them. I still think it was bad, but I can understand why they did it. I probably would help them. My goal will be to read more carefully.

The initial amount of time given to self-reflection and debriefing in the early months, and the sustained practice throughout the year, contribute greatly to the quality of response in literature circles. In order to prevent the self-reflection process from becoming laborious, time given to clarify personal thoughts in writing is short, perhaps 10 to 15 minutes. Oral reflections in our class usually take longer, since the children enjoy discussing strengths, examining attitudes and feelings, and generating ideas for improvement. To encourage such reflection, I am careful not to criticize or evaluate their reflections. Instead, I listen, clarify, and reflect their ideas in order to create a safe, risk-taking environment.

Nurturing Reflective and Thoughtful Response

Students need time to consider their feelings and to think about a book at their own pace. The students created the following definitions:

>**Reflective/thinking:** *The act of studying, pondering and thinking carefully.*

>**Thoughtful response:** *To communicate one's ideas in a clear, detailed manner through conversation, writing, or an aesthetic response.*

I ask the students to come prepared for literature circles with a response that clearly and sincerely expresses their reactions and questions about the book. Students may or may not refer to their responses during literature circles, but having the time to think carefully before the discussion increases student confidence and ensures that each student has something to contribute to the group. Initially, I have the students focus on thoughtful oral and written responses. Gradually we incorporate artistic response such as illustrations, three-dimensional scenes, and poetry, as Lisa Norwick and Barry Hoonan describe in Chapters 10 and 11. The students look forward to seeing how classmates chose to respond to books. Such responses are wonderful springboards for literature circle discussions. Both the written responses and illustrations become more expressive as the students continue to learn about depth and detail.

During our first literature circles, children often made quick judgment statements such as, "I liked the book," or "It was good." Few backed up their judgments with reasons or examples. Challenging a child to consider "why" she thinks something and to seek greater depth can be a delicate task. The child may take your challenge to be an insinuation that her thinking is not up to par, or that your thinking is better. In order to encourage children to seek greater depth, not only must you believe all children are valuable, important human beings capable of great thought, but you must also genuinely convince the children that this is true. Of course, the students have to want to improve their ability to express and probe themselves. Many children are uncomfortable about articulating their feelings in the beginning, both in writing and orally, since for so long they have relied on a teacher to come up with the questions and correct answers. I find that using sample journal responses from previous students is a valuable learning tool. Using student models, I label statements of elaboration and clarification, and point out details that support an opinion. Later, when the students write their own responses, they know my expectations. While they are writing or creating their literature responses, I use "Post-it" notes or hold private conferences in which I usually ask, "Tell me more. Help me to understand. Explain what you mean." Beneath my prompts lies my faith in their ability to prepare high-quality responses.

Initially, I use structured prompts and then gradually remove the prompts as students become more skilled. I consistently encourage students to back up their reaction statements by selecting interesting ideas, passages, plot changes, vocabulary, or descriptions of characters or settings from the book to share with their group. As a class, we create a list of prompts, which students keep in their reading notebook (see Figure 8-5). (See Chapter 4 for ways to encourage deeper response in emergent readers.)

Journal Prompts

- What was your reaction? Why?
- Do you like the book? Why or why not?
- Do you think this story could really happen?
- Who is your favorite character and why?
- Who do the characters remind you of?
- Why do you think (a character) did . . .?
- What would you have done?
- What was your favorite part?

Figure 8-5 Journal Prompts

During literature circles, my role is to observe and record what I see and hear. I record examples of effective group dynamics and depth of response. I try to take five journals home each evening so that I can review them and assess student growth. The response journals contain a wealth of information about individual student comprehension and attitudes. I use my observations to assess students' growth for several purposes:

- to plan future mini-lessons
- to help students learn more effectively
- to evaluate my teaching and student learning
- to establish priorities and set goals
- to communicate academic and personal growth with students and parents

Benefits of Literature Circles

I believe literature circles are invaluable. Literary conversations reveal so much about the personal characteristics of each student that otherwise may have been missed. Students' interests and quality of thinking become visible, as does their confidence and knowledge of learning. With that confidence comes a higher responsibility toward learning. All students have a voice and they have opportunities to use that voice often. When students share very personal thoughts, ideas, and feelings, a stronger bond develops among class members. Students are intrigued by the different points of view expressed during a literature discussion. I've often observed during literature circles that students increase their understanding of an idea by talking it out with someone else. Literature circles using informational books move students beyond basic recall and detachment, toward a deeper understanding of causal relationship and deeper reasoning. Informational literature circles give students a personal orientation rather than submerging them in trivial facts and dates.

Refreshing ideas and risk-taking are frequently the norm, as students' confidence in their own voice grows with each literature circle. Sometimes quiet children or ones who struggle in school will surprise me with the quality of their responses. The positive reaction of the group enhances those children's sense of self, to the point where they may voice their ideas again and again.

One of the wonders of literature circles is how students can put themselves into a story. They become the characters they read about; they experience the book as if they are there. The intensity of their involvement reflects both their development and the growing responsibility they feel for their own learning, as well as their love of reading. Providing children with the time to talk about books is perhaps one of the most satisfying experiences I have had as a teacher. The value of literature circles is captured in a poem written by Anna-Lisa, a student from our class:

We read the same books,
And I've heard your ideas,
And I wonder, why do we
Think so differently?

We read the same books,
And I've heard your ideas,
And I wonder, why do we
Think so alike?

I wonder if these questions
Will ever be answered, but
wondering about these answers
causes me to know who I am.

References

Dahl, Roald. (1984). *Boy.* New York: Penguin.

Filipovic, Zlata. (1994). *Zlata's Diary: A Child's Life in Sarajevo.* New York: Viking.

Goodlad, John. (1984). *A Place Called School.* New York: McGraw-Hill.

Hyman, Trina Schart. (1981). *Trina Schart Hyman: Self–Portrait.* New York: Addison–Wesley.

Lindberg, Anne Morrow. (1955). *Gift from the Sea.* New York: Pantheon.

Routman, Regie. (1991). *Invitations: Changing as Teachers and Learners K–12.* Portsmouth, NH: Heinemann.

Taylor, Mildred. (1976). *Roll of Thunder, Hear My Cry.* New York: Puffin.

Chapter 9

Choosing Books for Literature Circles

*⊅ Great
Book lists in
this chapter.*

Dianne Monson

When I recommend books for literature circles, I know they must be the best books available, those that we want to be sure children come into contact with. That presents a special challenge because these must be books that deal with themes children care about and they must also represent excellence in writing and illustrating. In this chapter, I will highlight four genres of children's literature often used for literature circles and discuss the qualities we need to keep in mind when we select books for literature discussion. I will also point out some of the characteristics that make each type of literature unique and show how children may be encouraged to include these in their journals and discussions. In order to demonstrate the qualities of good literature, I will discuss books that I think of as landmarks, books that I tend to use as a measuring stick for others of that genre. By showing you my preferences, I hope to encourage you to define your own set of standards and to identify your own best examples of literature to use as standards for book selection. I will also include short lists of recently published books that you might want to consider when you put together your classroom book sets. You may also want to explore the list of books provided in the annotated bibliography for additional titles.

To decide whether a book is of high quality, I like to ask three questions:

1. Does the book succeed in arousing my emotions and will it arouse children's emotions?
2. Is the book well-written?
3. Is the book meaningful?

These questions (Purves & Monson, 1984, p. 152) take into account the underlying characteristics of good writing. The first question is very important because it indicates that, in fiction and biography, the characters and their actions must engage us; in informational material, the topic must be intriguing enough to capture and keep our attention.

The second question involves the techniques that an author uses to construct the piece. Quality fiction includes excellent use of description to create believable settings and the effective use of a combination of description and dialogue to reveal characterization. In informational books, quality relates to skillful use of words to convey information clearly, and carefully chosen illustrative material that enhances the information presented in the text.

The third question gets at the importance of themes that deal with universals of life in a way that children can relate to.

These questions are useful for us in book selection and, in time, they may become important questions for students to discuss as they critically examine books they are reading. Although the first question pertains more to fiction and biography than to informational books, all three can help to describe any book we truly value.

When we select picture books, we must be sure the illustrations are beautifully designed, with appropriate attention given to line, color, and the balance of text and pictures on each page. Since we want students to have book experiences that involve the senses and evoke images, it is especially important that the illustrations match the tone of the story. A lively, humorous story often calls for illustrations in a cartoon-like style with vivid colors. Harry Allard and James Marshall's *Miss Nelson is Missing* (1977) is a good example of that. The more subtle humor of Cynthia Rylant's *The Relatives Came* (1985) is underscored by Stephen Gammell's amusing illustrations done in quiet colors, but showing the rollicking good time had by all. The serious images suggested in David Adler's *A Picture Biography of Anne Frank* (1993) are rendered in painterly style by Karen Ritz. Her illustrations are detailed enough to evoke a clear sense of time and place and the portrait style lets us know much about Anne Frank and the people she lived with. In all of these books, the artistic style is so well suited to the text that the total effect is a book that children can respond to visually as well as emotionally. You might want to keep these qualities in mind as you select picture books for discussion.

Selecting Traditional Literature

In discussing types of children's books, it makes sense to begin with traditional literature, since the storytelling style of the oral tradition underlies all of literature. Traditional literature embraces a wide range of material, including folk tales, fables, myths and legends, and it deals with elemental feelings—those universal beliefs and emotions that cut across cultures and take many forms, including fear, love, hate, wisdom, and foolishness. Let's see how it works when we apply the three selection questions to traditional literature.

Does the book succeed in arousing my emotions?

So many themes in folk literature are emotionally laden. The age-old tales seem as entertaining to us today as they were to the folk who told the stories hundreds of years ago. As readers we are interested in folk characters who have a problem to solve or a quest to make. We want to relive the adventure with them, perhaps because we can see something of our own lives in these folk characters and their challenges. We also enjoy stories that bring to mind similar tales from other cultures. The intellectual stimulation of comparing *Lon Po Po* (Young, 1989) to *Little Red Riding Hood*, for example, adds to the fun of the story.

Is the story well written?

Traditional tales are meant to be told or read aloud, so the style of writing is very important. The stories children really enjoy hearing and reading capture the oral tradition in storytelling style. In some cases, the language reflects the old-time style of talk. That produces memorable phrases like this ending to *The Three Billy Goats Gruff*, "so, snip, snap, snout, my tale's told out," in Marcia Brown's version (1957), a retelling that is faithful to the original Norwegian text. To assess the quality of writing style, always read part of the story aloud. If the reading goes smoothly and has a comfortable storytelling feel to it, chances are the reteller has done a good job with style. A related criterion for selecting a folk tale is that it must be an authentic interpretation of the original version. That means that the reteller should give us some indication of the source of the original tale, as Paul Goble does in the introductory material to his retellings of Lakota legends. Children can learn to search for this information, which may be included in a foreword or afterword, on the copyright page, or even on the jacket flap.

Since traditional literature is often published in picture book form, we want to be sure the illustrations are respectful to the text, capturing the mood of the story and including visual events that are authentically associated with the story and its origins.

One of Goble's books, *Dream Wolf* (1990), is a book I look to as an example of good literary and artistic strength. The text reads aloud in a natural, storytelling style. It carries the story line and brings a sense of adventure to the reading experience. The wonderful illustrations capture the cultural identity of the tale, with motifs and colors that are authentic. Indeed, the illustrations utilize many of the same colors and motifs that are evident in beadwork and other art produced by people of the Lakota nation.

Another measuring stick for me, from traditional literature, is John Steptoe's *Mufaro's Beautiful Daughters* (1987). The storyline is graceful and leads easily from one episode to the next. The illustrations are exceptional in design and capture the essential differences of the two girls, while they also present a lush African landscape that transports us to the time and place of the story.

Verna Aardema's *Why Mosquitoes Buzz in People's Ears* (1975), illustrated by Leo and Diane Dillon, does a remarkable job of recreating a story in a stylized fashion with illustrations that pull us into the sequence of happenings that make up that cumulative tale. Children who have some experience in visual literacy will notice the use of vibrant colors and strong lines in these illustrations, and the way movement in the pictures reflects and extends the movement from one page to the next in this sequential tale. The storytelling style of the tale is also noteworthy. In Aardema's retelling, the words used to describe the movements of the animals (as "wasa wusa" for the snake) add an interesting sound effect.

Is the book meaningful?

In judging folk literature, we can simply ask what the tale is all about. Does it tell a story of kindness repaid, as in *The Frog Prince*, or the triumph of wisdom over foolishness, as in *The Three Little Pigs*? Or is it a pourqoui tale that gives an interpretation of some natural event, as in Gerald McDermott's *Anansi the Spider* (1972), in which the ending tells us why the moon is in the sky each night? The meanings embedded in traditional literature are old understandings. When we select such literature, we ask only that the reteller has carefully researched the tale and retold it in clear and graceful prose so that the underlying theme is easy to comprehend.

Looking at the Structure of Traditional Literature

According to the framework of the Nebraska Literature Curriculum (1966), there are four motifs that serve as the underpinnings for all of literature: a journey from home and back, a journey from home to confrontation with a monster, the rescue from a harsh home, and the parable of the wise and foolish beast. It is easy to think of folk tales, myths, and legends that illustrate the journey theme, particularly when a monster is involved. Students may enjoy identifying these motifs and discussing them in literature circles. Such discussions can help to develop a sense of structure in stories.

The journey motif in *Little Red Riding Hood*, *Hansel and Gretel*, *Goldilocks*, and *The Three Little Pigs* provides a tension of events that keeps the stories moving. Children will enjoy looking for this motif in other stories. The rescue theme is clear in the many versions of Cinderella, including *Lon Po Po* (1989), retold and illustrated by Ed Young. The Fables of Aesop are probably the clearest examples of the wise/foolish beast conflict, but it is also easy to identify in stories like *The Three Little Pigs* and the tales about Anansi the spider from West Africa and the Caribbean. In addition to these motifs, folk tales are often characterized by repetition of three, four, or seven parallel events. The repetition helps to make the stories memorable for children who read or hear them and provides a framework for their own retellings. In conjunction with their reading for literature circles, children may enjoy making their own lists of stories with three, four, or seven repetitions and sharing them with others.

Figure 9-1 lists some recently published traditional literature worth considering for literature circle discussions.

Traditional Literature

Picture Books
Anansi and the Moss-covered Rock (1988)—Eric Kimmel
The Cat's Purr (1985)—Ashley Bryan
Dreamcatcher (1992)—Audrey Osofsky
Lon Po Po (1989)—Ed Young
Sungura and Leopard (1993)—Barbara Knutson

Picture Books for Older Readers
Dream Wolf (1990)—Paul Goble
Ladder to the Sky (1989)—Barbara Esbensen
Mufaro's Beautiful Daughters (1987)—John Steptoe
Raven (1993)—Gerald McDermott
The Woman Who Fell from the Sky (1993)—John Bierhorst

Collected Stories
The Dark Thirty (1992)—Patricia M. McKissack
Cut from the Same Cloth (1993)—Robert D. San Souci
The People Could Fly (1985)—Virginia Hamilton

Figure 9-1 Traditional Literature

Selecting Fantasy

As a genre, fantasy has several links to folk literature. Hans Christian Andersen's stories are the most important bridge between traditional literature and contemporary fantasy. They reflect the folk tales he heard as a child as well as the creations of his own fertile imagination. With his gift for storytelling, he produced such stories as *The Tin Soldier* and *The Little Fir Tree*, the first tales in which inanimate objects revealed their feelings through human speech. It is easy to see this influence on books of modern fantasy such as *The Tub People* (1989) by Pam Conrad and *The Velveteen Rabbit* (1922, 1975) by Marjorie Williams.

Just as traditional literature encompasses forms such as myths, legends, and fairy tales, fantasy also encompasses a variety of forms that include science fiction and high fantasy. In science fiction, the time is generally the future and the setting is often influenced by mechanization more sophisticated than what we now know to be possible. In high fantasy, the setting may be a new world, as in *A Wizard of Earthsea* (LeGuin, 1968). Here, the author has created a kingdom called Earthsea and it encompasses all of the story action. In other high fantasy, the setting is contemporary, but elements of the distant past are brought in through creation of a character who appears over many generations. Susan Cooper uses this technique in her series, *The Dark is Rising* (1973). Will's unusual vision sets him apart; his ability to cross the boundaries of time and place creates the fantasy in the story. These books are successful because the authors are completely consistent in their treatment of the qualities that maintain the fantasy world.

When we select fantasy, we must assess the author's effectiveness in creating a story with one or more elements of fantasy and keeping those elements consistent throughout the book. That consistency is most important, and it must show through in the illustrations as well as in the text. If we ask ourselves three criteria questions about books of fantasy, the answers might go something like this:

Does the book succeed in arousing my emotions?

A book like *Owen* (1993) by Kevin Henkes succeeds in arousing my sense of humor, as the neighborhood busybody tries to break Owen's dependence on having his blanket with him all the time. It also makes me feel sympathy for the poor little mouse and to recall objects that have been important to children I know. I think the book will arouse children's emotions on that basis, too.

On a deeper level, when I read *The Giver* (Lowry, 1993), I am drawn into Jonas's feelings and I experience anguish along with him as he tries to decide whether to run away from the community that has been his home. A well-written fantasy should offer characters and events we can relate to, even though it is necessary for us to suspend disbelief in order to enter into the fantasy world.

Is the book well written?

In order to write fantasy well, an author must create settings and characters so vividly that we believe in them. That presents a particular challenge when an author must give us the details to help us see the small world of Mary Norton's *The Borrowers* (1953) or a future world, as in John Christopher's *The White Mountains* (1967). Details are also important in describing characters such as Constance the Badger in *Redwall* (Jacques, 1986) or Pippi in *Pippi Longstocking* (Lindgren, 1950). Brian Jacques lets us learn about Constance's personality by showing how she interacts with the others in the band and how courageously she faces their enemies. Astrid Lindgren introduces us to the super girl Pippi through a series of humorous anecdotes that show how strong and independent she is. Both books have plenty of good, descriptive writing. In *Doctor De Soto* (1982), William Steig augments the descriptions of the mouse dentist and his wicked fox patient with illustrations in which facial expressions help to show what the two are like.

Structure of Fantasy

How does an author create a story that is fantastic rather than realistic? Generally speaking, authors have two devices at hand. They may choose to manipulate either a character, as in the creation of an imp in Susan Cooper's *The Boggart* (1993), or a set of characters, as in the small people in *The Borrowers* (Norton, 1953). The character(s) may be changed in size, they may take on the characteristics of supernatural beings, or assume powers beyond human nature, as in *Pippi Longstocking* (Lindgren, 1950). They may become lovable monsters like those in Maurice Sendak's *Where the Wild Things Are* (1963). When the author is able to give these characters enough personality so that we care about them, the result is a book that draws readers in so that they relive the story, without a thought as to whether it is real or fantastic. Children who come to the literature circle ready to talk about how the author makes the small people in *The Borrowers* seem real are beginning to be aware of the way authors use description and dialogue to create characters. They may bring examples of the description and dialogue to share in discussion.

In addition to manipulation of character forms, authors may also create fantasy by manipulating the time and place of a story, essentially the setting. For example, *Tom's Midnight Garden* (Pearce, 1958) becomes a fantasy because Tom discovers that when the old clock strikes thirteen, he can step into the back garden and see it as it was generations earlier. The setting of *The Giver* (Lowry, 1993) is clearly futuristic and the complete control of people's lives is one element of that time shift. So is the creation of the controlled environment in which Jonas and his family live. In *A Wrinkle in Time* (L'Engle, 1962), the fantasy element is developed through time shifts and creation of a fantastic place away from our planet. The boldness of those creations and their believability contribute to the strength of the story. Students may notice how the author enriches the fantasy with description of the setting, such as showing how small people in *The Borrowers* make use of old postage stamps or broken pieces of glass to decorate their homes. As they become aware of these details, record them in their journals, and share them in literature circles, they also appreciate how important setting is in fantasy.

Other books of fantasy you may want to consider for literature circle sets appear in Figure 9-2. When you read them, see how well you think they succeed in arousing your emotions and whether you find them well-written and meaningful.

Fantasy

Picture Books
A Bargain for Frances (1970)—Russell Hoban
The Boy Who Swallowed Snakes (1994)—Laurence Yep
Martha Calling (1994)—Susan Meddaugh
Owen (1993)—Kevin Henkes
Polar Express (1985)—Chris Van Allsburg

Picture Books for Older Readers
Bub or the Very Best Thing (1994)—Natalie Babbit
The King's Equal (1992)—Katherine Paterson
Swamp Angel (1994)—Susan Isaacs
Tar Beach (1991)—Faith Ringgold
Zeke Pippin (1994)—William Steig

Easy Chapter Books
Catwings Return (1989)—Ursula LeGuin
The Sherluck Bones Mystery—Detective Book 1
    (1981)—Jim & Mary Razzi
Stories about Rosie (1986)—Cynthia Voigt
When Bluebell Sang (1989)—Lisa Campbell Ernst

Chapter Books
The Boggart (1993)—Susan Cooper
Forest (1993)—Janet Lisle
The Giver (1993)—Lois Lowry
Maniac Magee (1990)—Jerry Spinelli
Pippi Longstocking (1950)—Astrid Lindgren
The Princess in the Pigpen (1989)—Jane Resh Thomas
A Taste of Smoke (1993)—Marion Dane Bauer
Tuck Everlasting (1975)—Natalie Babbit
The White Mountain (1967) and series—John Christopher

Figure 9-2 Fantasy

Selecting Realistic Fiction

Realistic fiction needs strong characters in order to be effective. In fact, these stories are often character-driven, with character behaviors and relationships among characters influencing the plot of the story. The problems and the way people try to deal with them emerge as story themes. Children can often relate to the characters in realistic fiction and to the problems they have to deal with, so these books are good choices for journaling and for literature circle discussions.

Realistic fiction includes historical fiction as well as contemporary fiction. Criteria for choosing the two types of literature are very similar, though the author's attention to details of setting is generally more important in historical fiction since it is necessary to establish a clear sense of time and place. One book of historical fiction that is often used for literature circles is Lois Lowry's *Number the Stars* (1989). Let us see how it is rated when we ask the three basic questions for book selection.

Does the book succeed in arousing my emotions?

The tension of the story and the wartime intrigue make this a fast-paced book that is likely to engage most readers. More important, Annemarie and Ellen, the two main characters, are very real people. Lois Lowry has shown us their strong friendship and also the things that both girls fear, the worries that haunt their everyday lives. I find that the key episodes evoke strong images in my mind and draw me into the events that are changing the lives of both girls.

Is the book well written?

Realistic fiction is judged by the quality of characterization and by the skill with which the author describes the setting and develops a strong story line in which each episode leads toward the resolution of the story conflict. Style is also important, because the dialogue must seem natural and the flow of language throughout must be smooth when read aloud.

Number the Stars is strong in all three areas. The characterization is marked by dialogue passages that really let us know how Ellen and Annemarie act toward one another and what they feel about the Nazi occupation of their country. The plot of the story, based on an actual event, is truly captivating. The scene where the soldiers come to search Annemarie's house is a stark depiction of tyrants invading the family's privacy. The later scene, where Annemarie brings the special handkerchief to the ship and is almost captured, is another gripping part of the story. All of the episodes link together so well that the story moves forward seamlessly. Lowry's description of wartime Denmark includes the kinds of details and anecdotes that children need in order to have some sense of what life was like under those circumstances.

Is the story meaningful?

The theme of the story is so clearly developed that the story will have meaning for most readers. The oppression of innocent people by the soldiers of a fascist government—the unmistakable opposition of good and evil—cannot be ignored. The theme is played out in the dangers encountered by people fleeing for their lives and by those trying to help them escape. The ending of the story is satisfying because the Rosens and others escaped. It is meaningful because their escape is a symbol of the triumph of right over wrong.

Structure of Realistic Fiction

The characteristics of good realistic fiction—characterization, plot, setting, and theme—provide the basis for response through journals as well as discussion. A book with strong characters presents us with people who are real to us, people we care about. We know about their joys and their fears. We know how they feel about one another. And, in well written works, we also notice how the major characters change over the period of the story. All of these can be important for children to discuss in literature circles.

Katherine Paterson's *The Great Gilly Hopkins* (1978) is a fine example of the development of characterization. Gilly is a very real girl, from her naughty behavior at the beginning of the story to the deep-down yearning for a mother she can only dream about. We watch her feelings toward Maime Trotter change from outright dislike at the outset, to acceptance and even dependency at the end of the story, as Gilly seeks to return to Trotter's loving home. That change, Gilly's maturing, is the mark of well-developed characterization. Paterson has included incidents in the story that help to reveal Gilly's point of view toward Trotter and toward other characters, as well. This revelation of feelings can be a powerful discussion focus, as students try to describe episodes of the story from Gilly's point of view and give examples of how the author lets us in on Gilly's feelings. Readers Theatre scripts, as described in Chapter 10, can also help children recognize Gilly's feelings and those of the people who must deal with her. As children are engaged in reading and interpreting dialogue, they enter into the lives of those characters and begin to feel as they feel.

Students may also find it interesting to look at changes in the characters' feelings from the beginning to the end of the book. For example, they can think of words and phrases to describe how Gilly feels about Trotter, William Ernest, Mr. Randolph and others at the beginning of the story, and how they feel about her. Then, they can do the same exercise after they finish the book. The changes in those descriptions will tell a lot about how Gilly has changed over the course of the story. Students can also read aloud passages that show how Gilly's attitudes have changed over time. As children record their responses in journals, those entries may also encourage discussion of why Gilly felt and acted as she did, and cause children to recognize that she had fears but tried to cover them up with her tough behavior. These and other strategies can help to engage children with the people and events that make realistic fiction come alive.

The books listed in Figure 9-3 may be among those you will want to consider when you add sets of realistic fiction titles to your classroom collection.

Selecting Informational Books

Informational books can provide good material for literature circle discussions, particularly those that deal with encompassing themes like ecology or episodes in the history of our country. *A River Ran Wild* (Cherry, 1992) is an informational book that I like because it contains many layers of information. It has also caught the attention of teachers who nominated it for the 1992 Teachers' Choices List of books that children should be introduced to. Let's see how well it fits our criteria for selection.

Does the book succeed in arousing my emotions?

Yes, it appeals to my concerns about ecology and extends my thinking by leading me backwards in time to look at conditions over several hundred years that have threatened the ecological balance of an area.

Is the book well written?

Since *A River Ran Wild* is an informational book, I will look at graphics and illustrations as well as text in answering the question. I'll also need to consider accuracy of text and illustrations. After studying the format of the book and reading sections of it aloud, I know I'd give it a strong rating. The information conveyed through the text is well documented, so I believe it is accurate. The information about community members involved in the drive to restore the Nashua River adds to the credibility of the book. The Author's Note at the beginning of the book gives important historical background; the Acknowledgments at the end indicate the range of specialists who contributed to the making of the book.

The artistic renderings of wildlife and the artifacts found in the region from early days are clearly presented and appear authentic. I also like the way the artist works these into frames around the paintings. The maps shown in the endpapers are very interesting, particularly because they are accompanied by a time line extending from prehistoric times through 1979. I also like the

---

Realistic Fiction

<u>Picture Books</u>

The Cabin Key (1994)—Gloria Rand
Owl Moon (1987)—Jane Yolen
Some Birthday! (1991)—Patricia Polacco
Sunshine Home (1994)—Eve Bunting
Up North at the Cabin (1992)—Marsha Chall
Where Are You Going, Manyoni? (1993)—Catherine Stock

<u>Picture Books for Older Readers</u>

Mirette on the High Wire (1992)—Emily Arnold McCully
Pepe the Lamplighter (1993)—Elisa Bartone
When Jo Louis Won the Title (1994)—Belinda Rochelle

<u>Easy Chapter Books</u>

The Comeback Dog (1981)—Jane Resh Thomas
Grandaddy and Janetta (1994)—Helen Griffith
The Hundred Dresses (1944, 1974)—Eleanor Estes
Maybe Yes, Maybe No, Maybe Maybe (1993)—Susan Patron
More Stories Julian Tells (1986)—Ann Cameron
Morning Girl (1992)—Michael Dorris
Much Ado about Aldo (1978)—Johanna Hurwitz
No One is Going to Nashville (1983)—Mavis Jukes
Sarah, Plain and Tall (1985)—Patricia MacLachlan
Skylark (1994)—Patricia MacLachlan

<u>Chapter Books</u>

Baby (1993)—Patricia MacLachlan
The Best School Day Ever (1994)—Barbara Robinson
Bound for Oregon (1994)—Jean van Leeuwen
Bull Run (1993)—Paul Fleischman
Crazy Lady! (1993)—Jane Conley
Dear Levi: Letters from the Overland Trail (1994)—
   Elvira Woodruff
Dear Mr. Henshaw (1983)—Beverly Cleary
Dragon's Gate (1993)—Laurence Yep
Flip-flop Girl (1994)—Katherine Paterson
The Great Gilly Hopkins (1978)—Katherine Paterson
Guests (1994)—Michael Dorris
Julie (1994)—Jean Craighead George
Lyddie (1991)—Katherine Paterson
Number the Stars (1989)—Lois Lowry
The Pool Party (1993)—Gary Soto
Shabanu (1989)—Suzanne Fisher Staples
Shiloh (1991)—Phyllis Reynolds Naylor

Figure 9-3 Realistic Fiction

way the author/illustrator has presented information skillfully through a combination of text and illustrations. She has managed to provide that information in a layered effect so that I can delve as deeply as I choose. This means that I can read the text and scan the full-color illustrations for basic information, or I can spend much more time studying the material presented in frames around the pictures. The illustrations, too, are of high quality. The full-color illustrations capture a sense of time and place that spans the centuries. The smaller, detailed drawings that frame the pictures reflect important details about implements used by the native people and the early settlers. This opportunity for intellectual stimulation will also be important for students who read and discuss the book in literature circles. They may be encouraged to use the library to find out more about the animals and artifacts shown in the pictures.

Is the book meaningful?

This question really asks whether the theme of the book is one that I care about. There is no doubt that the theme of ecology is a topic I want to read about and discuss with others. I hope that is also true for the students who will read and discuss this book, for it offers plenty of opportunity to bring ecology-based items from local news into the literature circle discussions.

   Now that I have satisfied my criteria for choosing this book, I need to consider how children can become involved as they read and discuss it. The historical dimension is important, so I want them to notice how the author shows change over time in that small river valley. They will see this through the illustrations and read about it in the text. Their journals may include entries that document important changes in the region from 1600 to the 1990s.

   As they look back at the historical trend, they will certainly find that factories contributed to the breakdown of the river ecology. People and housing developments have also affected rivers. Being aware of that might lead students to read newspaper articles or books like Molly Cone's *Come Back, Salmon* (1992).

   The abundance of wildlife in a region is an indication of the status of its ecosystem. Some students may be interested in learning more about the many birds and animals that inhabited the region before it was settled, and in finding out what wildlife still exists.

   A further extension would be to learn more about the implements that frame some pages in order to know what tools and household items were important to the native people of the region and to the immigrants who settled in the area. Children who read and keep journals on this book will find plenty of interesting themes and information to discuss.

   Other informational books that may provide good material for literature circles are shown in Figure 9-4.

Informational Books

Picture Books

The Great Kapok Tree (1990)—Lynne Cherry
In a Small, Small Pond (1993)—Denise Fleming
My Great Aunt Arizona (1992)—Gloria Houston

Picture Books for Older Readers

Come Back, Salmon (1992)—Molly Cone
Manatee on Location (1991)—Kathy Darling
A Picture Biography of Anne Frank (1993)—David Adler
Pueblo Boy: Growing Up in Two Worlds (1991)—Marcia
    Keegan
A River Ran Wild (1992)—Lynne Cherry
The Sacred Harvest (1992)—Gordon Reggiunti
Searching for Laura Ingalls (1993)—Kathryn Lasky &
    Maribah Knight
The Serengeti Migration: Africa's Animals on the Move
    (1994)—Lisa Lindblad
Ship (1993)—David Macaulay

Chapter Books

Across America on an Emigrant Train (1993)—Jim
    Murphy
Anne Frank: Beyond the Diary (1992)—R. van der Roll
    & R. Verhoeven
Greff, the Story of a Guide Dog (1982)—Patricia Curtis
Talking with Artists (1992)—Pat Cunningham

Figure 9-4 Informational Books

This brief overview of criteria for book selection can provide a framework for your own decisions about books for literature circles. For further guidance on selecting quality literature, you may want to refer to *A Critical Handbook of Children's Literature* (Lukens, 1995), *Essentials of Children's Literature* (Lynch-Brown & Tomlinson, 1993), and *Children and Books* (Sutherland & Arbuthnon, 1991).

As students become more sophisticated in reading critically, they may be able to use some of these criteria in selecting their own books. Teachers and students can begin to weave conversations about the qualities of genres into mini-lessons and literature circle discussions. With guidance, they may also be able to apply the criteria to their own writing, particularly at the stage of revising their work. Students may ultimately gain experience in noticing which authors are particularly good at developing the themes, characters, setting, and memorable language that make reading an important part of their lives.

References

Aardema, Verna. (1975). *Why Mosquitoes Buzz in People's Ears.* Illustrated by Leo and Diane Dillon. New York: Dial.

Adler, David A. (1993). A *Picture Biography of Anne Frank.* Illustrated by Karen Ritz. New York: Holiday House.

Allard, Harry. (1977). *Miss Nelson is Missing.* Illustrated by James Marshall. Boston: Houghton Mifflin.

Babbitt, Natalie. (1994). *Bub or the Very Best Thing.* New York: HarperCollins.

Babbitt, Natalie. (1975). *Tuck Everlasting.* New York: Farrar, Straus & Giroux.

Bartone, Elisa. (1993). *Peppe the Lamplighter.* Illustrated by Ted Lewin. New York: Lothrop, Lee & Shepard.

Bauer, Marion Dane. (1993). *A Taste of Smoke.* New York: Clarion.

Bierhorst, John. (1993). *The Woman Who Fell from the Sky.* Illustrated by Robert Andrew Parker. New York: Morrow Junior Books.

Brown, Marcia. (1957). *The Three Billy Goats Gruff.* New York: Harcourt Brace.

Bryan, Ashley. (1985). *The Cat's Purr.* New York: Atheneum.

Bunting, Eve. (1994). *Sunshine Home.* Illustrated by Diane de Groat. New York: Clarion.

Cameron, Ann. (1986). *More Stories Julian Tells.* Illustrated by Ann Strugnell. New York: Knopf.

Chall, Marsha. (1992). *Up North at the Cabin.* Illustrated by Steve Johnson. New York: Lothrop, Lee & Shepard.

Cherry, Lynne. (1992). *A River Ran Wild: An Environmental Story.* San Diego, CA: Harcourt Brace Jovanovich.

Cherry, Lynne. (1990). *The Great Kapok Tree.* San Diego, CA: Harcourt Brace Jovanovich.

Christopher, John. (1967). *The White Mountain.* New York: Macmillan.

Cleary, Beverly. (1983). *Dear Mr. Henshaw.* New York: Dell.

Cone, Molly. (1992). *Come Back, Salmon.* Photographs by Sidnee Wheelwright. San Francisco: Sierra Club Books for Children.

Conley, Jane. (1993). *Crazy Lady!* New York: HarperCollins.

Conrad, Pam. (1989). *The Tub People.* Illustrated by Richard Egielski. New York: Harper & Row.

Cooper, Susan. (1993). *The Boggart.* New York: Margaret McElderry Books.

Cooper, Susan. (1973). *The Dark is Rising.* New York: Macmillan.

Cunningham, Pat. (Ed.). (1992). *Talking with Artists.* New York: Bradbury.

Curtis, Patricia. (1982). *Greff, the Story of a Guide Dog.* Photographs by Mary Bloom. New York: Lodestar.

Darling, Kathy. (1991). *Manatee on Location*. Photographs by Tara Darling. New York: Lothrop, Lee & Shepard.

Dorris, Michael. (1994). *Guests*. New York: Hyperion.

Dorris, Michael. (1992). *Morning Girl*. New York: Hyperion.

Ernst, Lisa Campbell. (1989). *When Bluebell Sang*. New York: Bradbury.

Esbensen, Barbara. (1989). *Ladder to the Sky*. Illustrated by Helen K. Davie. Boston: Little, Brown.

Estes, Eleanor. (1944, 1974). *The Hundred Dresses*. Illustrated by Louis Slobodkin. New York: Harcourt Brace Jovanovich.

Fleischman, Paul. (1993). *Bull Run*. New York: HarperCollins.

Fleming, Denise. (1993). *In a Small, Small Pond*. New York: Holt.

George, Jean Craighead. (1994). *Julie*. New York: HarperCollins.

Goble, Paul. (1990). *Dream Wolf*. New York: Bradbury.

Griffith, Helen V. (1994). *Grandaddy and Janetta*. Illustrated by James Stevenson. New York: Greenwillow.

Hamilton, Virginia. (1985). *The People Could Fly*. Illustrated by Leo and Diane Dillon. New York: Knopf.

Henkes, Kevin. (1993). *Owen*. New York: Greenwillow.

Hoban, Russell. (1970). *A Bargain for Frances*. Illustrated by Lilian Hoban. New York: Harper & Row.

Houston, Gloria. (1992). *My Great Aunt Arizona*. Illustrated by Susan Condie Lamb. New York: HarperCollins.

Hurwitz, Johanna. (1978). *Much Ado about Aldo*. Illustrated by John Wallner. New York: Morrow.

Isaac, Susan. (1994). *Swamp Angel*. Illustrated by Paul Zelinski. New York: Dutton.

Jacques, Brian. (1986). *Redwall*. New York: Philomel.

Jukes, Mavis. (1983). *No One is Going to Nashville*. Illustrated by Lloyd Bloom. New York: Knopf.

Keegan, Marcia. (1991). *Pueblo Boy: Growing Up in Two Worlds*. New York: Cobblehill Books.

Kimmel, Eric. (1988). *Anansi and the Moss-Covered Rock*. Illustrated by Janet Stevens. New York: Holiday House.

Knutson, Barbara. (1993). *Sungura and Leopard*. Boston: Little, Brown.

Lasky, Kathryn & Knight, Maribah. (1993). *Searching for Laura Ingalls*. Photographs by Christopher G. Knight. New York: Macmillan.

LeGuin, Ursula. (1989). *Catwings Return*. Illustrated by S. D. Schindler. New York: Orchard.

LeGuin, Ursula. (1968). *A Wizard of Earthsea*. Berkeley, CA: Parnassus Press.

L'Engle, Madeleine. (1962). *A Wrinkle in Time*. New York: Farrar, Straus and Giroux.

Lindblad, Lisa. (1994). *The Serengeti Migration: Africa's Animals on the Move*. Photographs by Sven-Olof Lindblad. New York: Hyperion.

Lindgren, Astrid. (1950). *Pippi Longstockings*. New York: Viking.

Lisle, Janet. (1993). *Forest*. New York: Orchard.

Lowry, Lois. (1993). *The Giver*. Boston: Houghton Mifflin.

Lowry, Lois. (1989). *Number the Stars*. Boston: Houghton Mifflin.

Lukens, Rebecca. (1995). *A Critical Handbook of Children's Literature*. Fifth edition. New York: HarperCollins.

Lynch-Brown, Carol & Tomlinson, Carl. (1993). *Essentials of Children's Literature*. Glenview, IL: Scott Foresman.

Macaulay, David. (1993). *Ship*. Boston: Houghton Mifflin.

MacLachlan, Patricia. (1994). *Skylark*. New York: HarperCollins.

MacLachlan, Patricia. (1993). *Baby*. New York: HarperCollins.

MacLachlan, Patricia. (1985). *Sarah, Plain and Tall*. New York: Harper & Row.

McCully, Emily Arnold. (1992). *Mirette on the High Wire*. New York: Putnam.

McDermott, Gerald. (1993). *Raven*. San Diego: Harcourt Brace Jovanovich.

McDermott, Gerald. (1972). *Anansi the Spider: A Tale from the Ashanti*. New York: Holt, Rinehart & Winston.

McKissack, Patricia M. (1992). *The Dark Thirty*. Illustrated by Brian Pinkney. New York: Knopf.

Meddaugh, Susan. (1994). *Martha Calling*. Boston: Houghton Mifflin.

Murphy, Jim. (1993). *Across America on an Emigrant Train*. New York: Clarion.

Naylor, Phyllis Reynolds. (1991). *Shiloh*. New York: Dell.

The Nebraska Literature Curriculum. (1966). University of Nebraska Press.

Norton, Mary. (1953). *The Borrowers*. New York: Harcourt Brace.

Osofsky, Audrey. (1992). *Dreamcatcher*. Illustrated by Ed Young. New York: Orchard.

Paterson, Katherine. (1994). *Flip-Flop Girl*. New York: Lodestar.

Paterson, Katherine. (1992). *The King's Equal*. Illustrated by Vladimir Vagin. New York: HarperCollins.

Paterson, Katherine. (1991). *Lyddie*. New York: Lodestar.

Paterson, Katherine. (1978). *The Great Gilly Hopkins*. New York: Crowell.

Patron, Susan. (1993). *Maybe Yes, Maybe, Maybe Maybe*. Illustrated by Dorothy Donahue. New York: Orchard Books.

Pearce, Philippa. (1958). *Tom's Midnight Garden*. New York: Dell.

Polacco, Patricia. (1991). *Some Birthday*! New York: Simon & Schuster Books for Young Readers.

Purves, Alan & Monson, Dianne. (1984). *Experiencing Children's Literature*. Glenview, IL: Scott Foresman.

Rand, Gloria. (1994). *The Cabin Key*. Illustrated by Ted Rand. San Diego: Harcourt Brace.

Razzi, Jim & Razzi, Mary. (1981). *The Sherluck Bones Mystery—Detective Book 1*. Illustrated by New York: Bantam.

Reggiunti, Gordon. (1992). *The Sacred Harvest*. Photographs by Dale Kakkak. Minneapolis: Lerner Publications.

Ringgold, Faith. (1991). *Tar Beach*. New York: Crown.

Robinson, Barbara. (1994). *The Best School Day Ever*. New York: HarperCollins.

Rochelle, Belinda. (1994). *When Jo Louis Won the Title*. Illustrated by Larry Johnson. Boston: Houghton Mifflin.

Rylant, Cynthia. (1985). *The Relatives Came*. Illustrated by Stephen Gammell. New York: Bradbury.

San Souci, Robert D. (1993). *Cut from the Same Cloth*. Illustrated by Brian Pinkney. New York: Philomel.

Sendak, Maurice. (1963). *Where the Wild Things Are*. New York: Puffin.

Soto, Gary. (1993). *The Pool Party*. New York: Delacorte.

Spinelli, Jerry. (1990). *Maniac Magee*. New York: Harper-Collins.

Staples, Suzanne Fisher. (1989). *Shabanu*. New York: Alfred A. Knopf.

Steig, William. (1994). *Zeke Pippin*. New York: Harper.

Steig, William. (1982). *Dr. De Soto*. New York: Farrar, Straus & Giroux.

Steptoe, John. (1987). *Mufaro's Beautiful Daughter*. New York: Lothrop, Lee & Shepard.

Stock, Catherine. (1993). *Where Are You Going, Manyoni?* New York: Morrow Junior Books.

Sutherland, Zena & Arbuthnot, May Hill. (Eds.). (1991). *Children and Books*. Glenview, IL: Scott Foresman.

Thomas, Jane Resh. (1989). *The Princess in the Pigpen*. New York: Clarion.

Thomas, Jane Resh. (1981). *The Comeback Dog*. New York: Clarion.

Van Allsburg, Chris. (1985). *The Polar Express*. Boston: Houghton Mifflin.

van der Rol, Ruud & Verhoeven, Rian. (1992). *Anne Frank: Beyond the Diary*. New York: Viking.

van Leeuwen, Jean. (1994). *Bound for Oregon*. New York: Dial.

Voigt, Cynthia. (1986). *Stories about Rosie*. Illustrated by Dennis Kendrick. New York: Atheneum.

Williams, Margery. (1922, 1975). *The Velveteen Rabbit*. Illustrated by William Nicholson. New York: Avon.

Woodruff, Elvira. (1994). *Dear Levi: Letters from the Overland Trail*. Illustrated by Beth Peck. New York: Knopf.

Yep, Laurence. (1994). *The Boy Who Swallowed Snakes*. Illustrated by Jean and Mou-Sien Tseng. New York: Scholastic.

Yep, Laurence. (1993). *Dragon's Gate*. New York: HarperCollins.

Yolen, Jane. (1987). *Owl Moon*. Illustrated by John Schoenherr. New York: Philomel.

Young, Ed. (1989). *Lon Po Po: A Red-Riding Hood Story from China*. New York: Scholastic.

Chapter 10

Deepening Response Through the Arts

Lisa F. Norwick

The Island

The island,
There it sits,
In silence,
In peace.

The loons at its side.
The heron had cried,
The turtle takes its prey,
For this is the day.

A place to rest, to breathe.
To retrieve an animal's life,
not to take away
And while he sits and watches,
he studies.

For the island is him,
And Will is the island.

The island.

—Shawna Osborne (grade 6)
Reading response to *The Island*
(Paulsen, 1990)

I had just finished reading aloud *The Island* by Gary Paulsen. The next morning, Shawna approached me with an eager smile, asking if she could share a poem she had written the night before. She explained to the class that, while listening to the book, she had created a picture in her mind of what the island looked like and that she wanted to capture that picture in her poem. As Shawna read her poem, the students were drawn in by her language and the mood she created. Nick commented on how Shawna's poem left him with a memorable picture of Will's relationship with the many animals that lived on the island. Tara mentioned that Shawna's language helped her understand the peaceful feeling that Will must have felt while living on the island.

Shawna's poem is one example of how a reader can choose a scene that elicits a strong emotional reaction and bring it to life. Whenever I hear and see readers' voices and passions become the center of their responses to literature, I'm reminded of how quality books can kindle children's imagination.

Currently I teach in a multi-age classroom of third and fourth graders; previously I taught sixth graders. Literature circles have been a vital component of my reading and writing program with students of all ages. Previous chapters have illuminated the structure of literature circles in a variety of classrooms. In this chapter, I'll focus on how reading and writing can be enhanced through the visual and performing arts.

Introducing Writing and the Visual Arts

> I liked literature circles because you could show your feelings of the book to other people. I think drawing for the response is a good idea because it shows how you formed words into pictures in your mind. It's my favorite response because it's an interesting way of showing the parts of the book you liked best.
>
> —Anusuya (grade 3)

Reading Aloud to Build a Community

As I read aloud from *Stone Fox* (Gardiner, 1980), the children couldn't help but feel strong emotions as they listened to the story of Little Willy's struggle to save his grandfather's farm. After I turned the last page, we composed a poem together about the story. We negotiated meaning, choice of words, and organization of phrases.

After our poem was finished, I shared my drawing of Little Willy sitting on his grandfather's bed. I explained that I was touched by Little Willy's love and commitment to his grandfather and tried to capture that feeling in my picture. I asked the children if they would like to choose a scene from *Stone Fox* to illustrate. The students were enthusiastic about the idea and begin working on their own pictures. I watched the children plan drafts and make revisions before beginning their illustrations, as they decided how their pictures would represent what *Stone Fox* meant to them.

Throughout this process, I heard students making connections between Little Willy's ordeal of losing a pet and their own experiences. Throughout the year, we continued to discuss how illustrations enhanced our enjoyment of books and communicated our emotional response.

Many students selected their *Stone Fox* picture to put in their portfolio. When I asked Pete why he chose to include his picture, he confided, "Art is not my strength, but I surprised myself. I think that my picture gives a good representation of how the characters really felt at the end of the story. I had to really concentrate before I could do my drawing about how I could make them look the way I pictured them in my mind. Because Little Willy is not your normal kid; he is much more determined and serious and I wanted him to look that way in his picture."

Our classroom began to investigate the variety of ways in which people can respond to literature through our read aloud. *Stone Fox* provided the children with opportunities to discuss their varied interpretations, write a class poem, and create a visual representation of an event that was personally meaningful. As I observed the children, I saw exciting possibilities for continuing to explore the arts. The poetry and drawing fueled the children with enthusiasm about responding to literature through art.

Introducing Diverse Forms of Journal Responses

Through responding to literature, students gain a clearer understanding of literary elements, connections between books, and how a book connects with their own life. When we give learners choices and opportunities to use diverse forms of response, reading becomes more powerful and enjoyable. I find that as readers move from reading to responding in a variety of ways, they discover new meanings and expand their interpretations.

This year, I began literature circles in the fall with a unit on "Fantasy Animal Stories." I gave book talks on seven novels and the students chose the book they wanted to read. We gathered around our meeting area on the carpet to discuss how readers respond to literature and what they might include in their journal entries. The students began by telling me that a response should let people know what the book is about. When I asked how they could do that, Pete quickly raised his hand and said, "Well, you do that by writing a couple of paragraphs. And be sure to include the interesting parts, but don't give the ending away." I confirmed Pete's idea that writing is an excellent way to share his reaction. I asked the children, however, if they could also use art along with writing. By combining art and writing, students can communicate what their visual representation means to them personally.

My goal early in the year was to present many possible types of artistic and written journal entries and to offer an opportunity to try each type of response. We created a chart of possible journal choices, adding one new type of response to the chart each week. I used our read aloud to introduce and model each form of response, emphasizing the process involved. The new journal entry was presented in a mini-lesson on Monday and the students completed the response by Wednesday. The children chose their second journal response for the week, which was due on Friday. For their second response, they chose a journal entry from our class chart or tried a new idea of their own. After a variety of possibilities for journal entries had been presented, the students used our chart as a resource and chose both of their responses for the week. As I unlocked doors and gave students more ownership over their journal entries, their responses became more thoughtful and creative.

Each literature circle set lasts approximately three weeks. It takes about three literature circles sets to introduce, model, and explore the different types of journal responses.

Journal Response Possibilities

Diary Entry: Pretend you're one of the characters in your book and write a diary entry from that character. Remember to include the character's thoughts and feelings.

Illustration: Create an illustration showing a favorite or an important scene in your book. Use thought bubbles to show the character's thoughts, feelings, and/or actions. You may want to use a caption instead of thought bubbles to explain the scene's importance.

Interview: Interview a character from your book and respond as if you're the character.

Letter: Choose an audience of a friend or the author of your book. Write a letter to send in which you discuss the book and share your reactions. You can also write a letter to one of the characters in your book, asking them questions and sharing your thoughts about the book. Another option is to become one of the book's characters and write a letter they might send to another character, the author, or a character in a different book.

Mind Map: Make a mind map of memorable scenes, characters, or settings from your book. Try to find passages from your book to add to your mind map.

Pamphlet: Create a pamphlet about the characters in your book or about scenes that are important to you. Remember to include written descriptions, sharing your personal reactions.

Paragraph: Create your own questions or respond to a question from our class list. *(These are questions generated by the students.)*

Poetry: Write a poem about the characters, plot, setting, theme, or mood of your book. Include descriptive language so that your audience can create a mental picture of the book you're reading.

Pop-Up: Make a pop-up of a significant scene. Include a written description of your personal reaction when you read that part of the book.

Sketch-to-Stretch: (Harste, Short & Burke, 1988, pp. 353–357). Create a visual representation that expresses your feelings about the book, your understanding of the characters or conflicts that happen in the book. While creating your Sketch-to-Stretch, think about what stays with you from the book.

Summary and Reaction: Write a summary of key events from your book and discuss your reactions or thoughts about what you read.

Venn Diagram: Create a Venn diagram comparing two characters or two scenes from your literature circle book. You could also compare the characters or scenes from your literature circle book to those in another book. (*For an example of a Venn diagram, see* Invitations *(1991) by Regie Routman, p. 95.*)

Eliciting Depth in Journal Responses

After students explore a variety of ways to respond to literature, I begin to concentrate some of our mini-lessons on eliciting more depth in their journal entries. I want the children to gain a new perspective and appreciation of their book through their responses. I want my students to move beyond retelling to a more personal reaction to books. During mini-lessons, I ask the children what makes a good journal entry. After discussing our ideas, we generate a list.

In the fall our list is simple and includes some key ideas (Figure 10-1). Early in the year, most students concentrate on retelling the storyline and incorporate some description of the characters. At that time, my focus is on encouraging students to experiment with varied responses. By January, I focus more on eliciting personal and aesthetic responses.

Throughout the year, we revisit the list and expand on our ideas. The mini-lessons encourage students to reexamine their ideas and reflect on their journal entries. I explain that art involves making personal meaning. For example, I encourage the children to experiment with the use of color, line, texture, and space in their visual representations.

By the spring, our list looks much different than it did in the fall (Figure 10-2). I notice that the students have begun to internalize many of the ideas on our list. As students experiment with various ways of responding to literature, their journal entries become deeper and more personal. Their self-reflections about the entries they select to place in their portfolios also become more insightful. I discover children's responses are of a higher quality when I allow choice, model literature responses, focus on the process involved, and provide time for discussion.

Literature Circle Journal Entries

Fall, 1993

- Include what happened in the book
- Describe the characters
- Write nearly
- Add color to your picutres

Figure 10-1

Literature Circle Journal Entries

Spring, 1994

Depth/Content

- Go beyond retelling
- Reflect on the book and share your feelings
- Share why the scene was important to you
- Compare the book to your own life, someone you know, or another book
- Imagine another point of view. If you were one of the characters, what would you do?

Quality/Packaging

- Write neatly
- Pay attention to color, line, space, and texture
- Put detail into your pictures
- You may want to add a border

Figure 10-2

In the fall, Jenny, a fourth grader, was reading *The Cricket in Times Square* (Selden, 1981) and created a character mind map for her journal entry (Figure 10-3). Jenny's mind map described the main character, a mouse named Tucker. She listed examples of his actions and events in the story. Her descriptions were very concrete and, at this point in the year, did not reflect her personal reaction to the story or character.

As the year progressed, Jenny moved beyond describing characters to responding aesthetically and sharing her personal reactions. In April, Jenny read *Shiloh* (Naylor, 1991) as part of our theme of "Significant Characters." She created a pop-up journal response of a memorable scene in the novel. Jenny carefully added color, line, and details to her pop-up.

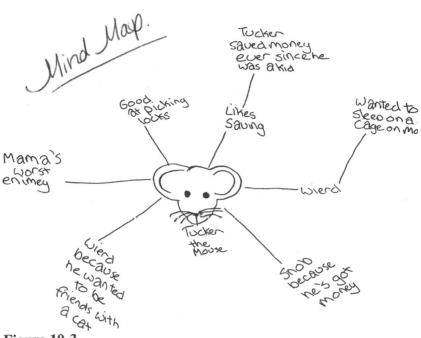

Mind Map.

Tucker saved money ever since he was a kid

Good at picking locks

Likes Saving

Wanted to sleep on a cage on mo

Mama's worst enimey

Wierd

Tucker the Mouse

Wierd because he wanted to be friends with a cat

Snob because he's got money

Figure 10-3

In her written reflection, Jenny shared her emotional reaction to the scene.

> I chose this scene because I sort of felt sorry for Shiloh. He had to sit out in the cold rain for twenty minutes. Shiloh is in a little pen because Marty found the dog after the dog ran away from Judd. Judd is the original owner of Shiloh. Marty built the pen because he didn't want Judd to beat the dog. Marty is the only one that knows Judd beats his dogs, that is why Marty wanted Shiloh. My favorite character is Shiloh.

Encouraging Student-Led Mini-lessons

I've recently discovered the power of having students lead mini-lessons. Children listen attentively as their peers share responses to literature, introduce new reading strategies, or explain how they prepare for literature circle meetings. I coach students before they share so that they will be sure to emphasize both their process and insights.

In response to *Tuck Everlasting* (Babbitt, 1975), Michael created a "Sketch to Stretch" (Harste, Short & Burke, 1988). I invited him to present his sketch in a mini-lesson, since his technique was very different from illustrating a scene (Figure 10-4). In addition, Michael had initiated this approach on his own; it wasn't an option we had thought to include on our chart. He explained how, at the beginning of the book, Babbitt compares the setting to the metaphor of a ferris wheel. The language intrigued Michael and he wanted to explore the rotation of the seasons. I hoped that Michael's mini-lesson on his rather abstract reflection would encourage students to risk moving beyond literal forms of illustration. When students show transparencies of their work and describe their creative process to their peers, they are encouraged to become more reflective and confident.

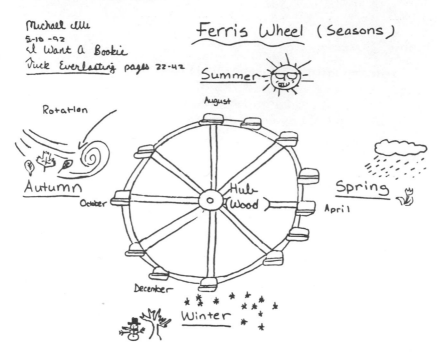

Figure 10-4.

Providing Feedback to Students

I collect students' journal responses twice a week and respond to them in writing. This provides an opportunity to touch base with each child individually, provide support when needed, and celebrate his or her growth. I concentrate on confirming, reflecting, and/or extending as I respond to their journal entries. Most often, I ask one of the following questions in order to nudge students to extend their thinking and share their personal reactions: "How did you feel while reading this part of your book?" "Has anything like this ever happened to you?" or "Do you have any questions or wonderings about your book?"

In our classroom community, when students are encouraged to respond to each other and to literature, they become empowered as readers, writers, and thinkers. As we explore diverse forms of response, we strive to become what C. S. Lewis terms "literary readers." Through exploring artistic and written responses to literature, we broaden our understandings, thoughts, and feelings about books and each other.

Weaving in the Performing Arts

> When Michelle and I did the puppet show we had to work
> hard on expression. That meant, we needed to understand
> how the characters felt so we could make it seem real. That
> helped me understand what was really happening. It made
> me appreciate the characters' feelings a lot more than when I
> just read the book.
>
> —Kirsten (grade 6)

After an artist in residence had visited our school, I became
interested in integrating the performing arts into my curriculum. A
drama specialist visited my classroom each day for four weeks.
During this time, we explored drama as a vehicle for communicat-
ing meaning. This experience gave me confidence and helped me
understand the important role drama could play in my classroom.

From this experience, through professional reading, and after
an interview with Sam Sebesta (author of Chapter 13), I learned
ways in which to integrate the performing arts. The purpose for
integrating the performing arts before reading is to motivate students and build background knowledge. During reading, the performing arts enhance enjoyment and comprehension. Involving
students in dramatic response after they have finished reading af-
fords them opportunities to further extend their appreciation and
interpretation of literature.

For students and teachers who have not had much experience, the performing arts can be intimidating. I always felt that my
strengths were in the visual arts and I never dabbled in drama. In
the past, I was much more comfortable with a paintbrush in my
hand than experimenting with mime. After reading *Creative Drama
in the Classroom* (McCaslin, 1991), I acquired valuable information for bringing authentic, rather than superficial, drama into the
classroom. I find it's important to begin investigating the performing arts early in the fall, in order to have the whole year in which to
grow as artists.

Mime

Mime is a good place to begin because it's easy and involves movement instead of verbal response. Sam Sebesta advises starting with
one important scene from the book and adding movements. When
children are reluctant to put large motions in their mime, Sam uses
encouraging statements, such as "Make a display" or "Double it."

I often use picture books or poetry with action in the narration for mime. For example, students choose significant characters and mime their actions from *All the Magic in the World*
(Hartmann, 1993). When Lena received her necklace from Joseph,
she "danced like the wind across the wheat fields." As they become comfortable with mime, I emphasize accuracy by having

students reread their chosen passage to include important details in their movement. My students loved making the characters visible through mime.

Story Theatre

We next explore Story Theatre. Again, I choose literature with action, but not too much dialogue. For example, when we read Gardiner's *Stone Fox* (Gardiner, 1980), small groups of children mimed the actions of Little Willy, his grandfather, and Stone Fox without narration. Each group picks a particular scene to portray. Students build their character as they reread their chapter in order to incorporate vivid details. With practice, students become comfortable with movements that bring their character to life. A student from each group provides the narration by reading aloud directly from the text as the others mime the actions of the characters. Story Theatre heightens students' enjoyment and understanding of both the plot and the characters' feelings.

Choral Reading

Building on students' skill at mime and story theatre, I introduce choral reading of predictable poems. I selected the following four poems that Shelley Harwayne recommended in *Lasting Impressions* (1992, pp. 15–18): "Marbles" by Kathleen Fraser, "Rules" by Karla Kuskin, "Street Song" by Myra Cohn Livingston, and "Talking" by Judith Viorst. I read the poems aloud, modeling pace, fluency, and expression. Next, I demonstrated the following choral arrangements: unison, line-at-a-time, refrain, and antiphonal. The children worked in groups of four, each group choosing one of the poems. The students experimented with different choral arrangements and prepared a performance. Through this process, they learn to rehearse, experiment with the sounds of language, and take pride in their accomplishments.

Readers Theatre

Readers Theatre is more appropriate for a story in which dialogue is part of the action and characters strongly interact with each other. In this form of dramatic response, students read from a written script but don't memorize their lines, use props or costumes, or add movement. The focus is on reading with expression. Readers Theatre is an excellent extension before children begin reading to whet their appetite for the book. Sam Sebesta recommends the following guidelines for Readers Theatre:

- Do not add movements; it makes it difficult for the children to follow their scripts.
- Provide children with plenty of time to practice before they read their part for the performance.
- The audience should not have a copy of the script.

The passages I select for Readers Theatre are meaningful enough to give an audience insight into the entire book. I choose selections with a strong emotional appeal that would stimulate the audience's imagination. After I create the script, students choose roles and read the dialogue as if they were the characters. A narrator then reads sections of the story that describe the action. Readers Theatre provides a safe way to take on the role of characters and is one of my students' favorite ways to respond to literature.

Improvisation

Improvisation is drama with dialogue, but without a script. One advantage to improvisation is that the dialogue is ad-libbed and does not have to be memorized or repeated the same way each time children perform the drama. I find that when using improvisation for puppet shows, students interpret the characters more personally than when they follow a script.

I modeled improvisation by inviting children to help me choose a significant scene from *Mufaro's Beautiful Daughters* (Steptoe, 1987). We created a mind map of important incidents that happened in our chosen scene, then we sequenced the events in the order they appeared in the book. The students practiced improvising the scene and concentrated on using dialogue they believed the actual characters might use. Once the children felt comfortable with their improvisation, they made puppets. Next, they practiced using both their puppets and improvisation. I provided guidance on speaking loudly and holding the puppets behind the stage so the audience could see them. Improvisation is a fun way for students to experiment with drama and share their interpretation of the book.

Music and Movement

I introduced music and movement by having the children mime *We Got Here Together* (Stafford, 1994) as I read the text aloud. The children needed guidance; it was not easy to capture the gentle movement of a raindrop or an air bubble rising from the ocean. Props became useful tools; for example, scarves became undulating waves or the fierce wind in the thunderstorm. After the children polished their actions, we dropped the narration and added music.

I keep a collection of instruments in my classroom. The children who do not mime actions in the story create music to enhance the performance. They concentrate on the rhythm of the author's words and the mood of the story when adding music to literature. Music and movement add creativity and enjoyment to literature.

Teacher's Role

My role in integrating the performing arts is crucial as I weave them into our reading program. I concentrate on creating a climate that communicates the message that my classroom is a safe place where children can take risks and learn together. The performing arts give students time to interpret quality literature as they encounter memorable characters and scenes. Sam Sebesta (1987) observes that,

> Teachers who successfully use drama techniques within the curriculum aren't likely to go outside the curriculum to find drama scripts, nor are they likely to devote large blocks of school time to polish a production to impress an audience. Drama in such classrooms is a process for teaching imagery, characterization, close reading for interpretation, and enhancing literary experience. (p. 83)

He recommends that whenever students grasp an idea, teachers stop the performance and "draw the curtain" in order to debrief the creative process. "Did the scene have credibility?" and "What are we after?" are two of Sam's favorite questions as he encourages children to self-reflect. He also suggests that teachers concentrate on questions that focus on the whole production instead of those directed to individual students. I also find that if I stop children too often to self-reflect, their reflections are not as meaningful. My role is to model, encourage, and applaud students' exploration through creative drama.

Involving children in drama early in the year provides a setting for future literature extensions. I view the performing arts as natural opportunities for children to express their images and perceptions of literary characters and scenes. Students gain confidence and useful oral language skills. In my classroom, the performing arts spark an interest that continues throughout the year.

Celebrating Through Writing, Visual Arts, and Performing Arts

> Writing is my favorite type of extension. Writing is a way of showing how I feel about a book. It also helps me appreciate the author more. Because when I write I try to do what the author did. I use words that give the audience a picture in their minds. I describe what happened and who the characters are and what they're thinking and feeling.
> —Pete (grade 4)

To culminate each literature circle set, students create extension projects. The purpose of the projects is to extend and enhance the children's enjoyment, appreciation, and understanding of literature. These projects give them a chance to revisit their book, make connections between the literature and their own lives, and gain a clearer picture of how all the books in our literature circle set were connected by a common theme.

If the project is not meaningful, it becomes a showcase product instead of a learning vehicle. I caution students to know why they are selecting a particular extension project before they begin. In Figure 10-5 I've listed the questions they should ask themselves about possible extension projects.

Questions for Extension Projects

- How closely does the extension project relate to the book?

- Does the extension project cause the student to revisit the book?

- What does the extension project do to enhance the reader's appreciation and understanding of the book?

- Does the response project use diverse forms of response to explore meaning?

- Does the extension project help the reader make connections with other books, with personal experiences, or across the curriculum?

(handwritten margin note: important elements for extension projects)

Figure 10-5 Questions for Extension Projects

Literature Circle Extension Possibilities

When students finish reading their literature circle books, I introduce extension projects. I explain the purpose for doing each project, describe the process involved, and often demonstrate the extension. I start with several projects and add new choices to the list after each successive literature circle, building on the students' ideas and interests. Each time, I include a variety of projects: verbal, nonverbal, musical, artistic, dramatic, and written. Students may choose from any project on the list of seven to ten possibilities; my only request is that the children try a project they haven't already explored. The students in each literature circle decide whether they are going to work as a group, break into smaller groups, or work individually.

The 26 projects listed below are suggestions that I have collected over the past five years from colleagues, students, and through professional reading. I have become more selective and only present projects to children that I truly believe are worthwhile. Not all of the projects are presented every year.

Literature Extension Possibilities

ABC Book: Create an ABC book, focusing on key events, characters, ideas, and information from your book. This may work best as a group project because the book will have 26 pages, one for each letter in the alphabet.

Accordion Book: Choose three to five significant scenes from your book. Make an illustrated book that reveals the sequence of your book's storyline. Include written descriptions: What's happening in the scene? Why is the scene important to you?

Commemorative Stamp: Select a key character or scene, or focus on an important theme from your book, and develop a stamp to commemorate that character, scene, or theme. Include a picture, a selected phrase, and the stamp's value to highlight your choice.*

Cube: Create a six-sided tagboard cube focusing on your favorite scenes or significant story events from your book.

Diorama: Make a diorama of one of your favorite scenes. Be sure to include a written explanation of the scene. You could also make a multi-sided diorama by connecting the back or sides of the diorama to display contrasting scenes or to present two points of view.*

Diary: Select a significant character in your book and write diary entries from his or her point of view. Include the character's thoughts, feelings, and insights.

Flannel Board Story: Select an important scene from your book. Recreate the scene using flannel, and be prepared to have the characters act out the scene on the board.

Jackdaw: Collect artifacts representing ideas, events, characters, and/or themes in your book. Next, build a display of these items. Label each artifact, sharing its importance to the book. You may also want to include a direct quotation from your book for some items.*

Journeyline: Develop a timeline sequencing the plot of your story, with key events highlighted by a brief explanation and small illustration. Or chart the character's journey through the course of your book, including high points and low points in his or her life.

Map: Design a map of the setting of your book. Include the main character's journey, important landmarks, and a key explaining the map. You may want to experiment with clay or salt dough for making your map.

Main Idea Belt: Create a belt section for each chapter or selected scenes in your book. Include an illustration of the event and a brief (one sentence or phrase) description of that scene. Connect your belt sections with string, yarn, or ribbon.*

Mime: Choose a significant scene from your book in which there is action but not too much dialogue. Create a mime of the characters' actions. Reread your chosen scene to include the important details in your movements. Write a summary of the book, giving an overview and why you chose that particular scene to mime. Read the summary to the audience before your performance.

Mural: Choose an important scene from your book. Create that scene on a mural. You may want to paint the background and use construction paper for the characters to make it multidimensional. Include a written description of the mural, explaining what's happening in the scene and why you selected it.

Musical Accompaniment: Choose a significant passage from your book. Practice reading fluently and with expression, capturing the mood of the passage. When you feel confident about reading the passage, record it on a tape recorder. Experiment with musical instruments to accompany your reading. While creating your musical accompaniment, focus on the rhythm of the author's word and the mood of your passage.

Pop-Up Book: Develop a pop-up book of memorable aspects of your literature circle book. Include a written explanation for each page, sharing your personal reactions.

Puppet Show: Choose an important scene from your book and write a script or use improvisation to capture the scene. Then make puppets for each character. You may also want to make puppets for important props.

Readers Theatre: Select an important scene from your book where there is action imbedded in the dialogue. Rewrite the scene as a Readers Theatre script. Either present it in front of the class or tape record it for presentation.

Riddle Character Book: Write and illustrate riddle poems about the characters in your book. A "Who Am I?" poem is a good pattern to use for the book. You may want to hide each character's picture under a flap so that your audience can try to guess who the characters are.

Scrapbook: Create a scrapbook that includes your favorite scenes or characters from your book. Include a written explanation for each page.

Song: Write a song about your book and share it with the class. You may want to use a melody from another song or create your own. Prepare a copy of the song for class members, so we can sing with you the second time around.

Story Banner: Create a story banner about an important aspect from your book. Illustrate your banner and include a border representing something significant from your book.

Story or Character Quilt: Create quilt squares that represent key aspects or characters in your book. Each quilt square needs to include an illustration and a written explanation (you can use direct quotes from the book if you'd like). Mount the squares on a piece of butcher paper or connect the squares with yarn. This is a good group project since your quilt should have between 16 and 25 squares.

Story Theatre: Choose an important scene from the book where there is action but not too much dialogue. Begin by miming the characters' actions. Reread the scene to include all the important details in your movements. After you have polished the scene and are comfortable with the mime, add the author's words.

Story Wheel: Make a story wheel that describes the key events in your book. Decide how many parts to break the story into by selecting and sequencing the most important events. Include illustrations and writing for each event.*

Tableaux: Select six to eight significant scenes from your book. Illustrate each scene and include a written description explaining why the scene is important to you. Sequence the scenes and mount them on butcher paper. Experiment with art materials that seem most appropriate to your book.

Talk Show: Become a radio announcer or talk show host/hostess. Write a script of questions the interviewer will ask a key character in your book. Remember to have the characters respond from their point of view. Either tape record or role play the interview.

* Examples of these extension projects are included at the end of this chapter.

Facilitating Extension Projects

A visiting teacher entered my room as the children were busy working on their extension projects. After looking around and talking with some of the children, she commented on how impressed she was with their engagement and projects. I could tell that she had some questions about what she had just observed. As the children left for recess, she asked, "How do you keep track of what all the students are doing? What if two or three groups are struggling? How do you provide support to all of them at once? Where do you get all your materials?" She shook her head and added, "I just don't know if I'm up to this." Her questions were ones I have worked through for the past five years and continue to ponder. I reassured her that my changes have taken many years.

Student planning needs to focus both on their purpose for doing the project and the process involved. Space is provided on a Literature Extension Planning Sheet (similar to Anne Klein's form on page 192 in Chapter 12) for students to create a draft of their project and note pages for future reference. I've discovered that when children spend quality time drafting their extension project, they don't run into as many roadblocks throughout the process. Their planning sheet is only a guideline; their final projects may change along the way. The purpose of this planning is to encourage children to think through their process before plunging into their projects.

On the planning sheet, students write a list of materials they will use for their project. They add a note describing materials they need that we don't have in our classroom publishing center. After school, I collect the materials the children requested, so that the next day they can immediately begin working on their projects.

Besides using planning sheets, I've also found that student-led mini-lessons are a powerful teaching tool for supporting readers in the process of creating their extensions. During student-led mini-lessons, children share their extensions, the process, helpful strategies they discovered, and their next steps. Having students share their discoveries is an extremely helpful troubleshooting tool for all the children in our class.

Following the mini-lesson, I schedule a two-hour block because students need large amounts of time to confer and work on their extensions. During this time, I often meet with groups of students who are struggling with similar problems. By focusing the conference on specific needs, I am able to listen carefully, let the children coach each other, and discover how I can help.

Widening the Audience

As the children put the finishing touches on their extension projects, we begin to plan our culminating celebration. We choose a date and make invitations to give to family members. On the day of our celebration, the children proudly display their work, turning our classroom into an art gallery. The children and their families gather near the front of the room to watch students present their performing arts extensions. After the presentations, children display their extension planning sheets alongside their project. Family members can wander around the classroom and admire the children's extensions. Comment cards are placed by each project so that peers and family members can write their comments.

Emphasizing the Process: Conscious Reflection

Pete and Charles created a puppet show from a scene in *Howliday Inn* (Howe, 1982). They debated which event would best convey the suspense of the book. After choosing the scene, they carefully planned the characters' actions, rereading and making many revisions along the way. As they began to improvise, they concentrated on fluency, using expression, and speaking as if they were the actual characters. During one of their practice sessions, I heard

Pete say, "This book really makes your brain think. The author sets it up so that a lot of the characters are suspected of committing the crime."

On the day of their performance, it was difficult to see their puppets, their voices were muffled because of the puppet stage, and they had a bit of stage fright. As I watched their puppet show, I reflected back to their process and how actively they had created meaning. After their performance, I asked Pete to share what he had learned by doing a puppet show. "I think Charles and I worked really hard to do our puppet show. It wasn't always easy to work together. And we had to do a lot of extra reading and practicing. Even though our performance wasn't the best in the class, we still learned a lot. Next time I write a story, I think I'll be able to use dialogue better because of all the dialogue we used in our puppet show." Pete's words reveal the importance of self-reflection and of emphasizing process as well as the product.

A crucial component of the performing and visual arts in the classroom is conscious reflection. Children gain clearer understandings when they step back and reflect. These are the three questions that I find elicit the most thoughtful responses from students:

1. How did using writing, visual arts, or performing arts as a response to literature enhance your appreciation and understanding of the book?
2. What is something about your extension you're proud of?
3. What is something you learned from another person's extension that you may include in your next project?

Closing Thoughts

Literature circles are rewarding times during which conversations and responses to books enlighten our lives. In our class, students respond to literature before, during, and after reading. We investigate meaning through writing, visual arts, and performing arts. It's not always easy; there are no teacher's guides or packaged materials. Together, we explore diverse forms of response and acquire clearer understandings of our world and ourselves. Responding to literature enriches our minds, imaginations, and hearts.

References

Alexander, Lloyd. (1965). *The Black Cauldron.* New York: Holt, Rinehart & Winston.

Babbitt. Natalie. (1975). *Tuck Everlasting.* New York: Farrar, Straus & Giroux.

DeFelice, Cynthia. (1990). New York: Avon.

Fraser, Kathleen. (1976). "Marbles." In Lee Bennett Hopkins & Misha Arenstein. (Eds.), *Potato Chips and a Slice of the Moon.* New York: Scholastic.

Gardiner, John Reynolds. (1980). *Stone Fox.* Illustrated by Marcia Sewell. New York: HarperCollins.

Harste, Jerome, Short, Kathy, & Burke, Carolyn. (1988). *Creating Classrooms for Authors.* Portsmouth, NH: Heinemann.

Hartmann, Wendy. (1993). *All the Magic in the World.* Illustrated by Niki Daly. New York: Dutton.

Harwayne, Shelley. (1992). *Lasting Impressions.* Portsmouth, NH: Heinemann.

Hotze, Sollace. (1988). *A Circle Unbroken.* New York: Clarion.

Howe, James. (1982). *Howliday Inn.* New York: Avon.

Kuskin, Karla. (1980). "Rules." In *Dogs & Dragons, Trees & Dreams.* New York: Harper & Row.

Livingston, Myra Cohn. (1974). "Street song." In *The Way Things Are and Other Poems.* New York: Holiday House.

McCaslin, Nellie. (1991). *Creative Drama in the Classroom,* Fifth edition. New York: Longman.

Naylor, Phyllis Reynolds. (1991). *Shiloh.* New York: Dell.

Paulsen, Gary. (1990). *The Island.* New York: Dell.

Routman, Regie. (1991). Invitations: Changing as Teachers and Learners K-12. Pourtsmouth, NH: Heinemann.

Sebesta, S. (1987). Enriching the arts and humanities through children's books. In B. Cullinan (Ed.), *Children's Literature in the Reading Program.* Newark, DE: International Reading Association, 77–88.

Selden, George. (1981). *The Cricket in Times Square.* New York: Dell.

Stafford, Kim. (1994). *We Got Here Together.* Illustrated by Debra Frasier. New York: Harcourt Brace.

Steptoe, John. (1987). *Mufaro's Beautiful Daughters.* New York: Scholastic.

Viorst, Judith. (1982). "Talking." In *If I Were in Charge of the World.* New York: Atheneum.

Wrede, Patricia. (1990). *Dealing with Dragons.* New York: Harcourt Brace Jovanovich.

Wrede, Patricia. (1991). *Searching for Dragons.* New York: Harcourt Brace Jovanovich.

Examples of Journal Responses and Extension Projects
By Lisa Norwick
Commemorative Stamp

<u>Commemorative stamps are a</u>
<u>favorite extension for children</u>
<u>of all ages</u>. After students have
created their stamps, they can
write a short paragraph describing why they chose that specific
character and how they decided
the value of the stamp. This
commemorative stamp was an
extension project that was done
after *A Circle Unbroken* was
read (Holtze, 1988).

<u>Diorama</u>

Dioramas can take
on many different
forms and use a variety of materials.
Lisa, a sixth
grader, created the
diorama on the top
left after reading
*Dealing with
Dragons* (Wrede,
1990). Lisa used a
wooden board that
she painted for the
base, heavy poster
board for the back
of her diorama,
and tissue paper to
make the sun and
bushes behind the
trees. Rosie, a
fourth grader, designed the diorama
on the bottom left
after reading *Weasel* (DeFelice,
1991). Rosie used
poster-board and
colored construction paper.

Jackdaw

Below is a jackdaw created by Kirsten, a sixth grader. Kirsten's jackdaw was an extension project created after reading *The Black Cauldron* (Alexander, 1965). Kirsten carefully chose important artifacts from the book. She used a variety of materials for creating the artifacts. For example, she used clay to make the cauldron and fabric for the harp.

Main Idea Belt

Main idea belts are best used as a literature extension after reading a book. Students create a belt section for key events in the book. They illustrate each event and write a brief description of the scene. The belt is connected with string, yarn, or ribbon. Below is a picture of a main idea belt.

Story Wheel

Kirsten, also created a story wheel as a literature extension project after reading *Shiloh* (Naylor, 1991). She chose eight key scenes, sequenced and illustrated the scenes, and then wrote a short description.

Chapter 11

Drawing on the Artist's Perspective:
Ventures into Meaning Making

Barry Hoonan

I am a doodler. I love sketching. My ideas come fast and furiously and I usually choose to draw in order to express what I'm thinking. Writing, on the other hand, is something I struggle with. My words sometimes fail to capture my thoughts. Knowing this about myself, it's easier to understand the importance of providing learners a variety of ways to respond to literature. I have learned that the arts help us construct meaning. They help us to see others' ideas as they are manifested; they give us opportunities to personalize meaning; and they help us derive meaning before, during, and even after the act of creation.

Let me begin with two stories from my fifth/sixth multi-age classroom to show the ways in which the performing and visual arts enhance meaning making.

The Story of *Popcorn Days and Buttermilk Nights*

After one literature circle group finished reading *Popcorn Days and Buttermilk Nights* (Paulsen, 1983), they decided to share the book with the class. Following a discussion about the main character (an adolescent involved in thievery and lying), they decided to present the book through Readers Theatre. "Where can we get something that looks like a horse? What could we use for grass? Lynden, can you help me highlight my parts of the story?" They ran down to the first grade classroom to borrow cowboy hats. They put scarves on the ground for grass. Even Katie and Lynden, who had never worked well together, found themselves working shoulder to shoulder.

What had started out as a self-conscious, anxious group of pre-adolescents turned into an energized, determined, thoughtful, and collaborative group. As they shared their reading with the class, it became evident that the students had commitment and investment in bringing this book to life for their peers. Breanne, Alex, and Allison had even memorized their portions of the text, in order to focus on the dramatization rather than the reading. The class was spellbound. Several students asked the group to repeat the name and author of the book, which launched an interest in other books by Gary Paulsen. When there was some free time at the end of the day, classmates requested another performance.

The dramatization of this book and the group's investment in the meaning they created gave us a deeper understanding of *Popcorn Days and Buttermilk Nights*. In contrast to the more traditional oral book report, this ten-minute presentation inspired the group with the power of drama.

The Story of *Roll of Thunder, Hear My Cry*

Our class had just returned from the Seattle Children's Theater's dramatic presentation of *Roll of Thunder, Hear My Cry* (Taylor, 1976). Following field trips, it was customary for my students to write in their journals for a designated period of time and to share their responses with the entire class. But this time, because of our collective quiet and aching mood, I requested that we each reflect in a visual medium other than narrative writing. I suggested some possibilities: painting, collage, chalk, ink, or clay. My original intent was to move beyond what had become a routine of jotting down superficial reactions. We had read *Roll of Thunder, Hear My Cry* and talked about it before seeing the play, and it had touched our hearts. The play, however, stunned this group of suburban students. I wanted to provide time for us to unravel our feelings.

The students worked for two hours with passionate involvement—both with the book and with each other—as they sorted out what was important. Bethany moved from classmate to classmate asking how they'd made sense of the book. She eventually drew black and red boxes in a frame with a caption about blacks being trapped inside; the illustration represented the lack of intellectual and especially physical freedom of the blacks in the story. Josh moved into the hall and worked for an hour on a four-line poem about his own inability to influence the important decisions that affected his life. Katie illustrated her mood by overlapping black and white tissue with more white than black. A few black spots speckled the white tissue, symbolizing how the whites controlled the blacks simply by intimidating a few.

Early in my teaching career, I sensed the potential the arts held for enhancing literature discussions. The artistic responses and conversations after both novels had been read were so rich that I knew it was important for me to explore the role of the arts in the classroom.

Articulating a Personal Definition of Literacy

Writing has always been important in our classroom. We write in learning logs and journals and publish a monthly magazine. We use writing as a way to show how we feel, what we comprehend when we read, and what we know while researching. Writing is important in creating a climate of trust and friendship; we use a message board and mailboxes for both public and personal displays of thoughts and feelings. Writing has reigned supreme—its place undiminished in importance. I now recognize the exclusive place writing held in my classroom as the predominant sign system.

In this chapter I use "the arts" and "sign systems" interchangeably. Art, music, dance, language, and mathematics are all sign systems that humans have developed to make sense of the world (Harste, Short & Burke, 1988).

My exclusive focus on writing did not fit with what I knew to be important in making sense of the world. I realized I had treated the arts as peripheral. Because I viewed the arts as enrichment, they were relegated to a back seat in my classroom.

I began to reflect on the ways learners in my class made meaning other than through reading and writing. When invited to choose their own form of response, students sometimes drew diagrams or sketches to show what they had learned. Some enjoyed acting out their ideas.

After reading Howard Gardner's *Frames of Mind* (1983), I began to question my narrow perspective on literacy. Gardner's work convinced me that new ways of knowing needed to be acknowledged and elevated in status. For example, Nels responded to *Chive* (Barre, 1993) on a xylophone. The "lived through experience" (Rosenblatt, 1978) would have been quite different if he had responded through writing. Nels was able to compose through music what he couldn't articulate in words. What we heard as the audience resonated through all of us. When learners share and express in a variety of ways and move across and between sign systems, they are able to "author" new insights and knowledge (Berghoff, 1993; Harste, 1993). Based on the theories of Gardner, Berghoff, and Harste, I began to encourage response through other sign systems during literature circles. I wondered how to invite students to respond to literature through movement, dance, art, music, poetry, or drama.

I decided to turn to professional artists in order to understand the theories I'd been exploring and to understand how artists make sense of their world. I was specifically interested in the ways artists would respond to literature.

Responding Through the Arts:
Literature Study with Artists

What do artists do when they explore literature? How do artists help us understand how to make meaning through the arts? These two questions intrigued me, so I invited four artist friends to listen to pieces of literature and to respond in the way—or sign system—they felt would best express their interpretation. I purposefully invited an architect, a chef, a ballet dancer, and a poet because I wanted a variety of responses. I selected five children's picture books, varying in topic and complexity. After we browsed the literature, they noted with surprise the intrigue and power of both the writing and illustrations. They commented that these books went far beyond entertaining just children; they were books that explored compelling themes for adults as well.

The first book we settled on reading aloud was Barry Moser's visually stunning folk ballad, *Polly Vaughn* (1992). This Appalachian Romeo and Juliet story focuses on the loss of a loved one in a tragic hunting accident. I read the book aloud and we then talked about the intriguing issues in the story and the powerful, eerie illustrations. Our conversation focused on the book's somber tone and the lack of likable characters. The "structure" of ballads came up toward the end of the discussion, no doubt because I was a teacher and that was a school way to talk about literature.

The group was quiet and subdued. Jennifer, the dancer, suggested that we listen to another book. The second book we chose was *Fly Away Home* (Bunting, 1991), a story dealing with a homeless family that lives in an airport. Our conversation turned to the current plight of the homeless. We wondered about whether homeless people really do occupy airports. The group marveled at the beautiful and moving illustrations, captured in watercolor browns and blues. We discussed the challenge and ramifications of living one's life while attempting to go unnoticed.

Our session ended with each person accepting the invitation to respond to either of the books through the sign system he or she understood best. I was intrigued by their reactions to this invitation. My friends responded as if it were a school assignment—something that had to be done "correctly." The chef wanted to know if she could write a response. I assured her that was fine, but that it might be more interesting for her to move beyond written language. The ambiguity of the assignment seemed unsettling. "But what do you want?" echoed throughout the room. I encouraged everyone to trust that they could make sense of the books through their own expertise and to share their responses the next week.

Response Through Dance

The following meeting began with Jennifer, the dancer, volunteering to dance her response to *Fly Away Home* (Bunting, 1991). With music from Annie Lennox's song "Little Bird" softly playing in the background, Jennifer enacted the playful movements of someone unencumbered and full of enthusiasm. Slowly, as the words of the song told of the flying away of a bird, Jennifer's actions became compressed, narrow, and slight. Her whole being turned from an exuberant ball of energy to a round-shouldered, hands-to-the-side minimalist.

The reaction to Jennifer's dance was quick and direct. Each person interjected different insights and connections. John, the architect, remarked that, when he heard the book, he concentrated on how people were free to fly, yet the boy and his father were stuck, without a destination. After Jennifer's dance, however, he understood the book with a new insight.

> When Jennifer danced, I felt a different sense. I felt this kid not only could not leave, but he could not enjoy himself because he was constrained by his own particular situation. And so the metaphor of the bird was not that he couldn't leave the airport, but that he couldn't leave his own inhibitions.

Jennifer, the dancer, said pensively:

> You each had a different angle on my general idea. I wasn't sure of my real idea . . . I was learning through the physical sense of the story. First, Lennox's song struck me . . . I wasn't sure why, I guess it was the image of the bird flying away. Then I thought about the little kid and what he'd like to be doing—but couldn't. Because if he was to act goofy like other kids, he'd be noticed . . . he'd be found.

The group was surprised at how instantaneous and effortless their insights had been generated. Making meaning of this text through movement brought the book alive for all of us.

Response Through Poetry

The metaphor of movement again connected us with *Fly Away Home*, as Barb, the poet, shared words from her own personal journey and her discomfort of living so near a family in need. Here is an excerpt from her poem, "Crossing Paths."

> Now, I turn left,
>   along my revised route,
>   avoiding Christina and her house.
> As long as I continue on my way,
>   I can push away my shame and nameless discomfort.
> We all long for something—
>   peace, love, a full stomach, inspiration,
>   the company of friends, mail in the box,
>   new shoes . . . more sleep.
> But comfort? Hope?
>   My heart, wrapped and wounded, aches with unfamiliar
>   feeling,
>   perhaps futility.

Barb read her poem twice. The poem directed us right into our own struggles and experiences of walking by panhandlers and seeing destitute families. She tapped our feeling of being at odds with the issue of giving in order to make ourselves feel better or trying to falsely remedy a very complex situation. Our conversation echoed of personal experiences and our feelings of helplessness. Barb commented that it was important for her to place the characters' experience into her own world. When she connected to something she knew personally, the characters became more real and the message more haunting.

> The act of writing this poem was triggered by a feeling . . .
> the sense of pain I experienced . . . pain for the child, the
> little boy in blue. And this triggered a picture of a child in
> my own neighborhood. And while my poem sounds so bleak,
> it's through this writing and subsequent conversations that
> I'm now better able to see the message of hope it entertains.

Response Through Cooking

In response to *Polly Vaughn* (Moser, 1992), Pat, the chef, presented a large sirloin roast, rare and bloody. She had wrapped the meat in a dirty white rope and had set the meat on a tray in a small, tarnished pan. We didn't know what to say. It took 30 seconds before anyone spoke. Barb offered her best guess as to what this meat represented: "The meat was a metaphor for violence." Unlike our reactions to the poetry and dance, our feeling was more somber and the reaction more visceral. We chose our words carefully and deliberately.

Response Through Visual Art

I responded to *Polly Vaughn*, presenting a mural that portrayed the disillusioned characters, using metaphors and headlines cut from the newspaper. The group's attention focused primarily on how the contemporary headline heightened the similarity of present times to the historical setting of the book. Pat commented that the headlines, "Teenagers' Clothes May Have Provoked Shooting," reminded her of the tragic similarity between the accidental death of Polly because of what she was wearing and recent shootings of teenagers for their designer clothes.

John, an architect and watercolor artist, had read *Fly Away Home* (Bunting, 1991), and ended the evening by sharing his sketch of a bird superimposed on an airplane. A tightly constrained male figure fit inside a narrow band placed between the bird and airplane. A giant dollar sign balanced at the top of the ink sketch (see Figure 11-1).

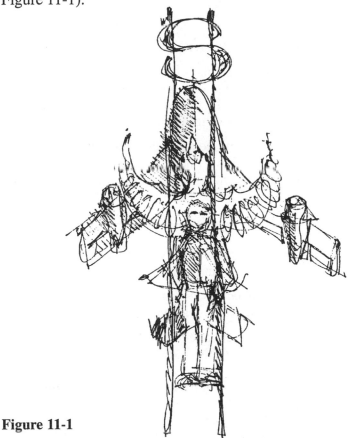

Figure 11-1

Our conversation ranged from the significance of money to its effect on a person's freedom. This last piece steered the night's talk to a symbolic finale. The sketch moved us into a discussion of the similarity between the two books and how powerfully the themes of violence and choice (or lack thereof) pervaded the art pieces and discussions.

Pat, the chef, who had initially felt reluctant about her participation, stood back to consider the experience. "I thought this was going to be quite nebulous. I was very uncertain about what we were doing or what you wanted. This has been fun. I think I've learned why this is valuable. It encouraged creativity . . . to think about what we wanted to think about, what stirred, what moved, and what touched us."

Initial Insights

The experience of responding to books through the arts was very powerful for all of us. As I first reflected on the experience and reread the work of Berghoff (1993) and Harste (1993), I had several insights:

- Exploring meaning through the arts created new possibilities for understanding the texts.

- Creating a personal response enabled each of us to respond to the stories in any one of a variety of ways. The open invitation encouraged the participants to draw from their own experiences and strengths.

- We learned more from one another's representations than any one of us could have understood alone. Each person had something important to share and, in doing so, extended the understanding of the books for each individual and the group. We knew more at the conclusion of the get-together than we did when we started.

- We not only interpreted the texts with new understandings, but we felt different about the book and our lives.

- Expression through the arts encourages a deeper, more emotional understanding or evocation.

- Our experience was enhanced by the power of multiple types of expressions "rubbed up against each other."

[handwritten margin note: advantages to using different modalities/Arts etc.]

John, the architect in our group, reflected this last point at the end of our meeting:

The different media have different ways of conveying meaning and they really are supportive of each other. In other words, the image Jennifer had in the dance was very different than the image created in the book, but they supported each other. The story and the meat metaphor really did too. Without reading the book, if I saw the meat or the dance or the sketch or this mural, would they have had as much meaning? Do the images stand alone? I think a lot of the pictures we see in a museum, for example, we see outside their context. Very seldom do we see art pieces rubbed up against each other.

Jennifer, the dancer, added further:

> The whole process opened up all these different doors
> into looking at these stories. It seemed to be just branch-
> ing off and getting into more depth and poignancy. It
> was a very helpful process for me to see that my dance
> helped reveal what I knew, as well as helped other people
> understand the book differently.

Her response is interesting, for she originally prefaced her
presentation by saying, "This is trite." Jennifer's way of understanding the world through movement had seldom been valued or
legitimized in school. Although she has choreographed numerous
contemporary dance pieces and is currently dancing for The Rus-
sian Ballet Company, she had never thought of herself as "knowing" through dance, or using her knowledge in relationship to
literature.

The potential for knowing increases because the arts help us
make meaning in deeper ways. Sometimes we are surprised by
what it is we know and don't know. Through artistic creation and
expression, we can begin to figure out what it is we are indeed
thinking and feeling. The "ah-ha" that comes from this process
emphasizes the value that exploring multiple sign systems can provide. Jennifer recognized this when she commented:

> You each had a different angle on my general idea. I
> wasn't sure of my real idea . . . I was learning through
> the physical sense of the story . . . But now I think I
> understand what I was trying to represent even more
> clearly.

Implications for the Classroom

What do these artists' perspectives mean for my classroom and
my literature program? In the next section, I'll share six key points
that I've learned from my classroom experience this past year.

Choose Quality Literature

Start with good literature. *The Giver* (1993) by Lois Lowry was an
irresistible choice. This book is so well written and highlights issues so compelling that my students couldn't stop talking about it.
There were no simplistic conclusions to our discussions of freedom, literacy, and human rights. We decided to explore our thoughts
through art.

In response to *The Giver*, Andrew held up a sketch of a boy
sitting several feet from the dinner table while the mother, father,
and sister sat nudged tightly to each side. "See, they're there, his
parents and sister. But they share because of rules. I haven't heard

anyone say they love each other." He added, "It doesn't seem like love exists in this place. In fact, I'm not sure Jonas really lives in a family."

Figure 11-2

I shared my own sketch (Figure 11-2), explaining "All I could think about was how courageous and persevering the boy was. Guided by a sense of memory and drive, he continued up the snowy hill. I wonder if the sledding incident frightened or excited him."

Art provided a natural medium for response to the powerful themes and unanswered questions at the end of *The Giver*.

 Stay Open to Many Ways of Responding

While both student and teacher demonstrations provide students with potential ideas, I've learned that the more experience students have with multiple response invitations, the greater the chance students will push into new territory. I've learned that it's sometimes wisest to follow the students' leads. They are naturally curious and some are compelled to do it their own way.

For instance, early in the year, I noticed Todd crumpling a piece of brown construction paper. Later that day, he asked if he could leave the room to rub dirt and grass on his wadded paper. I watched uneasily as he even tried burning the corners of the paper. During our read-aloud time, Todd continued his work, coloring elaborate patterns on a second small sheet of white paper. At the end of the day, students shared some of their responses to *Afternoon of the Elves* (Lisle, 1989). Todd asked to present first. He held up the book he had made with its rugged, wrinkled cover (Figure 11-3). He spoke with confidence and new-found insight as he opened his book and shared the delicately drawn pattern.

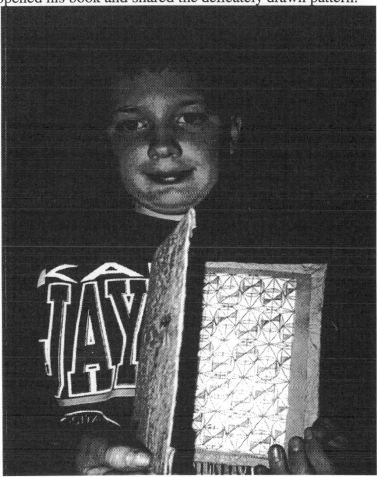

Figure 11-3

As Todd explained, pointing to the book's cover, "This is Sara-Kate as people see her. Ragged and unkempt. But this is what they should see." Todd opened his book and shared the delicately drawn pattern. "You can't tell a book by its cover," he added.

What had appeared from a distance as a day of nonsensical starts and stops for Todd was just the opposite. It was a day of making meaning.

Value All Responses

My experience with both students and adults is that there are some forms of response that lend themselves to more in-depth discussions, while others promote introspection, quiet, and even confusion, qualities rarely recognized or validated in literature discussion groups. For example, illustrations and sketches often provide a context for everyone in the group to see what's there, make interpretations, and spark new ideas. But sometimes it's more challenging to interpret forms like poetry, music, and clay. I described earlier how the experience with the chef's response left the group silent and challenged. Similarly, our classroom experiences with poetry and clay evoked discomfort.

This was painfully evident when Michael presented his sculpture from *Charley Skedaddle* (Beatty, 1987).

> No one knew what to say when they saw my black and white statue. I knew the darkness of Charley was his gang side. The white—that was him at home, in the city, being a normal person. When he's in war, he's caught as a spy and you see, he's against everybody . . . He's both light and dark. He's not always good, not always bad. I mean, what would I write about Charley. I thought I made sense with my statue. I hoped others got it.

Going out on a limb with a new form of expression is not only scary, it's demanding of everyone in the group. When Michael played a dissonant arrangement on the xylophone, in response to *North to Freedom* (Holm, 1974), he gave the group a new form of expression—wordless and powerful. Art often pulls meaning from something outside the realm of words. We must trust and value these wordless occasions.

Participate in the Making of Meaning

It's important for me to be fully involved in the process alongside my students. By doing so, I not only *gain* personal value from the experience, but I *give* value to the experience. Students see that I am invested in the making of meaning through the exploration of literature and the exploration of the arts. Not only do I act as a catalyst, I learn firsthand what it means to know more about an idea or book from the process and discussion. This inside glimpse gives me credibility when I talk with parents about what's going on in my classroom.

Provide Shared Experiences as a Framework

Last year, when I merely offered open-ended invitations for response, students rarely ventured into poetry or music. I began using our read-aloud to highlight specific types of response. For instance, when I read *Number the Stars* (Lowry, 1989), I stopped

after the first few chapters and modeled my reaction through poetry. I then invited students to create their own poetic interpretation. I found that this direct focus on poetry provided the foundation
on which students could build. I also modeled sketch-to-stretch
(Harste, Short & Burke, 1988), dramatic tableaux, and the use of
drums. These demonstrations, coupled with layers of students' responses such as Nel's musical interpretation, Jenny's poetry, and Todd's
artistic metaphor, created an archive of potential artistic responses.

Provide Opportunities to Share Insights into Both Process and Product

While writing this chapter, I interviewed students about their response to literature. By listening to students, I not only validated
their work, I also validated their meaning making process. I asked
students why they used poetry as a response and what it afforded
them. Several articulated the chanciness of poetry; it allowed them
to take risks and venture into more open-ended interpretations.
For example, Jenny explained, "Poetry allows me to be on the
edge. It puts me out on the line. People give me looks when they
don't understand my poem. What's important is that I get what
I'm thinking."

Occasionally, I invite students up to the "Artist's Chair" to
display their work, share their interpretation, and give tips on their
artistic process. Highlighting both the students' products and processes validates and elevates the importance of the arts as a tool in
constructing meaning.

Final Thoughts

Jennifer, the dancer, ended the artists' evening of response to literature with her reflections:

> Creating the movement of the little boy made me think
> how it must feel like to be him and actually to physically
> walk through an airport. It's difficult and different to
> imagine yourself doing it. I know I will never forget the
> story. You do more thinking when you create something
> of your own out of it. It becomes ingrained in you.

The arts are participatory; they engage us and help us experience the world in new and refreshing ways. The issue I find myself
grappling with is not finding importance in the arts, but in understanding the difference between *doing* art through projects and
assignments, rather than responding and exploring meaning *through*
art. For me there is a distinction. We now value a variety of responses in our literature program. Because of this, our conversations have become more varied and the possibilities for creating
meaning multiply with each new experience.

Pat, the chef, captured my growing delight about the role of the arts in my classroom:

> I think the really nice thing about this project is you don't need to be an artist. You don't need to be a scientist . . . just a human being. And that's valuable. We got such very different responses. It would be interesting to see what thirty different kids would come up with. It would be phenomenal!

My goal this year has been to explore the role of the arts in school. I have embraced a definition of literacy that recognizes the power of understanding through art or dance or drama in the same way it recognizes the importance of understanding through writing. I have begun to redefine how the arts can enhance and inspire ventures into meaning making.

Note: Special thanks to my colleague, Kathy Egawa, who worked with me through the many drafts of this chapter.

References

Barre, Shelley. (1993). *Chive*. New York: Simon & Schuster.

Beatty, Patricia. (1987). *Charley Skedaddle*. New York: William Morrow.

Berghoff, Beth. (1993). *Multiple Sign Systems and Curriculum: Moving Toward Whole Literacy in a First Grade*. Unpublished manuscript.

Bunting, Eve. (1991). *Fly Away Home*. Illustrated by Ronald Himler. New York: Clarion.

Gardner, Howard. (1983). *Frames of Mind: The Theory of Multiple Intelligences*. New York: Basic Books.

Harste, Jerome. (1993). Literacy as curricular conversations about knowledge, inquiry, and morality. In Martha Ruddell & Robert Ruddell (Eds.), *Theoretical Models and Processes of Reading*, Fourth edition. Newark, DE: International Reading Association, 1220–1242.

Harste, Jerome, Short, Kathy, & Burke, Carolyn. (1988). *Creating Classrooms for Authors: The Reading-Writing Connection*. Portsmouth, NH: Heinemann.

Holm, Anne. (1974). *North to Freedom*. New York: Harcourt.

Lisle, Janet Taylor. (1989). *Afternoon of the Elves*. New York: Orchard.

Lowry, Lois. (1993). *The Giver*. Boston: Houghton Mifflin.

Lowry, Lois. (1989). *Number the Stars*. New York: Dell.

Moser, Barry. (1992). *Polly Vaughn*. Boston: Little, Brown.

Paulsen, Gary. (1983). *Popcorn Days and Buttermilk Nights*. New York: Penguin.

Rosenblatt, Louise. (1978). *The Reader, the Text, the Poem: Transactional Theory of the Literary Work*. Carbondale, IL: Southern Illinois Press.

Taylor, Mildred. (1976). *Roll of Thunder, Hear My Cry*. New York: Puffin.

Chapter 12

Literature Circles:
Assessment and Evaluation

Bonnie Campbell Hill

In previous chapters, you have read how communities of readers discuss, respond to, and extend their interpretations of literature. Observing these classrooms in action is inspiring, but how can we capture the quality of these interactions? What do the students' oral, written, and artistic/dramatic responses reveal about their developing understanding of story structure and elements of literature? How can we describe children's growth as readers to parents and administrators? And how can we involve students in assessing their growing understanding of literature, themselves, and the world around them?

Once you incorporate literature circles into your classroom, you will probably be delighted with your students' responses to literature. At the same time, you may feel a need for tools to assess their attitudes, reading strategies, levels of response, and amount and range of reading.

Ideally, assessment should be woven into the fabric of classroom instruction so that you don't have to stop teaching in order to evaluate learning. Assessment should involve an on-going collection of various types of information in order to help you teach responsively. Equally important, assessment should include the voices of students as they reflect upon their own growth.

The teachers in this book have developed many assessment forms and techniques that they have piloted in their classrooms. These teachers continue to create new forms and modify others, sometimes asking students for input. Several authors of this book contributed to *Practical Aspects of Authentic Assessment: Putting the Pieces Together* (Hill & Ruptic, 1994), and many of the forms and ideas in this chapter evolved from that book. Other books that teachers have found helpful for assessing literature circles and reading have been *Grand Conversations* (Peterson & Eeds, 1990), *Portfolio Assessment in the Reading-Writing Classroom* (Tierney, Carter & Desai, 1991), and *Assessment and Evaluation in Whole Language Programs* (Harp, 1993).

We've tried to trace the sources of our ideas, although in some cases, the forms have gone through so many revisions that they bear little resemblance to the original. We all find, however, that the forms we use most are the ones we develop ourselves. It's important not to inundate your students or yourself with too many forms. Our purpose is to offer a framework from which you can build. Select a few new ideas and don't become overwhelmed! Assessment should provide an organized way of collecting information to inform instruction. In this chapter, we'll explore six aspects of assessing literature circles and response:

- Assessing oral response
- Assessing extensive reading
- Assessing participation
- Assessing written response
- Assessing artistic and dramatic response
- Evaluation and portfolios

Assessing Oral Response

Discussions are one of the most exciting aspects of literature circles, yet oral responses are challenging to record and assess. With several groups meeting at once and comments bouncing back and forth, it's difficult to document even a fraction of the interactions. Many teachers have discovered the effectiveness of taking anecdotal notes that provide information for assessment and instruction. In *Portfolio Portraits* (1992), Cindy Matthews states that "Anecdotal records readjust the teacher's vision of who and where the student is and sharpens teachers' insight into how each student travels along his or her own path to learning" (p. 169).

First, it's important to decide your purpose for taking anecdotal notes. Most of the teachers in this book use anecdotal notes to provide information about students in order to:

- give immediate feedback after literature circle discussions
- plan instruction
- assess students' strengths, abilities, attitudes, and needs as readers/writers
- prepare for parent conferences and write narrative progress reports
- provide documentation for staffings or referrals

Next, you'll need to determine a manageable method for recording information and maintaining anecdotal records. While many of us have tried various systems, whenever we had to recopy information into a notebook or onto index cards, the notes piled up on our desks and were no longer useful. Once you decide how to take notes, it's also important to establish a realistic and predictable schedule. We've found that our skills as observers and the quality of our notes improve with practice.

Anecdotal Notes After Discussions

Christy Clausen developed a simple system for taking anecdotal notes in her first-grade classroom. As she described in Chapter 2, she meets with two literature groups each day. She finds that it's too difficult to listen attentively to her first graders and take notes at the same time, so she writes anecdotal comments immediately after discussions.

Christy modified the grid in *Assessment and Evaluation in Whole Language Programs* (Harp, 1993, p. 195) to note specific types of interactions during literature circles. She keeps a clipboard with blank forms on her desk and, after each discussion, jots down brief notations about children's participation, levels of response, or insights (Figure 12-1). For instance, when Christy listened to a discussion about *Leo the Late Bloomer* (Kraus, 1971), she recorded Courtney's comments ("Blooming shouldn't be forced. Kids shouldn't be forced to learn.") with a note about how this student was making connections between literature and her own ideas.

Anecdotal Notes During Discussions

Since Christy is fortunate to have adults in the classroom during literature circles, she enlists their help with anecdotal records. The reading specialist uses Christy's form, but has also added a key in order to be able to quickly note categories of students' responses (Figure 12-2). This "shorthand" form is easier to complete during the discussions and reflects Christy's focus and expectations. She finds that many of the specialist's observations confirm and support her own. Christy tucks the forms in her teacher's notebook for later reference when she writes comments on narrative report cards and when talking with parents during conferences.

"Post-it" Notes → for recording Anecdotal Records

Re-copying information always seems inefficient, so teachers are delighted with the idea of using "Post-it" notes to record information. Many of the teachers in this book use a grid with rectangles the size of small "Post-it" notes and write the names of their students above each rectangle. The teachers take anecdotal notes

Literature Discussion Notes

Book Title_____ Date_____

Record student responses that indicate any of the following:
showing enjoyment, sharing reactions, seeking meaning from
illustrations, drawing conclusions, elaborating, justifying,
explaining, expressing feelings, relating to personal
experiences, going beyond "I like" statements, making
predictions, asking questions, discussing literary elements

use for anecdotal Records →

Adapted from *Assessment and Evaluation in Whole Language Programs*
(Harp, 1993).

Figure 12-1 Literature Discussion Notes.

during or after literature circles on small "Post-it" notes, then affix
the note to the form under the child's name (Hill & Ruptic, 1994,
pp. 53–60).

Lisa Norwick keeps her grid on a clipboard as she observes
literature circles in her third/fourth grade multi-age classroom.
Since her literature circles are student-led, she jots down quick
notes as she listens to small group discussions. Figure 12-3a shows
an example of Lisa's notes for three groups that were reading

Literature Discussion Notes

Book Title_____Date_____

Record student responses that indicated any of the following:

1. shows enjoyment
2. shares reaction
3. seeks meaning from illustrations
4. draws conclusions
5. elaborates
6. justifies
7. explains

8. expresses feelings
9. relates to personal experiences
10. goes beyond "I like"
11. makes predictions
12. asks questions
13. discussing literary elements

Audrey	3, 4, 8, 1, 9, 2

Figure 12-2 Codes for Literature Discussion Notes

different novels. Notice that her anecdotal notes are very brief, yet, over time, help paint a picture of students as readers and literature circle members.

Lisa keeps a teacher's notebook for assessment purposes—a three-ring binder with tabs marking a section for each child. She places a blank anecdotal notes grid in each child's section. At the end of the week, she transfers each child's "Post-it" note from the class grid to his or her section in her teacher's notebook. In Figure 12-3b, you can see an example of Lisa's anecdotal notes about Nancy that capture her growth as a reader and group participant from October to January.

Refining Anecdotal Notes

When Lisa first began taking anecdotal notes, she found that trying to capture the animated discussions of 20 to 35 students throughout the day was overwhelming. She decided to focus on only a few children each day and concentrate on taking notes just during literature circles. As you can see by her notes about Nancy, her focused observations provide *specific* information about students' growth and needs. Each week, Lisa takes anecdotal notes on one or two of the areas listed in Figure 12-4.

Lisa keeps this list tucked under the anecdotal note grid on her clipboard. As she takes notes, she refers to the list in order to keep her observations focused and informative. After each literature circle discussion, Lisa shares her insights with the students. For instance, she might say, "Good readers often make connections between what they read and other books or real life. Today during your literature circles, I'll be listening for the connections you make." At other times, her insights might lead to mini-lessons.

ANECDOTAL RECORDS for _Literature Circles_

Michelle	Lani	Kylie	Ashleigh
Family Apart 1-11 Focuses on the authors' craft – dialogue + description	1-11 Evaluates characters actions, comparing herself to them	1-11 Connects with main characters struggles	1-11 acted out her favorite scene. very enthusiastic
Jeff	Brock	John	Dagny
Shiloh 1-11 Made a great prediction that generated a lot of discussion	1-11 asked Questions focuses on the plot	1-11 a bit more focused today responded to others	1-11 Read a Key scene she had marked to clarify discussion
Nancy	Skyler		
1-11 Responded thoughtfully to others	1-11 Very animated and enthusiastic Discussion centers around Brock and him		
Jonathan	James	Christy	Jennifer
Task of Blackboards 1-11 Reacts to humor Retells favorite parts, responds to others Keeps the group going	1-11 Shares opinion and justifies it using information from the book	1-11 Quiet Participant Positive Body language; needs encouragement to share ideas	1-11 Summarizes Key scenes Responds to others

Figure 12-3a Class Anecdotal Notes

ANECDOTAL RECORDS for _Nancy_

10-5 Not focused, didn't participate until the end	10-12 Came prepared, marked 3 passages she wanted to discuss	10-12 Comments focus on retelling and reacting to the humor	10-19 Is beginning to respond to others
10-19 Mainly responds to others when they're discussing a character	10-24 Planning for a puppet show, rereading for details	10-27 Discuss using improvisation, pretending you're the character	11-2 Presented puppet show, captured characters' struggle
11-30 Quiet participant, needs encouragement	12-7 More involved, shared her point of view + reread key scene	12-7 Making progress on responding to others	12-14 Very enthusiastic, connected with other members, asking them questions
12-21 Shares what she'd do if she were the main character, sparked a great discussion	1-11 Responded thoughtfully to others		

Figure 12-3b. Individual Anecdotal Notes

This year Patti Kamber has elicited parent help in taking anecdotal notes. In September she meets with volunteers to talk about literature circles and their role as observers. She finds their perspective invaluable. For example, this winter when her fifth graders were discussing *The Fighting Ground* (Avi, 1984), Patti asked one parent to take notes on students' questions that sparked good conversations, while she listened for in-depth responses. Parents share their observations during the debriefings and Patti keeps their notes, along with her own, in her teacher's notebook. Parents have thoroughly enjoyed this new role and often are amazed by the quality of conversation during literature circles.

Mini-Lessons

When a child tries a new form of response to literature or a new reading/writing strategy, Lisa Norwick may ask the student to share his or her insight with the class. For instance, when Johnathon didn't know the meaning of *chlorphyl* in his literature circle novel, he discovered that the author defined the word later in the text. After he shared his strategy, "reading-on" was added to the class list of effective reading strategies. If Lisa asks a student to prepare a mini-lesson on a written response or drawing, she makes a transparency of the entry for the student to refer to while explaining his or her response. These student-led mini-lessons enhance self-esteem and provide concrete, attainable models for their peers.

Anectodal Notes about Literature Circles

- Asking questions
- Listening actively to others
- Responding thoughtfully to others
- Making predicitons
- Retelling the main idea or supporting details
- Responding to the author's craft
- Using the text to support ideas and opinions
- Responding to elements of literature
- Making personal connections to their lives
- Making connections to other books and authors
- Reflecting on their reading and setting goals

Figure 12-4 Anecdotal Notes about Literature Circles

Both Lisa Norwick and Anne Klein keep a running list of mini-lessons (teacher-led and student-led) in their plan book or in the front of their teacher's notebook (Figure 12-5). They find that maintaining an on-going list keeps them organized and provides a record of what they have taught (and re-taught). It is also particularly helpful in showing student teachers, administrators, and parents how they teach skills within the context of a literature-based program.

MINI-LESSONS

Date   *T/S

*Teacher-Led or Student-Led Mini-Lesson

Figure 12-5 Mini-Lessons Record

Assessing Extensive Reading

Observing literature circle discussions provides information about *intensive* reading. However, we also need information about students' *extensive* reading. In the next chapter, Sam Sebesta cautions that reading assessment should not only assess comprehension, but should also examine the amount and range of students' reading in and out of school. If our goal is to nurture lifelong readers, we need a way to discover whether literature circle books and discussions entice children to read more.

Reading Logs

Many teachers have a collection of reading logs where students can record the books they read independently. In this chapter, we've provided two examples of reading logs, one primary and one intermediate (Figure 12-6 and 12-7). As students look back at their logs, they can begin to detect reading patterns and preferences. We've found the logs helpful in holding students accountable for their reading and in looking at the types of books and authors they select.

For young students, particularly at the beginning of the year, recording a book's title and author can be a time-consuming and laborious task. It's important that recording books doesn't become so burdensome that student reading diminishes. It's also important to keep the logs from becoming competitive or from emphasizing *quantity* over *quality*.

Reading logs can become dead-end exercises. In order for booklists to be meaningful to students, you might want to provide time in class for students to share their logs with partners or in small groups. You could also ask children once a month to refer to their logs and draw a picture or write about their recent favorite book or chapter. In some classrooms, students keep a class log of favorite books, listing titles, authors, and genres, along with brief evaluations. Before they go to the library, Lisa asks her students to turn to their reading log in their portfolios and talk about the books they've read recently. Such informal book talks contribute a great deal to developing a community of readers in which students enthusiastically exchange books and titles.

Reading Conferences

Many primary teachers conduct weekly reading conferences, meeting with four or five students each day. They may meet more frequently with less-proficient readers. Most teachers conduct reading conferences about the books students are reading independently, rather than about literature circle books. Some teachers, however, have students bring their literature circle response journals to the conference and discuss the entries. You can amass a wealth of in-

READING LOG

Name _____

Month/Year _____

Date	Title	How much did you like it? A Little Some A Lot
		1 2 3 4 5
		1 2 3 4 5
		1 2 3 4 5
		1 2 3 4 5
		1 2 3 4 5
		1 2 3 4 5

Figure 12-6 Primary Reading Log

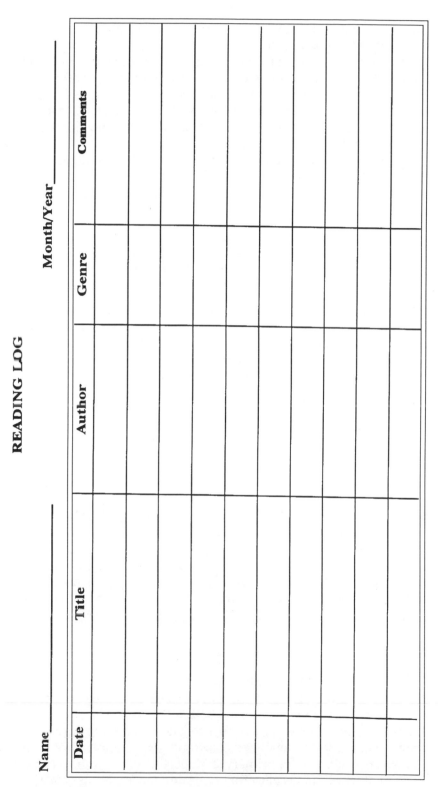

Figure 12-7 Intermediate Reading Log

formation using anecdotal notes during reading conferences about titles, attitudes, reading strategies, and areas for instruction. We've found, however, that we often end up writing the same comments over and over as we listen to children during reading conferences. In order to save time, several teachers have created assessment forms that document frequently observed behaviors and strategies. You can check off common observations, then use anecdotal notes more sparingly.

Lisa Norwick confers with her intermediate students about their independent reading every two or three weeks and meets weekly with less-proficient readers. She uses these conferences to:

- assess students' strengths and needs
- teach strategies
- help students develop background knowledge
- discuss literature circle participation and journal entries

She modified a reading conference form (Hill & Ruptic, 1994, p. 109) for use with her intermediate students. As she listens to her students read aloud and talk about their books, she records their reading strategies, fluency, and comprehension. Information from this form helps Lisa plan instruction and complete progress reports. We've provided an example of Lisa's notes in order for you to see how she can quickly check the boxes, note the strategy she taught, and add one quick comment each time she confers with a student (Figure 12-8).

Assessing Participation

Many of the teachers who have written chapters in this book used a form similar to one in *Grand Conversations* (Peterson and Eeds, 1990, p. 71) when they began assessing literature circles. However, as they became more comfortable with literature circles and saw that students were responsibly engaged, they relied on anecdotal notes for their observations and let students assess their own participation.

Self-Evaluation with Primary Students

The Daily Literature Study Record in *Grand Conversations* (Peterson & Eeds, 1990, p. 66) is often used to assess participation, particularly in classrooms where teachers are just beginning literature circles. Over time, most teachers adapt the form to fit their particular grade level and classroom expectations. We've included an adaptation for primary students that uses symbols (faces) instead of words and is easy for beginning readers/writers to complete (Figure 12-9).

Name __Nancy__

READING CONFERENCE RECORD

Reading Strategies	Date: 9-12 Title: Boxcar Children	Date: 9-21 Title: Burnicula	Date: 10-3 Title: Holiday Inn →	Date: 10-20 Title:
Rereads	||	|||	THL	||||
Skips/Returns	✓	✓+	+	+
Uses Context Clues	✓	✓	✓+	✓+
Decodes	too much	too much	✓	✓+
Knows Sight Words	+	+	+	+
Replaces Unknown Words				
Miscues Preserve Meaning	✓	✓	✓+	
Appropriate Level	just right	just right	just right	just right
Reads Fluently	✓	✓	✓+	✓
Literal Comprehension	+	+	+	+
Interpretive Comprehension	✓	✓	✓+	✓+
Strategy Taught		Check: Does this make sense?		Replace unknown word

Key: + consistently ✓ sometimes

Comments:
9-12 Reads word by word, stops flow when she comes to an unknown word.

9-21 Worked on rereading + using context words to figure out unknown words.

10-3 Rereading more often when text doesn't make sense.

10-21 Didn't focus as much on decoding; reread when text didn't make sense. Only skipped words which it didn't interfere with meaning.

Figure 12-8 Reading Conference Form

Literature Circle Evaluation

Name_____

Evaluate yourself each day on your participation during literature circles.

I did my best ☺

I did O.K. ☺

Not this time. ☹

Date	Finished Reading	Date	Finished Writing	Date	Participated in Discussion	Listened Well

Comments:

Figure 12-9 Literature Circle Evaluation Form.

Once a week, Christy Clausen's first graders reflect on their participation, then fill out a self-evaluation form (Figure 12-10). Using this form holds students accountable, while not overwhelming the youngsters with a great deal of writing. As they become adept at using the form, Christy adds space for children to write their goals for the next literature circle set.

Self-Evaluation with Intermediate Students

Lisa Norwick and her third/fourth graders spend several mini-lessons at the beginning of the year analyzing effective literature circle discussions. Lisa takes careful anecdotal notes during literature circle discussions and shares her insights. She then provides a simple debriefing form that asks two basic questions: What did you do well during today's discussion? What is your goal for next time? The form includes specific prompts (for example, asked good questions, listened actively). Once students have internalized these techniques, Lisa removes the prompts (Figure 12-11).

Literature Circle Self-Evaluation

Name_____ Date_____

Title_____

1. I read my book   yes   no

2. I marked places in my book   yes   no

3. I brought my book on Monday   yes   no

4. I shared my book with others   yes   no

5. I thought this book was:

   Not So Good   O.K.   Very Good

Figure 12-10 Primary Literature Circle Self-Evaluation Form

Lisa Norwick has adapted another form (Hill & Ruptic, 1994, p. 145) that students can use to reflect upon their participation during literature circle discussions (Figure 12-12). At other times, she asks students to give written feedback to others in their literature circle group. She finds it helpful to vary the forms so that students' responses don't become rote. After students understand the three forms, Lisa leaves copies of each at the writing center. Her students can choose the form they want to use for their self-reflections. She sees significant improvement in literature circle discussions as students learn to step back and examine their participation and set goals.

Patti Kamber's more detailed Literature Circle Debriefing form (Figure 12-13) provides a scaffolding for response. She uses this form weekly during literature circles at the beginning of the year and her mini-lessons focus on each of the questions. Patti reinforces effective listening and speaking during oral debriefings at the end of each discussion. These conversations also help students learn to set specific goals. For instance, one student articulated a specific goal in these terms: "I need to get to the point because my group got a little bored. I guess I'm thinking while I'm talking instead of before I talk. Next time, I think I can get to the

LITERATURE CIRCLE SELF-REFLECTION

Name_____ Date_____

Title_____ Author_____

What did I do well today during our literature circle meeting?
(asked good questions, listened actively, responded to others, reread, took a risk, compared
the book to my experiences, compared the book to another book)

_____

_____

_____

_____

_____

_____

_____

What do I still need to work on during literature circle meetings?

_____

_____

_____

_____

_____

_____

Figure 12-11 Intermediate Literature Circle Self-Reflection Form.

point by using my notes a little more. This can be tricky!" Both
Patti and Lisa find that as the year progresses, their students internalize the questions and are able to write thoughtful reflections
and set goals without the forms.

Peer Evaluation

Many of the authors of this book describe how debriefing conversations after literature circles help children become more effective
listeners and speakers. Peer response is effective because it's usually immediate and honest. The challenge is to encourage students
to give honest feedback to one another, while still remaining supportive. At the beginning of the year, Anne Klein presents several
mini-lessons on constructive feedback, then introduces a Discussion Summary form (Figure 12-14) that students complete once
every week or two. At other times, she simply asks students to
write positive comments to group members on a blank piece of

Literature Circle Debriefing

Name_____ Date_____

Title_____ Author_____

Today's discussion was_____

_____

because_____

_____

My involvement/participation was_____

_____

I could improve by _____

_____

_____

Figure 12-12 Literature Circle Debriefing Form

paper. For example, Fabienne's group members commented, "You helped me remember words and descriptive passages in *Monkey Island*" and "You really helped me understand the book better. I liked how you did your entries. They were very understanding." Students keep these forms and comments in their literature circle folders, which are later placed inside their portfolios to share with parents.

Retrospective Self-Evaluation: End of Literature Circle Set

At the end of each literature circle set, Anne Klein's students complete a Literature Circle Self-Evaluation form (Figure 12-15). She finds that the numerical scale and simple questions make the form easy to complete and help students become accountable for being prepared and participating in discussions. She refers to these forms when helping students set goals and when writing comments on progress reports.

Literature Circle Debriefing

Name_____ Date_____

How much did you participate in the discussion today?

about the right amount   too much   not at all   too little

_____

What was an important contribution you made to the discussion?

_____

_____

What was an important idea expressed by someone else in the group during the discussion? (Identify the person and tell what he/she said.)

_____

_____

What group strategies did your group use well? What strategies did you struggle with?
(participating, staying on topic, contributing appropriate information, encouraging others to contribute, listening carefully, making good eye contact, being considerate of others' opinions, asking for clarification, summarizing, using appropriate voice levels)

_____

_____

_____

Suggestions/comments/goals for next literature circle discussion?

_____

_____

_____

_____

Figure 12-13 Literature Circle Debriefing Form

Retrospective Self-Evaluation: End of the Year

Although on-going assessment is essential, evaluating a new program is equally important. Christy Clausen gives her first graders a form at the end of the year so that she can discover what children learned and enjoyed about literature circles (Figure 12-16). She finds the results informative when it comes to fine-tuning her literature circles the following year.

We've presented a variety of ways to involve students in assessing oral response and participation during literature circles through daily debriefings, peer evaluations, and retrospective self-evaluations. It's important, however, not to overwhelm your students with forms. Select a few that work well and vary them from time to time. As students become comfortable with oral and written reflections, they will become more effective as literature circle participants.

Discussion Summary

Name_____   Date_____

Book_____   Author_____

Please summarize what **you** did and/or learned today during your literature circle discussion.

_____

_____

_____

_____

_____

_____

Comments from other group members:

1._____

_____

_____

2._____

_____

_____

3._____

_____

_____

Figure 12-14 Discussion Summary Form.

Assessing Written Response

Many teachers incorporate response forms or journals into their reading program. Some write brief notes in the margins of student journals, at the end of an entry, or on "Post-it" notes. Teachers comment to show they've read the entries, to affirm effort, and to ask questions that deepen students' responses. Others jot anecdotal notes as they read responses, noting whether students merely summarize the plot or make connections and understand the book at a deeper level. However, many teachers wish they had a tool to record the developmental growth of students' written response to literature.

Growth Over Time

Patti Kamber developed a Literature Circle Response Log that she uses at the beginning of the year to structure students' written re-

Literature Circles
Self-Evaluation

Name_____   Date_____

Book_____   Author_____

1 = Never 2 = Occasionally 3 = Sometimes 4 = Almost all the time 5 = Always

_____ I had my novel and response journal ready.
_____ I was quiet and listening for directions.
_____ I wrote thoughtfully in my response journal.
_____ I dated my entries.
_____ I wrote down quotes, new/interesting words, or items to discuss.
_____ I stayed on task during reading and discussion sessions.
_____ I listened well to others.
_____ I took an active role during discussions by asking questions and talking about the
       book.
_____ I was cooperative and participated in the extension activity.

What did you like most about this book?_____

_____

_____

What are your goals for the next literature circle set?_____

_____

_____

Literature Extension Activity

What went well?_____

_____

What are your goals for your next extension activity?_____

_____

Teacher Comments:_____

_____

Figure 12-15 Literature Circle Self-Evaluation Form

sponses (Hill & Ruptic, 1994, p. 141). The form includes room to write (1) a brief summary, (2) a personal reaction, (3) questions for discussion, and (4) a goal for the next meeting. Patti's students bring their logs to literature circle discussions. The written responses and questions stimulate conversation as they learn the fundamentals of student-led discussions. Many teachers have found this form very useful, particularly when they first begin literature circles. Comparing fall and spring entries often reveals significant growth in the complexity and depth of understanding.

Literature Circle Evaluation
(End of the Year)

Name_____ Date_____

1. Did you enjoy Literature Circles this year? _____

2. Which of the following did you like doing?

    _____ Reading at home with your parents
    _____ Talking about the book at school
    _____ Writing in your journal
    _____ Signing up on Friday
    _____ Choosing your first/second choice
    _____ Doing a project with the book

3. What were your favorite books?

_____

_____

_____

_____

4. What did you learn from Literature Circles?

_____

_____

_____

Figure 12-16 Literature Circle Evaluation Form (End of the Year)

Assessing Written Response of Primary Students

Christy Clausen encourages her first graders to talk about their books before they respond in their journals. The oral conversations provide scaffolding for children's writing and drawings. Their entries range from simple drawings to adding details, captions, and eventually sentences about their literature circle books. Young children's journal entries can show substantial changes from month to month. Christy uses anecdotal notes to record their:

- understanding of the book
- growing ability to articulate ideas
- developmental level of entries
- patterns of responses
- growth as writers and artists

A powerful evaluation technique is simply to place weekly samples side by side in front of students and ask them to tell you what they notice about their growth as readers and writers. These oral reflections about concrete examples are the first steps for young students as they begin to learn the language of self-reflection.

Christy also uses the Assessing Student's Written Response form (Figure 12-17) to document children's growth in responding to literature. The five categories reflect how children move from simply retelling a story, to being able to support their reactions, summarize, make connections to their lives and other books, and evaluate literature. Every week or two, Christy places a tally beside the levels of response evidenced in students' journals and makes brief comments about entries. She keeps individual forms in her teacher's notebook.

The next form incorporates the same five categories but provides a way to capture a larger picture of the developmental patterns of response within your whole class (Figure 12-18). You can record information on this form once in the fall (using a •) and once in the spring (using an X) to provide a broad picture of reading and writing development in your classroom.

Assessing Written Response of Intermediate Students

Lisa Norwick and Anne Klein use a more detailed form with their intermediate students to assess written response (Figure 12-19). Since their students take several weeks to complete a book, these teachers evaluate only the first and last journal entry for each literature circle set.

This form includes eight levels of response, as well as space to note effort and identify efferent and aesthetic responses. The categories are meant to be developmental, although the types of responses are also affected by maturity, experience in talking about books, genre, and where readers are in the book. For example, students tend to retell and summarize more at the beginning of a novel. Lisa and Anne keep a copy of this form in each child's section of their teacher's notebooks. They use the information to encourage more insightful responses, plan mini-lessons, and help students set goals.

Assessing Artistic and Dramatic Response

In the previous two chapters, Lisa and Barry Hoonan write persuasively of the power of making meaning through the performing

Assessing Student's Written Response

Name_____

Date	Literal	Supports	Summarizes	Connects	Evaluates	COMMENTS

Figure 12-17 Assessing Students' Written Response Form

Patterns of Written Response

Name	Literal	Supports	Summarizes	Connects	Evaluates

key: fall = ●   spring = X

Figure 12-18 Patterns of Written Response Form

arts. It's important, however, to move beyond superficial dioramas and skits to responses that help students deepen their understanding of a book. How can artistic response be assessed? What
are the criteria for evaluation? The key is to involve students in
articulating their processes and evaluating their own projects.

Assessing Artistic and Dramatic Response with Primary Students

Primary students often clamor to respond to a book they enjoy.
The teacher's main role is to be an enthusiastic audience and to
nudge those children who are capable of more effort. Christy jots
quick anecdotal notes as her first graders are working on weekly
extension projects She asks them questions such as, "What project
are you doing today? How does this relate to the story?" She records
their responses on "Post-it" notes, which she later transfers to individual pages in her teacher's notebook.

Assessing Written Response

Name __Erica__

Date	10-5	10-21	11-30	12-23	1-11	2-4
Title	Holiday Inn →	→	StoneEx →	→	Shiloh →	→
Reacts (It was funny.)	✓	✓				
Retells (literal level)						
Supports/Justifies (I like it because…)		✓	✓	✓		✓
Summarizes/Synthesizes				✓		✓
Connects (to experience/books/authors)					✓	✓
Discusses elements of literature (point of view, setting, characters…)			✓	✓		
Generalizes about theme or author's craft (interpretive level)						
Evaluates/Analyzes						
Effort (+ or -)	+	+	-	+	-	+
Aesthetic/Efferent (A/E)	A	E	A	A	A+E	A+E

Comments:

10-5   Picture w/ thought bubble : Very colorful + detailed

10-21 Letter to Main Character : Retold key scenes + asked questions

10-30 Pamphlet about characters

12-23 Bookmark about Little Willy

1-11   Summary/Reaction : very little reaction

2-4   Sketch with thought bubbles and description of situation

Figure 12-19 Assessing Written Response Form (Intermediate)

Assessing Artistic and Dramatic Response with Intermediate Students

Anne Klein's intermediate students also enjoy creating artistic and dramatic response projects. Before they embark on creating scripts, props, or sculptures, she asks them to complete an Extension Planning and Evaluation form (Figure 12-20). She's found that the form helps children reach consensus on what aspect of the book they will highlight and how they plan to work as a team, and also helps them remember that their project should focus on a significant aspect of the book.

Extension Planning and Evaluation

Title_____ Author_____
Group Members: Teacher Comments

_____   _____
                                      _____
_____   _____
                                      _____
_____   _____
                                      _____
_____   _____
                                      _____
_____   _____
                                      _____
_____   _____

What *part(s)* of the book do you plan on sharing with the class? Write specific chapters/page numbers.

_____

Describe in detail what you plan on doing as a group to share the book.

_____

_____

_____

How will your project reflect an important part of the book?_____

_____

_____

List the supplies you'll need that aren't already available in the room:

_____

_____

General Feedback:

Figure 12-20 Extension Planning and Evaluation Form

As Anne's students explore different ways to respond to literature, they talk about quality of response and the criteria for evaluation. The class discusses

- voice level
- display of material
- clarity and organization of presentation
- creativity
- how response extends meaning

After students share their extension projects, Anne writes a brief note for each group member at the top of the page and a general comment to the group at the bottom of the form.

Lisa's intermediate students complete a similar Literature Project Self-Reflection (not included here) after they have shared their artistic or dramatic projects with the class at the end of a literature circle set. The form contains three questions:

1. How did using the performing or visual arts enhance your appreciation of the book?

2. What is something about your extension project that you're proud of?

3. What is something you learned from another person's extension that you may include in your next project?

For example, when Lisa taught sixth graders, Kirsten wrote, "When me and Michelle did the puppet show, we had to work hard on expression. That meant we needed to understand how the characters felt so we could make it seem real. That helped me understand what was really happening. It made me appreciate their feelings a lot more than when I just read the book." The questions on the form nudge students to reflect upon both their processes and products and to stretch their ability to respond through the performing arts. Lisa finds that discussions about process and criteria, as well as the modeling during student-led mini-lessons, are the keys to eliciting quality projects and reflections.

The class is spellbound when Katie interviews family members from Patricia MacLachlan's book *Baby* (1993) and are moved by Mark's jackdaw of *Nightjohn* (Paulsen, 1993). How can pieces like these be included in students' portfolios? Both Anne and Lisa have recently begun taking photographs in order to capture students' dramatic and artistic responses. They've developed a form (Figure 12-21) with space for students to describe their process, how the project reflects a significant part of the book, and evaluate quality and effort. Students can place the photographs and reflections in their portfolios to share with families.

RESPONSE PROJECT

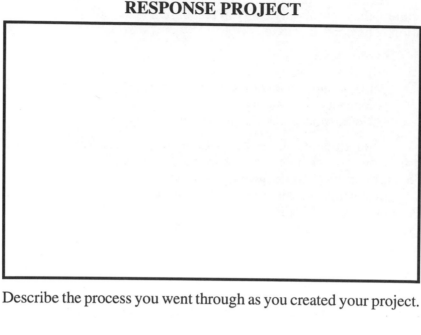

Describe the process you went through as you created your project.

How does it reflect an important aspect of the book?

How does this project show quality and effort?

Comments, feelings, or reflections:

Figure 12-21. Response Project Form.

Evaluation and Portfolios

All of the teachers in this book use a variety of forms to assess growth in reading, response to literature, and participation. Anecdotal notes document behavior and capture conversation. Reading logs and surveys provide information about attitudes, interests, and independent reading. During reading conferences, both anecdotal notes and conference forms can provide documentation of decoding skills, reading strategies, and comprehension. Teachers can also use diagnostic tools such as retelling, running records (Clay, 1993), or miscue analysis (Goodman, 1969). It's also important, however, to invite students inside the assessment process through self-evaluation and portfolios.

Many of the teachers in this book use a combination of data sources to evaluate students on a developmental reading continuum developed by a teacher in Bainbridge Island, Washington *(Practical Aspects of Authentic Assessment: Putting the Pieces Together,* Hill & Ruptic, 1994, pp. 235–242). (See Figure 12-22.) Teachers use colored pens to highlight students' growth each trimester: yellow for fall, blue for winter, and pink for spring. For instance, in the fall Lisa used a yellow highlighter to mark that Tanya was beginning to read easy chapter books and read to herself for brief periods of time. By spring, Lisa noted with a pink marker Tanya's growing ability to read more challenging novels for longer periods of time.

The descriptors on the continuum are ideal for mini-lessons as students become aware of their own development as readers and the criteria for evaluation. In many schools, teachers use the reading continuum as part of their progress report. Other teachers use the continuum to supplement their report card, while some only use it for diagnostic purposes. Many teachers, students, and parents find that the continuum provides clear benchmarks for identifying growth in reading.

Portfolio Entries

Portfolios are organized collections of work and reflections that celebrate learning and highlight directions for growth. We highly recommend *Portfolio Portraits* (Graves & Sunstein, 1992) as a reference that captures the heart of student-owned portfolios. Portfolios can provide evidence of students' development as readers through logs, samples of written or artistic response to literature, photographs of dramatic responses, peer evaluations, and self-evaluations.

Many of the authors of this book include student portfolios in their assessment programs. In this section, we'll focus on portfolio entries that relate specifically to reading and literature circles, although portfolios can also include documentation of learning in other content areas.

Lisa Norwick devotes several mini-lessons to helping her students learn to select portfolio entries. She begins with a simple half-sheet form with the question, "Why did you choose this piece for your portfolio?" Students brainstorm possible answers and talk about entries that move beyond "I chose it because I like it."

After students become comfortable describing why they selected a journal sample or response project for their portfolio, Lisa introduces another reflection form that asks, "What is the process you went through while creating this piece?" Students may choose either form for portfolio entries. One by one, she introduces and models each of the reflections listed in Figure 12-23.

Reading Continuum

Ages 4 - 6 Preconventional	5 - 7 Emergent	5 - 8 Developing	6 - 9 Beginning	7 - 9 Expanding
• Holds book, correctly turns pages. • Chooses book and has favorites. • Shows start/end of book. • Focuses on print. • Knows some letter names. • Interested in environmental print.	• Pretends to read. • Uses illustrations to tell story. • Participates in reading of familiar books. • Knows most letter sounds. • Recognizes names/words in context. • Memorizes pattern and familiar books. • Rhymes and plays with words.	• Sees self as reader. • Reads books with word patterns. • Knows most letter sounds. • Retells main idea of text. • Recognizes simple words. • Relies on print and illustrations.	• Reads early-reader books. • Relies on print more than illustrations. • Uses sentence structure clues. • Uses meaning clues. • Uses phonetic clues. • Retells beginning, middle, end. • Recognizes names, words by sight. • Begins to read silently. • Understands basic punctuation.	• Reads beginning chapter books. • Reads and finishes a variety of materials. • Uses reading strategies appropriately. • Retells plot, characters and events. • Recognizes different types of books. • Makes connections between reading, writing, and experiences. • Silent reads for short periods.

Ages 8 - 10 Bridging	9 - 12 Fluent	10 - 13 Proficient	12 - Adult Independent
• Begins medium level chapter books. • Reads and finishes a variety of materials with guidance. • Reads and understands most new words. • Uses reference materials to locate information with guidance. • Increases knowledge of literary elements and genres. • Silent reads for extended periods.	• Reads most young adult literature. • Selects, reads and finishes a wide variety of materials. • Uses reference materials independently. • Understands literary elements and genres. • Begins to interpret deeper meaning in young adult literature with frequent guidance. • Participates in guided literary discussions.	• Reads complex young adult literature. • Moves between many genres with ease. • Integrates non-fiction information to develop a deeper understanding. • Interprets sophisticated meaning in young adult literature with guidance. • Participates in complex literary discussions.	• Voluntarily reads and understands a wide variety of complex and sophisticated materials with ease. • Evaluates, interprets and analyzes literary elements critically.

Source: Practical Aspects of Authentic Assessment: Putting the Pieces Together, Hill and Ruptic 1994.

Figure 12-22 Reading Continuum

Portfolio Reflections

Why did you choose this piece for your portfolio?

What is the process you went through while creating this piece?

Why is this piece important to you?

What risks did you take while developing this piece?

How does this piece show what you have learned?

Why was this piece an experiment for you? What did you learn from your experiment?

Who or what influenced you to create this piece?

Do you have any wonderings or questions about this piece?

If you were going to re-do this piece, what would you do differently next time?

Figure 12-23 Portfolio Reflections

Lisa also color-codes portfolio reflection slips, using the same colors she used on the continuum: yellow for fall, blue for winter, and pink for spring. As students and their families glance through the portfolios, the color-coding helps them visually note the changes over time in both the quality of entries and the thoughtfulness of the reflections.

Assessment Challenges and Celebrations

The forms in this chapter are working well for us now. We will continue to adapt them to meet the needs of our students, and as we learn more about assessment, literature circles, reading development, and reader response. However, we want to issue some words of warning about overusing forms. All of these forms lying side by side in this chapter may give the impression that there is "a form for every occasion!" Our hope is that you will select the two or three techniques and forms that will provide the most helpful information for you and your students. We encourage you to modify these forms and develop new assessment techniques and strategies of your own. Send us copies of your forms, along with your name, grade level, and address, so that our book can become a forum for the on-going sharing of ideas. As technology changes, we hope we'll soon be able to share more of these via the "information highway."

As we wrote this book, we hesitated to put assessment in a separate chapter, because assessment and instruction should be seamless. We also worried about including so many forms. Our hope was that you would choose a few and adapt them to meet your own group of students. Assessment forms can provide a scaffolding as students begin to internalize the process of reflection. Eventually you may be able to simply use blank paper for debriefings and self-assessment. Our goal should be to help students learn to evaluate their own progress.

> Clearly, learners know themselves better than anybody else. If we teachers include them as participants in the evaluation of their own learning, not only will they gain more control of their own study and development, but also we will have a better understanding of them as learners and as people. Learner-centered assessment should be considered a necessary part of student-centered instruction. (Fu, 1992, p. 183)

As you incorporate literature circles in your classroom, we hope the assessment forms and ideas we've presented will encourage you to weave together your insights alongside those of your students.

References

Avi. (1984). *The Fighting Ground.* New York: Lippincott.

Clay, Marie. (1993). *An Observation Survey of Early Literary Achievement.* Portsmouth, NH: Heinemann.

Fu, Dan-Ling. (1992). One bilingual child talks about his portfolio. In Donald Graves and Bonnie Sunstein (Eds.), *Portfolio Portraits.* Portsmouth, NH: Heinemann, 171–183.

Goodman, Ken. (1969). Analysis of reading miscues: Applied psycholinguistics. *Reading Research Quarterly,* 5 (1), 652–658.

Graves, Donald & Sunstein, Bonnie. (Eds). (1992). *Portfolio Portraits.* Portsmouth, NH: Heinemann.

Harp, Bill. (1993). *Assessment and Evaluation in Whole Language Programs.* Norwood, MA: Christopher-Gordon.

Hill, Bonnie & Ruptic, Cynthia. (1994). *Practical Aspects of Authentic Assessment: Putting the Pieces Together.* Norwood, MA: Christopher-Gordon.

Kraus, Robert. (1971). *Leo the Late Bloomer.* Illustrated by Jose Aruego. New York: Windmill Books.

MacLachlan, Patricia. (1993). *Baby.* New York: Delacorte.

Matthews, Cindy. (1992). An alternative portfolio: Gathering one child's literacies. In Donald Graves and Bonnie Sunstein (Eds.), *Portfolio Portraits.* Portsmouth, NH: Heinemann, 158–170.

Paulsen, Gary. (1993). *Nightjohn.* New York: Delacorte.

Peterson, Ralph & Eeds, Maryann. (1990). *Grand Conversations: Literature Circles in Action.* New York: Scholastic.

Tierney, Robert, Carter, Mark & Desai, Laura. (1991). *Portfolio Assessment in the Reading-Writing Classroom.* Norwood, MA: Christopher-Gordon.

Chapter 13

Goals and Assessment:
How They Go in Circles

Sam Sebesta

Years ago I was assigned to interview gifted readers. They were seventh and eighth graders who scored at the top in reading achievement tests. They could read college texts fast and with good comprehension. I was supposed to find out what enabled them to do that.

Those interviews showed me two kinds of gifted readers. One kind remembered pleasant times associated with reading right from the start, with plenty of easy reading to practice on. They recalled specific books, times, and places that were milestones in their progress. Many said they went on reading binges. They'd get interested in a topic and read everything they could find about it.

In contrast, a small but consistent group of adolescent gifted readers told me that reading held little interest for them. From the beginning, they'd learned the strategies for reading school assignments and especially for taking tests. Reading was a job, no more. One of this group candidly told me, "I don't read for fun. I get my kicks from TV."

The achievement tests and informal reading inventories that identified these gifted readers didn't distinguish between the two groups. Nor did these measures show the motives and interests of average and below-average readers. In the past, some people assumed that reading achievement and reading enthusiasm are causally linked: if you increase achievement, then enthusiasm will follow. My interviews didn't support that notion. Nor did the study of Lamme (1976), which revealed a group of low-achieving middle graders who nevertheless loved to read and often found more time to read than their high-achieving classmates.

What I'm suggesting here is not isolated conjecture. Our concept of reading, whether for some utilitarian purpose or personal enlightenment, has broadened and deepened. So, too, have our ideas on how to assess reading. In the early 1800s, the Blue-back Speller days, assessment of reading meant "toe the line and talk from the book" (Smith, 1934)—in other words, oral reading accuracy. In the twentieth century, assessment has evolved. The question now asked is, "Can the student decode accurately, then answer questions that show literal comprehension and some degree of inference?" Recent assessment includes open-ended items to see, for instance, whether a student can retell a story or apply what has been read in order to discuss an issue. The evolution has been toward authenticity: Can the reader use reading in life-like situations?

All to the good, I think. Yet there's a missing link. That second group of gifted readers I interviewed still might do quite well according to this broadened assessment. That group of enthusiastic but "low" readers identified by Lamme might still do poorly. But in real life, in the years ahead of them, these two groups might surprise us despite our so-called authentic assessment. It is doubtful that readers who lack enthusiasm and a sense of the personal worth of reading will step into the role of mature, lifelong readers. Conversely, the reader who is self-motivated and persistent may well continue to find reading a pleasure and benefit despite continuing difficulty.

Authentic assessment, then, means more than evidence of skill in inference and problem-solving in life-like situations. It requires that we attend to attitudes and interests. And since modern authentic assessment is continuous and cooperative, this means that these factors are imbedded in what we do. We don't stop the curriculum to say, "Now we'll do a lesson to raise your attitude and extend your interests and then we'll test for results." Instead, we assess as we go along to see if these factors are intrinsic to what we're doing. As teachers, we are not alone in this endeavor. Students self-assess their attitudes and interests, collecting evidence and planning growth.

From this perspective, the chapters in this book are fascinating assessment documents. Think for a moment about the evidence they contain:

- Students quickly scoot their chairs into the literature circle. They're eager to get started.

- Students listen to each others' interpretations. So carefully do they consider others' opinions that sometimes they change their own!

- Students monitor their participation, suggesting specifically how they can change and do better.

- Teachers change their procedure on the basis of what's going on, not according to a preset plan.

There is evidence, too, of comprehension and literary understanding. Students can retell plot, for instance, but, more important, they can focus on incidents in order to discuss characters, cause-effect, and significance or theme. Evidence emerges to show that these students are developing intertextuality—that is, they can compare books or pit one text against another to arrive at a conclusion or judgment. Perhaps they are developing abilities that were not within the scope of closed assessment of a couple of decades ago.

Authentic Assessment in Literature Circles: The Beginnings

To participate in modern authentic assessment requires more than collecting evidence and bringing it to bear on predetermined objectives or goals. In many of the chapters in this book you will find something more: a spirit of evolution. Teachers and their students are searching beyond the boundaries of correct comprehension, literary analysis, and general attitudes. They are exploring the range and depth of response, a domain neglected in assessment. They are assessing a meta-level: children's movement toward self-selection and self-determination. Within the dynamics of literature circles, they are evolving and clarifying the traditional objectives and goals of literacy—and it's high time someone did that!

Here's an example. In first grades throughout the country, the tradition has been to teach with materials labeled as suitable for first-grade readability. Even the supplementary and series books for early grades carry an RL (Reading Level) designation. Gradually, Big Books and picture books with more difficult text have found their way from the library corner to a more central place in instruction. Teacher reactions have varied, but they still include doubt ("That book is too difficult. Those are not first-grade words."). Yet first-grade interests seem to be winning out over what was once believed to be first-grade vocabulary and first-grade sentence length. Recently I stumbled (literally) upon an informal literature circle of first graders absorbed in text and pictures of *Ship* by David Macaulay (1993), a fictional but precise account of the discovery and assembly of a fifteenth century caravel by modern scientists. Later a mother of one of this group remarked, "My son says he's going to be a marine archeologist. Where did he get that?" I wonder.

So assessment may no longer be authentic if it is tied to a predetermined objective such as "to read the words on the first-grade list." It will have to be more open, more evolving, and more responsive to what students can do in the wide, wide world of literacy. And such assessment should have repercussions on what we do in literature circles, including selection of materials. That is why the judgment of first-grade teacher Margee Morfitt (Chapter 3) seems especially sound: "Choosing books with sufficient depth to allow for insights and discussion is a more important selection criterion than readability."

Now, in the rest of this chapter I'd like to assist this spirit of evolution. I'll focus on three areas, although these by no means cover all the concerns of literacy or the creative and sometimes unique ways literature circle proponents attempt to solve them. But these three areas must be considered. The first, which I'll label Wide Reading, subsumes variety and taste. In my experience, assessment of variety and taste in reading is frequently mentioned but often neglected. Its importance is perhaps best explored in a full-blown study done several decades ago: *Maturity in Reading, Its Nature and Appraisal* (Gray & Rogers, 1956). The second, Reader Response, is derived from transactional theory (Rosenblatt, 1983), perhaps the most powerful rationale for literature circles. The third is to consider the issue of Achievement Testing: Should these tests have a place in this book or should they not? I may be wrong about them, but at least I'll be giving readers of this book something more to debate!

Wide Reading

In literature circles, students read whole books and, in most classes, a substantial number of them. A valid claim is that more reading gets done than in most other programs, certainly more than in basal reader programs where actual reading often is confined to excerpts and skills materials. If by wide reading we mean the amount of material covered, then surely we have evidence that literature circles contribute to that goal. Our assessment includes lists of books read in the circles and evidence from discussions, journals, and projects to show that the books were read thoroughly.

But I would not stop at that point. Let's look for more evidence of extended reading and the influence of literature circles on free reading. Here is an example. A group of students reads Paula Fox's *Monkey Island* (1991) and gives it the thorough going-over that we've come to expect in the literature circle. They are not certain that young Clay acted wisely when his mother deserted him in the welfare hotel. What should he have done? They are not quite convinced by the ending. Is it credible?

Now we've reached a crossroads that ought to be assessed carefully. Does a core book such as *Monkey Island* lead to extended reading? Readers might consult *No Place to Be: Voices of Homeless Children* (Berck, 1992), for instance, to discover alternatives to Clay's decision. Does a core book plus extended reading influence free reading? In our example, we might find students turning to Dean Hughes' intriguing *Family Pose* (1989) about a homeless central character, for all or part of their free, or independent, reading. What I'm suggesting is that we find out whether students, grouped or individually, seek other novels, nonfiction, or poetry on the topic of homelessness, sometimes trying to find answers to their puzzlements.

My own observations cause me to think that this goal and its assessment are important. I have observed literature circle classrooms in which the core book or set of books aroused so much interest and enthusiasm that you can bet your bottom dollar they spilled over into students' free reading, perhaps for years to come. But I have also observed classes in which the core book had no influence on free reading, neither on the amount of it nor on choices. Hence the need to assess this matter.

What about the range of selections used in literature circles? Does the range represent wide reading? Here's a challenge indeed for teachers' self-assessment. Some classes seem to limit literature circles to "novel units," confining choices to fiction. After all, there seems to be ample variety in fiction: modern realism, high adventure, fantasy, science fiction, and historical fiction. But the wide reading goal surely ought to include some recent biographies, such as those by Russell Freedman and Jean Fritz, and inquiry-based informational nonfiction, such as books by Patricia Lauber, David Macaulay, James Cross Giblin, and Milton Meltzer. Poetry? It would seem that literature circle interaction is an ideal place for recent poetry anthologies, from Arnold Adoff to Jack Prelutsky.

The research regarding reading interests shows that, traditionally, they narrow over the years. A typical reader, as he or she grows older, may confine selections to one genre—to modern realistic fiction, for instance, or to high fantasy. At the same time, interest in other genres—notably poetry and historical fiction—steadily lowers until these become avoidances for many readers. Now, we might hope that literature circles will come to the rescue. How might we find out? First, let us assess the literature circle core book choices. Do they represent all genres, say, over a year's reading? Second, let's see if the spin-offs (the extended reading and free reading that literature circle participants do) begin to reflect this range.

Logs, journals, and conversations can reveal such information about genre representation in core reading, choices in extended reading, and the amount and variety in free reading (Anderson, Wilson, & Fielding, 1988).

Reader Response

There appear to be two ways of teaching literature. Each has its own goal and the goals are as far apart as the goal posts on a football field. Text analysis, which is considered traditional, teaches us to probe text to figure out and appreciate what the author intended. What, exactly, is the setting and how does the author convey it? What are the techniques used to reveal character, and are the characters rounded and dynamic or static? Can we make a story grammar diagram to show conflict and outcome? Can we elucidate the author's theme? Safe and mainly efferent, text analysis is at the center of many published literature guides and perhaps the instructional focus of some literature circle classrooms. If so, the goal seems apparent. Assessment can be an on-going look at evidence: Do students grow in their ability to spot literary elements? Are they able to find, in their discussion and writing, a unification of elements?

Viewed this way, literary instruction doesn't differ from that used for any other subject. There's a body of information to be imparted, absorbed, and (we hope) applied.

The alternative view? We begin not with analysis of text but with the reader's response. We encourage the reader or readers to give free rein to their thoughts and feelings as they read. We don't impose a purpose for reading other than to encourage surrender to the literary experience. Rosenblatt (1983) calls this stage *evocation*. Without evocation, say reader response proponents, little else of real value can happen in the reading of literature. A parallel example would be a trip to Greece. For the avid tourist, the Parthenon summons up emotions and associations until, perhaps, she finds herself seemingly in the midst of ancient Athens, discovering gleaming marble and painted statues long since blemished and golden Athena supreme on her throne. That, for our hypothetical tourist, is evocation. Without evocation, she might just as well have stayed home and stared at a map.

Simple as it sounds, evocation can be difficult. Some of us do not willfully or willingly invest our emotions or tangle intellectually with text. Is that because we were never encouraged to do so? After all, there are reading programs that place no priority on evocation.

A central goal, then, of literature circles is to nurture evocation. In these chapters you find ways that this is done, ways to change stock responses ("I liked the book. It was fun.") to living response. Thus Patti Kamber (Chapter 8) describes her method: "I ask the students to come prepared . . . with a response that clearly and sincerely expresses their reactions and questions about the book." Journal writing and brief exchanges with a buddy may generate evocation, later to be expanded in the literature circle. Lisa Norwick (Chapter 10) and Barry Hoonan (Chapter 11) give evidence that activities in visual and performing arts may help unleash evocation.

This stage of reader response must be assessed, although the task is not as easy as ticking off incidents in a retell test. Yet, surprisingly, researchers and evaluators have opened up to accept what was once rejected as subjective evidence. Recorded dialogue or videotapes of literature circle activity can be used to sample evocation. So can children's self-reports, exemplified in these chapters. And, as an important spin-off of our success in nurturing evocation, we should be able to discover and assess an increase in the amount and quality of voluntary reading.

That isn't all. A skillful teacher who is guiding literature circle discussions will encourage *reflection*. Here the readers examine those thoughts and feelings that were their first response. They listen to others' views. They think back over what they have read or they re-read and re-experience. Their response now is more considered, more searching. Here, it seems to me, is where literature circle interaction plays its most significant role.

In the opening of Chapter 14, Nancy Johnson samples the dialogue that grew out of Naylor's *Shiloh* (1991), the reflection that follows initial evocation. Notice that it contains controversy, with an issue at the heart of it: Do we *hate* a wrong-doer (Judd, the dog-abuser) or do we examine his motives and, maybe, feel sorry for him? Likewise, citing evidence, students may argue, the reasons for Teresa's anger in Jane Resh Thomas's *Lights on the River* (1994). As a migrant worker who lives in a chicken house, will this anger help Teresa or hinder her? As you examine the reflection stage of reader response recorded in this book or present in literature circles around you, notice that (1) it is more likely to occur during interaction, hence helping justify literature circle discussion, and (2) it is often the result of good teaching in which alternative views and substantiation are encouraged.

Let me give you a complete example of reader response theory in action. In a first grade classroom, I presented an old story *Millions of Cats* (Gág, 1928, 1977). The children dramatized the story as I told it, elaborating its bare detail with their knowledge of cats—how they look and how they behave. The fray at the end—the cats quarreled until they destroyed each other—caused so much furor that we decided to choreograph it: that is, we figured out symbolic movements, put them into slow-motion, and backed them up with music. I doubt that the cast of *Cats* on Broadway had a better time of it. We certainly seemed to have accomplished evocation! But I began to worry about a story that seems to solve its problem with mass violence.

I needn't have worried, though. When we sat down to talk about what we'd done, the first reaction was, "I was a good cat. I shouldn't have got ate up." I refrained from saying that sometimes bad things happen to good cats and asked, instead, what *ought* to happen in the story. Solutions included founding a cat shelter, starting a cat chorus to raise money, and taking the cats back home again. Disagreement and justification followed. Later we acted, sketched, and painted some of these alternatives and, even later, we could refer to them as our prototype when we discussed alternative outcomes for other stories, histories, and biographies.

To sum up the theory and practice of reader response: Readers or listeners are encouraged to invest their feelings and thoughts in an all-out transaction with literature, then to reflect upon the experience. These are two intertwined stages, which may be called—at least for assessment purposes—*evocation* and *reflection*. As response deepens, as it is likely to do in literature circles, it may evolve in a number of ways. Readers may consider what ought to happen, what is likely to happen, and how this literary experience touches upon their own lives. This, I think, is the essence of reader response theory, and its application to literature circle technique and assessment seems significant.

The two theories for teaching literature—analysis of text and reader-centered response—are, as I've mentioned, a contrast. But I believe the crucial difference is in the order of their use. Reader response begins with evocation and reflection and a complete concentration on what the reader is experiencing, not with "What is the text stating and how did the author use literary techniques to do this?" Only after the transaction (the evocation and reflection) do we begin such a text analysis.

Let's return again to the *Millions of Cats* example in a first-grade classroom. As we further explore the story, we may ask, How did Wanda Gág keep us busy as we read the book? I may point out that she gave us a refrain to chant every time we came upon it. Are there other stories with refrains? Could students use a refrain in a story they are composing? *Millions of Cats* is a journey story. It goes from here to there and back again. Are there other journey stories? Why? Can children find journey stories in real life? In this way, elements of style and plot structure are woven into the discussion—but not until after the selection has been experienced. Gradually, then, we can name and examine literary elements and authors' techniques for using them (Lukens, 1995). But now literary analysis serves reader response. It is no longer a litany of literary craft but, instead, a set of tools to assist evocation and reflection.

From the perspective of assessment, we look for concrete, supportable signs of evocation—for example, when students display their enthusiasm while reading fantasy or poetry. We examine samples of dialogue journals, and visual and dramatic extensions, for evidence of reflection, including unforced reflections about how the literary experience applies to the readers' own lives. We discover whether students can use literary terms and concepts to probe text and enhance response. Several reader response scholars provide taxonomies for assessing response (Zarrillo, 1991; Cox & Many, 1992; Hancock, 1993) and these, too, may be useful as we study and report this crucial area of literature circles.

Another Look at Achievement Testing

In this book there is little mention, if any, of achievement testing. Maybe the teachers who authored these chapters believe that the chief goals of literature circles are not the goals of achievement tests. That's a refreshing thought.

After all, achievement testing grew up in an age of calibration. If you could measure the output of two hybrids of corn or how much torque to put on a crankshaft, perhaps you could also devise a way to calibrate reading performance. Then you could compare reading gains using Method A versus Method B. You could report reading achievement to a public asking for accountability.

The tests themselves are based on factor analysis. Researchers such as Davis (1973) listed factors they thought crucial in reading comprehension. They created test items loaded with these factors, administered the tests, and discovered that, sure enough, the results revealed significant differences in the comprehension of readers. From such studies came assessment of reading achievement, including grade level and percentile reporting.

Now, it is apparent that such tests do not assess wide reading or reader response. Some critics say that they don't effectively measure reading comprehension either, not in an authentic way. There are indeed many arguments against them. Before we consign them to the shredder, however, let's pause to consider.

First, consider tradition. Tradition in teaching reading has favored systematized prescriptive programs (Sebesta, 1994). In the 1950s came a movement to challenge those programs: Individualized Reading. Here, suddenly, was a reading method based on self-selected whole books—literature rather than textbooks. Of course, there was sharp debate. Reading experts took sides, expertly defending their opinions. Numerous articles containing that debate appeared in the 1950s, especially in *Elementary English*. But the trump card—the evidence that gave Individualized Reading its best advantage—was the repeated finding that IR students matched against basal program students did as well or better on achievement tests. That finding, I'm sorry to say, carried more weight in the education community than some related evidence, such as that IR students developed higher attitudes. I believe a similar case can be made for other holistic methods, including Language Experience and some recent literature-based programs.

The point is that achievement test results have, at least in the past, added support for programs whose philosophy parallels that of literature circles. Granted that the tests are limited, they still carry clout!

Second, consider your district and community. Is achievement testing required? If so, is it accompanied by portfolios and other evidence of achievement? If the answer to the first question is yes and the answer to the second question is no, then consider some more. It might be better to retain the testing and add evidence about wide reading, reader response, and other literature circle variables. Evidence indicates that students in literature-based classrooms will do as well or better on standardized tests. An all-out campaign to shred achievement tests might not be the way to reform assessment, at least at the start.

I'm merely suggesting. Meanwhile, you must consider whether or how achievement tests fit or don't fit into your literature circle assessment. If they do, then here are two warnings:

(1) Give your students some instruction on test format. Reading workbooks and black-line masters used in basal programs have one debatable virtue: they give practice on test format, including multiple choice items and cloze. A few minutes a day for a week will give your literature circle students this practice. Tell them why.

(2) Use achievement results, if at all, to assess reading programs, not individuals. As I've implied at the start of this chapter, the match between an individual's achievement test score and her or his real reading in the wide, wide world may be far from authentic.

Seven Guidelines for Literature Circle Assessment

1. Include interests and attitudes toward reading in your assessment. They're as likely to predict lifelong, mature reading as anything else you could assess.

2. Assess the amount and quality of extended reading and free reading, not just the books that were covered in literature circles.

3. Find out whether all genres are included in literature circle selection. Are these genres represented in students' reading choices?

4. Examine evidence of evocation. Does reader response begin with surrender to the book?

5. Assess reflective thinking: the search for meaning as students consider their literary experiences, including their weighing of alternatives and application to their own lives. Difficult as this may be, it is a crucial measure of the effect of literature circles.

6. Observe students' growth in ability to discern literary elements and techniques as they read and in their own writing process.

7. Consider achievement tests with caution. Are they required in your situation? If so, what is the purpose? What else will be done in assessment, along the guidelines listed above, to balance their effect?

Figure 13-1 Seven Guidelines for Literature Circle Assessment

The guidelines listed in Figure 13-1 will help us reach the heart of the literature circle process, whose goals and outcomes are directed at literary experience that is not text-bound but reader-centered. For, as British critic Elaine Moss (1978) observed: "A book by itself is nothing—a film shown in an empty cinema: one can only assess its value by the light it brings to a child's eye" (p. 142).

References

Anderson, Richard C., Wilson, Paul T., & Fielding, Linda G. (1988). Growth in reading and how children spend their time outside of school. *Reading Research Quarterly, 23*, 285–303.

Berck, Judith. (1992). *No Place to Be: Voices of Homeless Children*. Boston: Houghton Mifflin.

Cox, Carole & Many, Joyce. (1992). Toward an understanding of the aesthetic response to literature. *Language Arts,* 69 (1), 28–33.

Davis, F. (1973). Psychometric research on comprehension in reading. *Reading Research Quarterly, 7*, 628–678.

Fox, Paula. (1991). *Monkey Island*. New York: Greenwillow.

Gág, Wanda. (1928, 1977). *Millions of Cats*. New York: Putnam.

Goble, Paul. (1990). *Dream Wolf*. New York: Bradbury.

Gray, William & Rogers, Bernice. (1956). *Maturity in Reading, Its Nature and Appraisal*. Chicago: The University of Chicago Press.

Hancock, Marjorie. (1993). Exploring the meaning-making process through the content of literature response journals: A case study investigation. *Research in the Teaching of English, 27*, 335–368.

Hughes, Dean. (1989). *Family Pose*. New York: Atheneum.

Lamme, Linda. (1976). Are reading habits and abilities related? *The Reading Teacher, 30,* 21–27.

Lukens, Rebecca. (1995). *A Critical Handbook of Children's Literature*. Fifth edition. New York: HarperCollins.

Macaulay, David. (1993). *Ship*. Boston: Houghton Mifflin.

Moss, Elaine. (1978). The "Peppermint" lesson. In Margaret Meek, Aidan Warlow & Griselda Barton (Eds.), *The Cool Web*. New York: Atheneum, 140–142.

Naylor, Phyllis Reynolds. (1991). *Shiloh*. New York: Dell.

Rosenblatt, Louise. (1983). *Literature as Exploration*. Fourth edition. (First edition published in 1938.) New York: The Modern Language Association of America.

Sebesta, Sam Leaton. (1994). Why I work on basal readers. *Journal of Children's Literature, 20* (2), 45–48.

Smith, Nila Banton. (1934). *American Reading Instruction*. New York: Silver, Burdett.

Thomas, Jane Resh. (1994). *Lights on the River.* Illustrated by
    Michael Dooling. New York: Hyperion.
Zarrillo, James. (1991). Theory becomes practice: Aesthetic teach-
    ing with literature. *The New Advocate, 4* (4), 221–234.

Chapter 14

Time Changes Everything:
One Teacher's Story

Nancy J. Johnson

Their conversation seems to start even before they scoot their chairs into place. Just what starts the discussion—or who starts it—isn't important to these five readers. What matters is the notion that there will be time to meet and talk . . . and talk they do!

> "I *hate* Judd Travers. I can't *believe* somebody can be that mean to their own dogs."

> "Yeah, why does he have them in the first place? Doesn't he want to take care of them? Dogs know when you don't like them. His dogs must know he doesn't like them."

> "No wonder they growl and seem scary. If you were treated that way maybe you'd be mean too."

This is my second year in Lisa Norwick's classroom. Last year, I observed the action of literature circles with Lisa's sixth graders. This year it's with third and fourth graders. Some things have changed a great deal. Other things have simply been fine-tuned. Today, as I sit back and reread the transcribed conversations about *Shiloh* (Naylor, 1991), I again hear these readers' voices, feel their frustration with "bad guys" like Judd Travers, and revel in their passion toward books and stories that move them to gut-level response. And I think of how fortunate these young readers are to be in a classroom where literary discussions are valued and honored; where time is set aside every day to talk about what *they* need to talk about; where varied response forms are both encouraged and valued.

How is it that these young readers can gather on the floor and carry on such natural conversations about books? What kind of structure is necessary for such discussions to take place, especially given the nature of everything else occurring in the classroom? Is this outcome possible the first time a teacher tries literature circles? What happens in classrooms to get to this point? What did literature circles look like and sound like during Lisa's first year? What were her first steps? How did these plans change over time, across grade levels, and throughout the course of the school year?

Although previous chapters indirectly address these concerns, my focus is on the evolution of literature circles in one teacher's classroom. The more I observed in Lisa's classroom, the more I became intrigued by the process of teacher change that results from conscious and thoughtful decision making. This is the pedagogical story of how Lisa's focus changed from just trying to survive to responsive teaching.

Year One—Surviving and Feeling Secure

Lisa's first year of teaching occurred in a fourth grade classroom, where reading materials consisted of the district-adopted basal and three classroom novels. Students were expected to read the basal from cover to cover. Lisa began each story with a vocabulary lesson as suggested in the teacher's manual. Students read the selection, then completed a worksheet that focused on a specific skill. At the end of each quarter, students endured the basal's forty-question multiple choice test. These reading rituals in Lisa's room during her first year can still be seen in many classrooms across the country. A basal for every student, a teacher (and a teacher's manual) directing the show, and reading time chopped into the suggested pieces recommended by the publisher.

Like many of us, Lisa relied primarily on the basal during her first year of teaching. That spring, she introduced three novels, not because of any philosophy, but because students had completed their reading text. She chose the three books—*The Hundred Dresses* (Estes, 1944), *Snow Treasure* (McSwigan, 1942), and *The Whipping Boy* (Fleischman, 1986)—because her school already owned class sets of them. Each novel was accompanied by a teacher's manual and teaching materials prepared by a group of teachers in the district. As a class, students read each novel together and Lisa orchestrated the reading instruction time as outlined in the accompanying manuals. The components were similar to those used with the basal: strong teacher direction, vocabulary lessons, skill worksheets, and questions at the end of each chapter.

At the end of her first year, Lisa wasn't happy with the way she was teaching reading, but couldn't pinpoint the cause of her dissatisfaction. She knew her students weren't very enthusiastic about reading. She was also aware that their lack of enthusiasm contrasted with her goal of creating a classroom where students enjoyed books and learning. Yet her inexperience and her trust in the published materials left her with inadequate resources for change.

Recently I asked Lisa to reflect on her first year of teaching. She acknowledged the tensions that set the stage for changes during her second year.

> For as young and inexperienced as I was, I have to give myself credit for realizing I wasn't achieving my goal . . . I made all the decisions based on what the teacher's manual said. I think I felt so pressured to have my students do well on the tests that I let the tests take priority over developing a love for reading. Using the basals gave me a sense of security. After all, if they did well on the tests, then they were learning to read, right? I was too tied to the program to understand what was really important for the readers . . . I think some kids may have disliked the novel even more than the basal because the story took even longer to read. Can you imagine telling a fourth grade boy he has to read *The Hundred Dresses* and complete all the worksheets? My only saving grace with some of these kids was they really liked me. There- fore, they could tolerate being told what to read and how to respond to the story.

Changes during Lisa's second year were prompted by her participation in a class about planning a reading workshop. She also read *In the Middle: Writing, Reading and Learning with Ado- lescents* (Atwell, 1987). The class, Nancie Atwell's book, and her own nagging concerns prompted and supported her changes.

Year Two—Experiencing Cognitive Dissonance

Change was in the air the autumn of Lisa's second year of teach- ing. This year marked her return to two classrooms—her own fourth grade classroom and a local university classroom where she began her master's program in reading/language arts.

Year two brought more children's literature into Lisa's class- room. After meeting with her principal and talking about her goals for reading, she received permission to tuck away her classroom set of basals and use her workbook money for class novels. Based on books she thought her students would enjoy, Lisa selected six novel sets: *The Borrowers* (Norton, 1953), *James and the Giant Peach* (Dahl, 1961), *Harriet the Spy* (Fitzhugh, 1964), *How to Eat Fried Worms* (Rockwell, 1973), *Snow Treasure* (McSwigan, 1942), and *The Whipping Boy* (Fleischman, 1986). Students were placed in heterogeneous literature groups that remained permanent the entire school year. When asked about this decision, Lisa responded,

"The literature groups were like a base group; when I was in a book club, I stayed with the same people the whole year." Choosing the novels and groupings set the foundation; next, Lisa focused on structure.

Beginning Literature Circles

Lisa carefully designed her reading time during this second year. Literature groups met on Mondays, Tuesdays, and Wednesdays for 30 minutes. On Thursdays and Fridays, students were allowed to select books for independent reading. On those days, they also responded in writing to the books they chose.

The protocol for Monday, Tuesday, and Wednesday was predictable; literature groups read, conferred, and responded to their books. Lisa met with each group once a week for 30 minutes; two groups met each day. She selected how many pages the groups read for each meeting. Students recorded their assigned pages on a laminated calendar posted in the back of the classroom. Lisa also assigned the responses she wanted from the students. Each day was carefully organized; at the time, Lisa felt most comfortable with clear management and organization.

In addition to setting the schedule, Lisa also served as group leader. Each time she met with a literature group, she supported students through each chapter with a guided reading activity, most often following a DRTA (directed reading thinking activity) format. She asked the majority of the questions. Discussions were mostly teacher-directed and Lisa consciously focused on asking questions at the literal, re-organizational, and inferential levels of comprehension. Lisa assigned journal entries, relying a great deal on the list of questions for intermediate readers in the appendix of *Read On: A Conference Approach to Reading* (Hornsby, Sukarna, & Parry, 1986, pp. 160–162). Her major focus at this time was on providing students with the tools to become strategic readers.

Lisa also introduced her students to the notion of literature extensions. These projects weren't yet related to the literature circle selections; instead, they were connected to independent reading selections. Once a quarter, each student was required to complete one extension project on a book of their choice. These projects were treated as homework assignments and, when completed, students brought them to school to share with the whole class. At this time, there were no culminating projects at the end of each literature set. When a group completed their novel, they simply decided which one of the remaining sets of novels they would like to read next, and the cycle started all over again.

In retrospect, Lisa recognized a few problems with her daily schedule and reading requirements. One problem was requiring a written response for independent reading books. Although the focus for choice reading was enjoyment, students still had to complete a response to *prove* they'd been reading. Unintentionally, Lisa had changed the focus of independent reading time from extensive to intensive reading. The change was subtle, but significant.

Another problem was her requirement that students complete extension projects at home. If she had provided time for students to work in class and collaborate on projects, they could have shared their processes. Had she based extension projects on their literature circle novels, they could have talked about the book as they worked to deepen their understanding. As Lisa reflects on her role at this time, she states:

> Basically this second year I was in a period of cognitive dissonance, knowing I wanted to do something different. I wanted the kids to read a whole text and enjoy it. Nobody in my school was doing literature circles; everybody was in the basal. I didn't have anybody to draw on. I'd just started my master's and began to understand the reading process and that teaching should focus on strategies, not isolated skills. . . . I think I chose to structure my class the way I did because I felt I needed to be in control of their reading *at least* one day a week. That day we read together as a group; we didn't have a lot of time to discuss the story. I have now learned what a powerful comprehension tool discussion is. I wish I could tell you it all came together for me my second year, but it didn't.

While Lisa's cognitive dissonance was uncomfortable, it served as the catalyst for additional changes. During this time, Lisa read *Grand Conversations: Literature Groups in Action* (Peterson & Eeds, 1990). The combination of cognitive dissonance and a renewed focus enabled her to rethink her goals, her classroom structures, and how to engage students even more, using authentic literature.

Year Three—Beginning to Let Go

Lisa's third year of teaching involved big changes and continued growth. Not only did her grade level change, so too did the structure of literature circles as well as her teaching role. She was still taking graduate classes and continued to read professional books, journals, and children's literature. After two years of teaching fourth graders, Lisa moved to a sixth grade position. And then more changes began.

Adjusting the Schedule

During her third year, Lisa re-adjusted her schedule for intensive and extensive reading. This year Monday, Wednesday, and Friday became literature circle days; Tuesday and Thursday were choice reading days. The change in schedule helped to weave extensive and intensive reading days together. Having extensive reading days on alternating days provided students with more flexibility. When readers needed additional time to complete their literature circle book, they used extensive reading days.

Lisa also made other changes. First, she omitted required journal entries for extensive reading. In addition, she decided to make literature groups flexible rather than permanent. The reason for these changes? As Lisa stated, "By not requiring journal entries for choice reading, the focus became one of enjoyment. Students didn't have to prove anything to me. I didn't place students in permanent literature circles because I got a little smarter and realized it's very difficult to expect that students would stay a cohesive group all year long."

Each week, the literature circles met with Lisa on one designated day. The students decided what book to read and how many pages they'd read each time. This year marked the beginning of literature circle meetings as student-led literary discussions. Students completed their reading, selected a meaningful passage to share, and wrote in their journals *before* they came to the literature circle. The writing and thoughtful revisiting of the books served as a springboard for their discussion.

Changing the Teacher's Role

Lisa's role during discussion started changing, from being a teacher who controlled the reading and discussing to being a teacher with a less dominating presence. She continued to sit in on the literature circle meetings, interjecting questions and comments to keep the discussion flowing; however, she talked less, controlled less, and served more as a facilitator. Letting go of control isn't easy for those who cut their teaching teeth on basals and scripted teaching manuals. Lisa returned to *Grand Conversations* (1990) as she began to trust her students to take more control of their literary discussions. In addition, she began meeting with other teachers who used literature circles in their classrooms. For the first time, she had colleagues who shared similar interests and an equal passion for literature.

Plunging into Literature and Response

The move to sixth grade prompted Lisa to delve into young adult literature. Armed with recent reading from her children's literature class, suggestions in *Children's Literature in the Elementary School* (Huck, Heppler, & Hickman, 1987), and *Children's Literature in the Reading Program* (Cullinan, 1987), and recommendations from colleagues, Lisa made her initial selections for literature circles. Again, Lisa's principal allowed her to use her work-book funds to purchase novel sets. She purchased four genre study sets: two science fiction novels, *The White Mountains* (Christopher, 1967) and *The City of Gold and Lead* (Christopher, 1967); two contemporary fiction novels, *Bridge to Terabithia* (Paterson, 1972) and *Hatchet* (Paulsen, 1987); two historical fiction novels, *A Family Apart* (Nixon, 1987) and *Roll of Thunder, Hear My Cry* (Taylor, 1976); and two fantasy novels, *Tuck Everlasting* (Babbitt, 1975) and *The Black Cauldron* (Alexander, 1965).

Lisa also changed the students' focus for response to literature. Early in the year, most literary responses were written. By December she began to encourage students to use more diverse forms of response during and after their reading. She introduced each idea through mini-lessons, using the class read aloud book. Students then tried her suggestion for one of their two required weekly responses. As Lisa described in Chapter 10, she and her students developed a list of these diverse response forms that they posted in the room. When I asked Lisa how her students reacted to this new focus, she noted that they were more invested in their work and enjoyed the creativity. In addition, their responses were more fun to read.

Lisa also re-thought how she wanted students to respond *after* reading. She prepared a menu of choices that encouraged artistic response (for example, re-casting the novel as an alphabet book, scrapbook, or tableaux). Students chose a project or created one of their own, working either individually or in groups. At the end of the literature set, extension projects were celebrated with the whole class.

The changes Lisa made during this year were consciously crafted. She and her students experienced success with their new focus on diverse forms of response and extension projects. Lisa's reflections shifted to several new areas of concern:

> Extension projects presented some difficulty, because all five different literature circles were on different schedules. One or two groups were working on their extension projects while the other literature circles needed a quiet atmosphere for reading. Management was a bit tricky at times because of this. Since books weren't organized around a theme, the opportunity for readers to discuss their books with other literature circles didn't happen very often. And when it did happen, it was more of a surface conversation or a retelling of their novel, rather than anything with much depth. Also, I didn't have my students do any type of written self-reflection; all were done orally. I wish I had known more.

Year Four—Stepping Back

The desire to address these areas of concern served as an impetus for Lisa's next changes. As she continued working with sixth graders, she became more aware of literature that elicited genuine response. She began to trust students more as they made choices. Her role began to change. It was a year of stepping back in order to move forward.

During the summer, Lisa read *Creating Classrooms for Authors* (Harste, Short, & Burke, 1988), *In the Middle* (Atwell, 1987), and *The Whole Story* (Cambourne, 1988). She also continued her graduate coursework. She joined the study group of fifty teachers, described by Sarah Owens in Chapter 1, who were intrigued by literature circles. The group met monthly throughout the school year, shared ideas, supported each other, offered book talks, and passed along tried-and-true tips and suggestions. Lisa presented two or three times to the whole group, which offered her a chance to step back and reflect on her beliefs and practices.

Continuing to Make Changes

Lisa's teaching role during literature circles continued to evolve. In order to encourage students to direct their own literature circle discussions, she asked them to bring questions prompted by the reading, as well as passages to share. By spring, she had stepped outside the literature circles completely. She allowed her students to direct their own discussions, ask their own questions, and determine their own topics of focus. Lisa considered this a significant change:

> I'll never forget the first day I let go. I was so excited when I witnessed my students' reactions to the book and to each other. Their conversations took on a new spirit. They shared parts that were important to them, argued, asked questions, and most importantly enjoyed themselves . . . and they didn't need me to sit in with them for this to happen.

As Lisa stepped out of the literature circles, she found time for more observations, took more anecdotal notes, and gained a better perspective of what was happening during students' discussions.

Moving Students to Center-Stage

In addition to student-led literature circles, Lisa also tried student-led mini-lessons. She recognized that if students were put in the role of teacher, they would have to understand their thought process well enough to communicate it to others. Lisa noted:

Student-led mini-lessons became a teaching tool for them, to reinforce their own learning. Plus some kids pay better attention to their peers than they do to many adults, especially at that age. Just believing the kids made a big difference. As they began to teach the mini-lessons, they discovered they really knew something valuable and could share that with each other. I realized I was not the only teacher in this room.

Changing the Shape of Response

At the beginning of the year, Lisa again introduced the list of response forms. By February, the students had exhausted the ideas on the list. Although they were still required to complete two responses each week, she allowed students to choose both responses. The result was a focus on aesthetic and artistic responses *during* reading, as well as for extension projects. For example, Kelly crafted a pop-up page to depict a significant scene from *Dealing with Dragons* (Wrede, 1990) and shared her process during a mini-lesson. Kelly's mini-lesson was enough to trigger an enthusiastic production of pop-up responses the next few weeks, many quite complicated in design.

While most of the responses and extensions were written or artistic, none of the students had tried responses involving the performing arts. In her desire to offer students a wide range of possibilities, Lisa explored ways to encourage, support, and teach performing arts as a response to literature. She interviewed a local actor, playwright, and teacher of children's drama. Armed with his suggestions and information from Nellie McCaslin's *Creative Drama in the Classroom* (1991), Lisa stepped out of her comfort zone and organized a range of performing arts responses.

In the spring, students carefully planned, practiced, and performed scenes from the contemporary realistic novels they had been reading. They laughed as they observed a reenactment of the famous frogball scene from *Maniac Magee* (Spinelli, 1990). They reacted to abuse in scenes from *Cages* (Kehret, 1991). Solemnly they witnessed a gang member's struggle for control in a scene from *Scorpions* (Myers, 1988).

This became a pivotal year for Lisa as her students grew as passionate, responsive readers. She observed them talking about books outside of literature circles more often. These pre-adolescents took risks by responding to literature artistically, dramatically, and poetically.

Lisa started incorporating informal, classroom-based assessment tools to capture her students' interests, passions, strengths, and weaknesses as readers. Students surprised her with their honest perceptions in their written self-evaluations after literature circles. She also gained insights as students chose reading responses for their portfolios and wrote reflections following extension projects.

In June, Lisa accepted a new teaching position for the coming year in a multi-age third/fourth grade classroom. With a sense of confidence and enthusiasm, she revisited favorite books and talked to colleagues as she prepared for another year of change.

Year Five—Fine Tuning and Trusting the Community

Change has become a hallmark for Lisa. Not only did she change grade levels, she jumped into team teaching in a multi-age classroom. Lisa continued her professional growth as she completed her master's degree. She was greatly affected by books such as *Portfolio Portraits* (Graves & Sunstein, 1992), *Seeking Diversity: Language Arts with Adolescents* (Rief, 1991), and *The Whole Story* (Cambourne, 1988). Because of the change in grade level, she explored new areas of children's literature. Lisa also began her first forays into professional writing and presenting.

Adapting the Structure to Build Community

This year, Lisa decided to focus on getting to know her students before plunging into literature circles. She and her third/fourth graders spent the first four weeks sharing favorite books in a variety of ways. Lisa listened to each student read aloud and she took notes about their reading strategies and strengths. To learn more about her students as readers, Lisa prepared an interest inventory. Choosing the first theme was easy; these children loved animals. Lisa asked colleagues, librarians, and bookstore owners for suggested books on this topic. Her young students were delighted with the first literature circle because of its focus on animal fantasy stories.

Stepping Back In

In response to the needs of these students, Lisa extended the time devoted to scaffolding, especially during the first months of the school year. Scaffolding took many forms, though mostly it involved slowing down and not assuming that the same language and terminology used with sixth graders would make sense to these students. For example, in preparation for their first literature circle discussions, Lisa talked to the students about choosing a passage to share. She suggested that they choose their favorite part of the book or a part that described a literary element. They were confused because they didn't know how to find a passage to share. She resolved their confusion by explaining how they could mark a passage that made them laugh or caused them to be upset, sad, or confused. By focusing on their personal feelings about the book, they were able to choose passages with ease. For example, Shane, who was reading *Babe: The Gallant Pig* (King-Smith, 1985), marked a dozen passages that were important to him as a reader the very first week.

As in previous years, Lisa provided scaffolding through mini-lessons on organization and structure. She also included lessons about developing genuine response; the students' choices for response taught Lisa a great deal about their understanding as readers. She discovered that her students didn't produce earthshaking responses in the beginning. As the teacher, therefore, she recognized the need to be patient and give her students time.

Lisa also discovered that her students' needs during their initial involvement with literature circles necessitated a change in her role. At the beginning of the year, she sat on the periphery of literature circle discussions; she found it was not necessary to join every literature circle group. When a group needed her support and affirmation, however, she took a more active role in the discussions, directing comments about literary conversations and providing suggestions for more effective discussions. As groups became more independent, she was able to step outside the group and take anecdotal notes.

Incorporating Flexibility

As students became more comfortable with literature circles, a dramatic change occurred. During the past few years, Lisa had selected the day or days each literature circle met. An assigned day worked well at the beginning of this year, but as the children took more control of their discussions, they realized that they weren't always ready to discuss their book on the assigned day. So they negotiated with Lisa to meet at least once a week, letting the group members and their responses to the book determine when they would meet. The demands of some books and the needs of some readers caused a few literature circles to meet more than once a week. For the most part, one discussion a week seemed adequate. No longer did Lisa need to set their meeting schedules; instead, she relied on her students' judgment to make those decisions.

When I asked Lisa what she considered the biggest changes of the year, she focused on two key items: more involvement with the students in all aspects of literature circles and her continued changing role.

> My expectations for the kids are much more concrete now, less nebulous to them. I'm more able to articulate the process and expectations for the kids. By knowing my focus at the very first of the year I could become

more conscious of key areas where we needed work. For example, instead of doing just one mini-lesson on how to elicit depth of response in journal entries, we came back to it throughout the year. I involve the kids more with establishing criteria. I owe that learning to the ideas expressed in *Portfolio Portraits* (Graves & Sunstein, 1992).

Toward the end of this year, I overheard Lisa's discussion with two teachers who were visiting her classroom to gain an on-site sense of literature circles in action. She didn't promise that they would leave with all of their questions answered, yet she did offer collegial reassurance and some solid advice: "I know it can be scary to start a new program . . . what I've learned is that you need to trust your beliefs and your students."

Year Six: Looking Forward

As Lisa sets her sights on her sixth year of teaching, she's already experiencing some professional growing pains and asking questions that will, no doubt, result in further change. Two intriguing topics for Lisa are assessment, especially related to evaluating weekly journal entries, and enhancing self-reflection with her young students. Lisa's lingering questions for next year include, "How can drama be used before reading to enhance interest and meaning? How can I use nonfiction for literature circles? How about poetry? How can I link fiction during literature circles to our theme studies?"

Final Reflections

I've tried to capture a glimpse of literature circles in Lisa's classroom over a five-year period. What I've noticed is how her initial changes involved concrete concerns: "How do I get started? What literature do I use?" Over time, her concerns became more abstract: "How do I invite readers to respond with more depth? How do literature circles serve as a format for collaboration and sharing of meaning in other disciplines? Can movement and dance and the visual and performing arts be used as a during-reading response?" I have watched Lisa and many of the teachers who have written chapters in this book become thoughtful, responsive teachers.

Lisa's story reflects her changes—from teaching reading using a basal program, to whole class novels, to literature circles. Fortunately, she found support for her changes by surrounding herself with fine company—the company of top-notch professional and children's literature; the company of like-minded colleagues and administrators, supportive mentors, and parents; and the company of young learners. These eager readers, perhaps more than anything, remind her that her teaching will grow and change with the abilities, interests, needs, and spontaneous responses that they bring to the classroom community each and every year.

I'd like to return for a minute to the literature circles discussion about *Shiloh* (Naylor, 1991) in the spring of this school year. Toward the end of one lengthy discussion, the third and fourth grade readers queried:

> "Did any of you read the epilogue? I did and it makes me wonder what will happen ten years from now."

> "You read the epilogue? Are you already done with the book? I *never* read the end of the book until I'm done. I don't like to know what's going to happen."

> "Sometimes I do. The epilogue doesn't really give it away . . . not totally. I sometimes read the last page if I have to know what's going to happen. Then I don't have to worry about the character as much."

Whether you're an epilogue reader or not, it's often helpful to have a sense of the whole—of what literature circles can look like, how to organize for their success, even how to inspire genuine conversations. But, it's also a good idea to realize that you can't really know exactly what's going to happen from book to book, from student to student, even from year to year. We've all read many an epilogue, yet we still wonder . . . what will happen five years from now? Guaranteed, there will be change.

References

Alexander, Lloyd. (1965). *The Black Cauldron*. New York: Holt, Rinehart & Winston.

Atwell, Nancie. (1987). *In the Middle: Writing, Reading and Learning with Adolescents*. Portsmouth, NH: Heinemann.

Babbitt, Natalie. (1975). *Tuck Everlasting*. New York: Farrar, Straus & Giroux.

Cambourne, Brian. (1988). *The Whole Story: Natural Learning and the Acquisition of Literacy in the Classroom*. New York: Scholastic.

Christopher, John. (1967). *White Mountain*. New York: Collier.

Christopher, John. (1967). *The City of Gold and Lead*. New York: Collier.

Cullinan, Bernice. (Ed.). (1987). *Children's Literature in the Reading Program*. Newark, DE: International Reading Association.

Dahl, Roald. (1961). *James and the Giant Peach*. New York: Knopf.

Estes, Eleanor. (1944). *The Hundred Dresses*. New York: Harcourt Brace.

Fitzhugh, Louise. (1964). *Harriet the Spy*. New York: Harper & Row.

Fleischman, Sid. (1986). *The Whipping Boy*. New York: Greenwillow.

Graves, Donald & Sunstein, Bonnie. (Eds.). (1992). *Portfolio Portraits*. Portsmouth, NH: Heinemann.

Harste, Jerome, Short, Kathy & Burke, Carolyn. (1988). *Creating Classrooms for Authors: The Reading-Writing Connection*. Portsmouth, NH: Heinemann.

Hornsby, David, Sukarna, Deborah & Parry, Jo-Ann. (1986). *Read On: A Conference Approach to Reading*. Portsmouth, NH: Heinemann.

Huck, Charlotte, Hepler, Susan & Hickman, Janet. (1987). *Children's Literature in the Elementary School*. Fourth Edition. Chicago: Holt Rinehart Winston.

Kehret, Peg. (1991). *Cages*. New York: Atheneum.

King-Smith, Dick. (1985). *Babe: The Gallant Pig*. New York: Crown.

McCaslin, Nellie. (1991). *Creative Drama in the Classroom*. Fifth Edition. New York: Longman.

McSwigan. (1942). *Snow Treasure*. New York: Scholastic.

Myers, Walter Dean. (1988). *Scorpions*. New York: HarperCollins.

Naylor, Phyllis Reynolds. (1991). *Shiloh*. New York: Dell.

Nixon, Joan Lowry. (1987). *A Family Apart*. New York: Bantam.

Norton, Mary. (1953). *The Borrowers*. New York: Harcourt Brace.

Paterson, Katherine. (1972). *Bridge to Terabithia*. New York: Avon.

Paulsen, Gary. (1987). *Hatchet*. New York: Macmillan.

Peterson, Ralph & Eeds, Maryann. (1990). *Grand Conversations: Literature Circles in Action*. New York: Scholastic.

Rief, Linda. (1991). *Seeking Diversity: Language Arts with Adolescents*. Portsmouth, NH: Heinemann.

Rockwell, Thomas. (1973). *How to Eat Fried Worms*. New York: Dell.

Spinelli, Jerry. (1990). *Maniac Magee*. New York: HarperCollins.

Taylor, Mildred. (1976). *Roll of Thunder, Hear My Cry*. New York: Puffin.

Wrede, Patricia. (1990). *Dealing with Dragons*. New York: Harcourt Brace Jovanovich.

Closing Remarks

Our passion for books and children was probably evident as you read this book. The more we've explored the potential of literature circles and response, the more possibilities we've discovered. However, we're not the only ones who are enthusiastic. Students are powerful and articulate advocates for literature circles. We thought it fitting to close our book with their voices.

When we asked primary students for recommendations for literature circle books, their responses were informative. You might want to ask your own students for book suggestions.

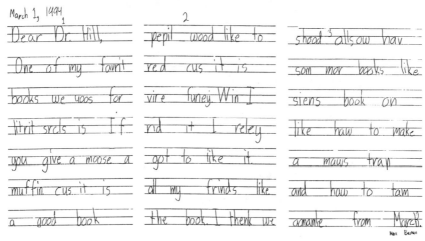

March 1, 1994

Dear Dr. Hill,
One of my favrit books we yoos for litrit srcls is If you give a moose a muffin cus it is a good book pepil wood like to red cus it is vire funey. Win I rid it I reley got to like it. all my frinds like the book. I thenk we shood allsow hav som mor books like siens book on like haw to make a maws trap and haw to tam anamle. from March.

Marc Bastian

Older students also offered recommendations. We end this book with our three favorite testimonials. Jennifer, a fourth grader, wrote:

> I believe that novels are better than textbooks because in textbooks, they tell you what happens but in novels you can capture the action first hand. You can be there. We are in the 90's now and the level of being able to read is very high, therefore kids will be reading more and we don't need low level questions to practice. This is taking away from our learning, it is pushing us down, forcing us to learn to read below level. We're not teaching kids to read, we're teaching them to hate reading.
>
> Novels make learning fun. They have educational value. Give us real books! Literature circles are one way to give students the experience of non-boring, action packed fun learning.

Another fourth grader, Ben, gave literature circles "a perfect 10" and outlined his rationale for enjoying reading novels.

5/7/4

Dear Dr. Hill,

I think that Lit. Circles are a great way to read novels. They may not let you read ahead or at your own pace, but they allow the fast readers free time, and the slow readers extra time. The books that Mrs. Sellers or you pick are superb. I think there are only minor flaws in the program, which don't really need to be fixed. Compared to Basal readers, Lit. Circles are a perfect 10. "Basals" are really boring and mediocre. Real books are just the opposite, superful and inventive. Basals are a leftover from the dark ages of American literature.

Sincerely,
Ben
McGreevy

April began her letter with "To Whom it may concern." Her first page defined literature circles, described the structure and expectations. We'll close the book with her remarks and recommendations.

I personnally like Literature circles. They give you a chance to read a great book but not just read. You can expand past the limits. I like the group cooperation. It all works out well without any shouting and everyone's opinion is counted, noticed, and well thought over.

Now for suggestions. I am charting it out for your benefit and ease.

Graph of Themes/Books

Theme	Books
Historical Fiction	Little house on the prairie
	Caddie Woodlawn
	Sarah, Plain and tall
	Little house in the big woods
Medieval Times	King arthur and knights
	Robin Hood
	Beauty
	The ordinary Princess
Twisted Fairy Tales	The ordinary Princess
	The telling of the tales
	Untold tales
	The Knights of the kitchen table
Indians	Indian in the cupboard
	Sing down the moon

I really like literature circles. Please do them.

Sincerly,
April Clark

From left to right: Sam L. Sebesta, Nancy J. Johnson, Dianne Monson, Lisa F. Norwick, Kary Brown, Katherine L. Schlick Noe, Bonnie Campbell Hill.

Sam L. Sebesta has taught courses in reader response and reading at the University of Washington for 32 years. He is well known for his work in a broad range of responses to literature as well as for his contributions as an author on a reading program. His extensive work in children's literature and the performing arts has had a profound impact on the authors of this book as well as on teachers and children throughout the country.

Nancy J. Johnson is associate professor of English Education at Western Washington University in Bellingham where she teaches courses in children's literature, writing, and integrated language arts processes. A former elementary and high school teacher, Nancy conducts inservice programs on reading, writing, and literature for teachers from kindergarten through high school. She is active in the Children's Literature Assembly of the National Council of Teachers of English, selecting Notable Children's Trade Books in the Language Arts.

Dianne Monson is professor of Children's Literature at the University of Minnesota. Her extensive professional contributions include numerous publications for children's literature textbooks and articles with a focus on genre studies and reader response. Her work in children's literature has earned the respect of educators at all levels.

Lisa F. Norwick is in her seventh year of teaching, with varied experience in the elementary grades. An active presenter at conferences and inservice workshops, Lisa's professional focus is on authentic assessment and extending literature response to include the performing arts. Her classroom was a site for a collaborative university-elementary school research project on literature circles.

Kary Brown is in her sixth year of teaching, refining literature circles with her fifth grade class in Kent, Washington. Kary emphasizes writing workshop and book making in her classrooms and has been invited to share her expertise with preservice teachers at local universities.

Katherine L. Schlick Noe taught at the high school level before joining Seattle University where she is an associate professor of reading and chairperson of the Curriculum and Instruction department. She teaches graduate courses and conducts workshops in integrative curriculum, children's literature, and content area reading. Her current research and professional interests focus on the role high quality literature plays in emergent literacy.

Bonnie Campbell Hill has extensive teaching experience at the elementary and university levels. She is an adjunct professor at Seattle Pacific University and Seattle University and provides consultation to school districts in the Puget Sound region. She is co-author of *Practical Aspects of Authentic Assessment;* published by Christopher-Gordon Publishers, Inc. in 1994.

From left to right: Anne Klein, Margee Morfitt, Penny Redman, Christy Clausen, Sarah Owens, Patricia Kamber, Barry Hoonan

Anne Klein has 11 years teaching experience, and is currently teaching in a multiage intermediate classroom in Edmonds, Washington. In addition to her interests in authentic assessment and the reading/writing process, Anne has been active in training teachers in her district to teach mathematics according to the Curriculum and Evaluation Standards developed by the National Council of Teachers of Mathematics.

Margee Morfitt has been teaching for nine years in first and second grades, as well as her current 1-2 mulitage classroom on Whidbey Island, Washington. She has most recently served as a primary grade representative on the district's language arts committee.

Penny Redman, who describes herself as a constant reader, has taught students in gifted and regular education programs in grades 1-6. Currently teaching fifth grade in Redmond, Washington, Penny had made many presentations at conferences and workshops.

Christy Clausen has been guiding first graders toward literacy for nine years in the Northshore School District outside of Seattle. Her classroom was a site for a collaborative university-elementary school research project on literature circles.

Sarah Owens has taught second through tenth grades and is currently teaching fourth grade in Edmonds, Washington. Sarah's professional efforts include weaving creative dramatics across her curriculum.

Patricia Kamber has taught for 15 years. Her current professional commitment is to engage students in critical, stimulating conversations about literature. She teaches 5th grade on Bainbridge Island, Washington where her classroom was a site for a collaborative university-elementary school research project on literature circles.

Barry Hoonan has been teaching for 13 years, including one year in Great Britain on a Fulbright Educational Exchange. His many professional interests include developing children's educational software and helping children and teachers engage in writing and responding to poetry.

Books for Literature Circles:
A Selected Annotated Bibliography

This annotated bibliography includes selected children's and young adult literature for literature circles. Each of these books has potential to spark rich discussion in grades 1–6 and meets the criteria for quality literature described in Chapters 4 and 9.

Although by no means exhaustive, this list should help you begin compiling your own. Rich sources of effective books for literature circles abound in libraries, journals, children's bookstores, and in colleagues' file cabinets. *BookLinks*, a journal published by the American Library Association, is just one of the places you will find ideas on themes and titles. As an example, look for Penny Bright's article on survival tales in the November, 1994, issue to enhance a theme study on Perseverance and Courage.

Organization

The bibliography is organized by themes, beginning with the very personal and moving out to a broader, more global focus on the world at large. These themes reflect the human challenges that face children and young adults. Within each theme, you will find books at various reading levels, representing emotional and physical challenges as well as ethnic, cultural, gender, and age diversity. Each of these themes could be used differently, depending on age level and experience of readers.

Each annotation describes how the book fits one theme, although most books have the potential to complement several themes. For example, *Bearstone* (Hobbs, 1989) appears under the theme Dealing with Personal Challenges, but would also be appropriate with the theme of Family Issues, Reaching Out to Others, Respecting Animals and Nature, or Perseverance and Courage.

Informational books, folk literature, and poetry are woven throughout the themes. Although we haven't provided content-specific bibliographies on topics such as Flight or Endangered Species, we encourage you to pursue literature circles using informational literature. You may also find that literature circles are a powerful way for children to share poetry and explore folk literature.

Codes/Key

Within each theme, the books are arranged in the following categories:

- **Picture Books**
- **Picture Books for Older Readers**
- **Easy Chapter Books**
- **Chapter Books**

It's worth noting that many picture books can be used effectively in literature circles with younger readers OR with older readers to introduce a theme (for example, using *Let the Celebrations Begin!* by Margaret Wild to introduce Challenges of War).

We've also included the following codes which appear at the end of some annotations:

- **IB = informational book**
- **P = poetry**
- **MR = for mature readers or teacher discretion** (Appropriate for independent readers who can handle more mature subject matter.)

Before You Begin

As we compiled this bibliography, we considered several factors that you may also find helpful as you select books for literature circles.

There is no such thing as a "grade level" book. Many of these titles are equally appealing and effective for readers at several grade levels. Even if a child has already read a book, that should not preclude you from using the book again for literature circles in later grades. None of us can experience everything in a book on the first reading. We bring different perspectives to a book as we mature. For these reasons, we have not placed grade level identifiers in this bibliography.

Be sure your selected books would work well in literature circles. Many of your favorite books may not elicit extended discussions and rich response. For example, a light and humorous chapter book or a pattern picture book may not be rich enough to sustain conversations.

Keep reading. It's important to keep up with newly published books as well as to keep reading ones you've missed. It's also important to rely on what you know about your students and their interests. You know far better than we ever could which themes, topics, characters, and plots will capture your students' interests.

Examine books for possible objections. You know your district's expectations and community standards and need to adapt our suggestions to fit what will work for you. Selecting literature brings with it the possibility that someone may feel that a book you've selected is inappropriate for children. Knowing your school's and district's policies on book challenges is crucial.

Organization of Annotated Bibliography

1. LOOKING INWARD

   A. Dealing with Personal Challenges
   B. Accepting Responsibility

2. REACHING OUT

   A. Perseverance and Courage
   B. Reaching Out to Others
   C. Respecting Animals and Nature

3. ROOTS AND RELATIONSHIPS

   A. Family Issues
   B. Generations Learning from One Another
   C. Challenges of Poverty
   D. Immigration and New Beginnings

4. WIDENING PERSPECTIVES

   A. Personal Explorations
   B. Justice and Prejudice
   C   Heroes and Heroines
   D. Exploration and Westward Expansion: Multiple Perspectives
   E. Cultural Conflicts
   F. Challenges of War
       Revolutionary War
       Civil War and Slavery
       WWII and Korean War
       Vietnam War and Southeast Asia

5. SPARKING THE IMAGINATION

   A. Tales and Twists
   B. Fantasy and Magic Journeys

6. MEETING AUTHORS AND ILLUSTRATORS

   A. Books About Authors/Illustrators

7. READING FOR PROFESSIONAL GROWTH

   A. Professional Books on Literature Circles and Response

1.   LOOKING INWARD

1. A. Dealing with Personal Challenges

Picture Books

Amazing Grace. (1991). By Mary Hoffman. Illustrated by Caroline Binch. New York: Dial. Grace loves all kinds of stories and is eager to try out for the lead role in Peter Pan. Despite her friends' doubts, Grace's mother and grandmother encourage her to be anything she wants to be.

Chrysanthemum. (1992). By Kevin Henkes. New York: Greenwillow. Chrysanthemum loves her name . . . until she starts school. This book touches upon the negative effects of teasing and the power of loving parents and teachers.

Everett Anderson's Goodbye. (1983). By Lucille Clifton. Illustrated by Ann Grifalconi. New York: Holt. In this simply told story, Everett Anderson begins to accept his father's death.

Hue Boy. (1993). By Rita Phillips Mitchell. Illustrated by Caroline Binch. New York: Penguin. Hue Boy and his mother worry that he is too small until a happy event shows them that size doesn't matter.

Ira Sleeps Over. (1972). By Bernard Waber. Boston: Houghton Mifflin. Although Ira looks forward to spending the night with his friend, Reggie, he worries about a secret too embarrassing to reveal.

The Leaving Morning. (1992). By Angela Johnson. Illustrated by David Soman. New York: Orchard. As a family prepares to move to a new home, a child leaves a reminder of herself in the old apartment.

Leo the Late Bloomer. (1971). By Robert Kraus. New York: Windmill. The more Leo's parents watch him anxiously, the more they notice he isn't growing in the same way as others. However, in his own good time, Leo does bloom.

Owen. (1993). By Kevin Henkes. New York: Greenwillow. Owen loves his blanket and takes it everywhere he goes. When school starts, he learns he can't take Fuzzy with him. His parents and neighbor join forces to come up with a solution.

Ruby the Copycat. (1991). By Peggy Rathmann. New York: Scholastic. Ruby is new to school and does everything Angela does. Angela thinks it's great . . . for a while. The teacher helps Ruby begin to realize that people will like her best when she is herself.

Sheila Rae, the Brave. (1987). By Kevin Henkes. New York: Viking Penguin. Louise is sure that her big sister, Sheila Rae, isn't afraid of anything. However, Louise ends up coming to the rescue of her big, brave sister.

The Shy Little Girl. (1970). By Phyllis Krasilovsky. Illustrated by Trina Schart Hyman. Boston: Houghton Mifflin. Sometimes it's hard to make friends when you're really shy. However, when Claudia moves to her school, Anne finds a friend and begins to blossom.

When Jo Louis Won the Title. (1994). By Belinda Rochelle. Illustrated by Larry Johnson. Boston: Houghton Mifflin. Jo hates being teased about her name until her grandfather explains she is named in honor of a famous athlete, Joe Louis.

Picture Books for Older Readers

The Black Snowman. (1989). By Phil Mendez. Illustrated by Carole Byard. New York: Scholastic. A magical black snowman helps a young boy accept himself and take pride in his African heritage.

Fire on the Mountain. (1994). By Jane Kurtz. Illustrated by E. B. Lewis. New York: Simon & Schuster. In this version of a traditional Ethiopian tale of courage, a young boy stands up to a wealthy man who tries to cheat him.

Hershel and the Hannukah Goblins. (1985). By Eric Kimmel. Illustrated by Trina Schart Hyman. New York: Scholastic. Hershel of Ostropol outwits a series of dreadful goblins and saves his Eastern European village.

Easy Chapter Books

The Chalk Box Kid. (1987). By Clyde Robert Bulla. Illustrated by Thomas Ellen. New York: Random House. Gregory Loney, feeling alone in his new neighborhood, finds solace drawing in an abandoned chalk factory behind his house.

Jim Abbott: Against All Odds. (1990). By Ellen Emerson White. New York: Scholastic. Jim Abbott plays baseball for the Toronto Blue Jays. . . with just one hand! He's one of the best pitchers in major league baseball despite the challenges he's had to overcome. IB

Kelly's Creek. (1975). By Doris Buchanan Smith. New York: Crowell. Kelly's teachers and family think he can't do anything and that he doesn't try. He knows he has a learning disability and truly does try. The only place where he finds friendship and understanding is in a Georgia tidal marsh where he befriends a scientist.

The Kid in the Red Jacket. (1987). By Barbara Park. New York: Knopf. Moving can be painful, as a boy discovers when he struggles to be known as something other than "the kid in the red jacket" at his new school.

The Skates of Uncle Richard. (1978). By Carol Fenner. Illustrated by Ati Forberg. New York: Knopf. Marsha longs to be a champion figure skater. When she receives some worn-out hockey skates for Christmas, she is disappointed until her uncle shows her how her dreams might come true.

A Taste of Blackberries. (1973). By Doris Buchanan Smith. New York: Crowell. A young boy must learn to accept his friend's death and go on with his life.

Chapter Books

Arly. (1989). By Robert Newton Peck. New York: Walker. Although Arly Poole seems bound to follow in his father's footsteps as a field worker in rural Florida during the Depression, his life changes forever when he encounters a school teacher who broadens his world. MR

Beardance. (1993). By Will Hobbs. New York: Macmillan. In this sequel to *Bearstone*, Cloyd lives with his friend Walter, who's determined to re-open an old gold mine. Cloyd's life becomes entangled with orphan grizzlies . . . perhaps the last in Colorado. He learns a great deal about bears, about friendship, and about himself.

Bearstone. (1989). By Will Hobbs. New York: Atheneum. After trouble at a group home for Indian boys, Cloyd is placed with a gruff old man in the Colorado mountains. The story touches on Cloyd's search for his identity with his Ute heritage and his developing friendship with the older man.

Boy. (1986). By Roald Dahl. New York: Penguin. The seeds of many Roald Dahl stories can be found in this autobiographical account of his childhood in Wales and Norway and his life at an English boarding school. MR

The Boy Who Loved Alligators. (1994). By Barbara Kennedy. New York: Atheneum. Left homeless by the death of his grandmother, Kim is sent to live temporarily with Billie, a single mother. Determined not to be sent away, Kim becomes useful, befriends the neighborhood grouch, and even tames a local alligator.

Crazy Lady! (1993). By Jane Conly. New York: HarperCollins. Maxine and her strange son are the object of teasing and ridicule in the neighborhood, but Vernon learns to see them differently. Despite his reluctance, he becomes entwined in their lives, learning about other people and himself along the way.

Dear Mr. Henshaw. (1983). By Beverly Cleary. New York: Dell. Leigh Botts copes with separation from his father by corresponding with his favorite children's author.

Dogsong. (1985). By Gary Paulsen. New York: Puffin. Russell tries to find his own "song" as he embarks on a journey with a dog team and sled. Full of realistic detail and adventure, this book touches upon issues of survival and growing up.

Flip-Flop Girl. (1994). By Katherine Paterson. New York: Lodestar. Uprooted after her father's death and struggling to adjust to a new school, Vinnie develops a rare friendship with another loner, but not without involvement in a situation she later regrets.

The Great Gilly Hopkins. (1978). By Katherine Paterson. New York: Crowell. Gilly is a tough kid who has been bounced from foster home to foster home. Despite her defenses, she's drawn into a family with a memorable foster mother, a blind neighbor, and a strange little boy. MR

Homesick: My Own Story. (1982). By Jean Fritz. New York: Yearling. Auto-biographical account of a children's author who grew up in China with missionary parents. The book captures the challenges she faces as she moves to the United States.

In the Year of the Boar and Jackie Robinson. (1984). By Bette Bao Lord. New York: Harper & Row. Shirley Temple Wong has just moved to Brooklyn from China and wants badly to fit into her school and her American dream.

Julie. (1994). By Jean Craighead George. New York: HarperCollins. Written 22 years after *Julie of the Wolves*, this sequel begins where the first novel left off. Julie struggles to come to terms with her new life and her Eskimo father and his "gussak" wife. Her life is intertwined with those of the wolves and the harsh beauty of the Alaskan tundra. This sequel is less a survival book and more a novel about growing up and dealing with personal challenges. MR

Just Call Me Stupid. (1993). By Tom Birdseye. New York: Holiday House. A fifth grader believes he is stupid because he has not learned to read. He comes to believe in himself and overcomes his terror of failure with the support of his next door neighbor.

Lyddie. (1991). By Katherine Paterson. New York: Puffin. Lyddie hopes to earn enough money in the textile mills to bring her brother and sisters back together. However, the conditions under which young women worked during the mid 1800s mean that her goal will be harder than she ever dreamed. MR

The Mozart Season. (1991). By Virginia Euwer Wolff. New York: Henry Holt. As she prepares for a violin competition, Allegra gains new perspectives on herself and those around her. MR

Nothing but the Truth. (1991). By Avi. New York: Avon. When Philip Malloy takes a stand for his rights, he learns a hard lesson about abuse of power and the fragile nature of truth. MR

Plain City. (1993). By Virginia Hamilton. New York: Scholastic. Buhlaire Sims must deal with an unexpected twist in her life when she discovers that her father, believed to have died in Vietnam, is still living. MR

Popcorn Days and Buttermilk Nights. (1983). By Gary Paulsen. New York: Penguin. To avoid reform school, Carley is sent to his uncle's family in the poverty of Minnesota farm country. Here he experiences exhausting work and a re-shaping of his life.

Scorpions. (1988). By Walter Dean Myers. New York: HarperCollins. Aspiring to lead the Scorpions spells trouble for Jamal. Street life and a gun pose a threat to him and his friend Tito. MR

See Ya, Simon. (1994). By David Hill. New York: Dutton. Set in New Zealand, this novel recounts the final year of Simon's struggle with muscular dystrophy. Told through his friend Nathan's eyes, this is a warm, humorous story of friendship, life, and death. MR

Thank You, Dr. Martin Luther King, Jr.! (1990). By Eleanora E. Tate. New York: Bantam. Although she feels her school's celebration of Black History Month focuses negative attention on her, a young girl finds pride in the contributions of many African Americans.

There's a Boy in the Girls' Bathroom. (1987). By Louis Sachar. New York: Knopf. Bradley Chalkers is a hard kid to like. Once the school counselor reaches out, Bradley begins to fit in and understand others.

1. B. Accepting Responsibility

Picture Books

The Eye of the Needle. (1990). By Teri Sloat. New York: Dutton. A Yupik boy learns a hard lesson about taking responsibility for his actions when his grandmother sends him to find food.

It Takes a Village. (1994). By Jane Cowen-Fletcher. New York: Scholastic. A child in Benin discovers that she is not the only one watching out for her younger brother.

A Promise is a Promise. (1988). By Robert Munsch, Michael Kusugak & Vladyana Krykorka. Toronto: Annick Press. An Inuit girl learns a lesson in keeping promises when she ventures alone out onto the forbidden ice.

Too Many Tamales. By Gary Soto. (1993). Illustrated by Ed Martinez. New York: G. P. Putnam's Sons. While Maria is happy to take part in the family Christmas traditions, she learns to take responsibility for her own mistakes.

Picture Books for Older Readers

A Day's Work. (1994). By Eve Bunting. Illustrated by Ronald Himler. New York: Clarion. Since his grandfather doesn't speak English, a young Mexican boy accompanies him as he seeks work. The boy learns a lesson in honesty from his grandfather.

Easy Chapter Books

Justin and the Best Biscuits in the World. (1986). By Mildred Pitts Walter. New York: Lothrop, Lee & Shepard. Justin struggles with his identity while surrounded by a family full of females. On a visit to his grandfather's ranch, he discovers "women's work" is even done by cowboys.

Keep Ms. Sugarman in the Fourth Grade. (1992). By Elizabeth Levy. Illustrated by Dave Henderson. New York: HarperCollins. Jackie begins to blossom in Ms. Sugarman's fourth-grade classroom. When this favorite teacher is promoted to principal, Jackie must deal with her sense of loss.

On My Honor. (1986). By Marion Dane Bauer. New York: Clarion. Joel dares his friend Tony to swim across the river. When he turns around, Tony isn't there. A short but compelling book about friendship, death, and truth.

Summer of the Swans. (1970). By Betsy Byars. New York: Viking. A girl gains new insight into herself and her family when her disabled brother gets lost.

Chapter Books

Among the Volcanoes. (1991). By Omar S. Castaneda. New York: Dell. Isabel must set aside her dreams of becoming a teacher when her mother's illness worsens and she must take care of her family. She learns to keep hold of her dreams in the face of personal and social obstacles. MR

The Giver. (1993). By Lois Lowry. Boston: Houghton Mifflin. A young boy has been chosen for a difficult and lonely job in his community. With echoes of *Brave New World* and *1984*, this intriguing Newbery winner can provide the sparks for powerful discussions about death, freedom and values. MR

Shiloh. (1991). By Phyllis Reynolds Naylor. New York: Dell. When Marty discovers that a neighbor is mistreating his dog, he faces some tough decisions. The novel provides impetus for discussions about animal rights, abuse, and right and wrong.

Toughboy and Sister. (1990). By Kirkpatrick Hill. New York: Puffin. When their father dies, Toughboy and his younger sister are stranded at a remote Athabascan fishing camp on the Yukon River and forced to take responsibility for each other's survival.

2. LOOKING OUTWARD

2. A. Perseverance and Courage

Picture Books

Lon Po Po: A Red-Riding Hood Story from China. (1989). By Ed Young. New York: Scholastic. The powerful, almost frightening watercolors enhance this Chinese folktale in which three children outwit the wolf.

Mirette on the High Wire. (1992). By Emily Arnold McCully. New York: Putnam. Mirette befriends the great high-wire walker, Bellini, who has lost his courage.

Sing to the Stars. (1994). By Mary Brigid Barrett. Illustrated by Sandra Speidel. New York: Little, Brown. Ephram must overcome his own fear of performance in order to help his friend, a famous pianist, who is unwilling to return to the stage because of his blindness.

Easy Chapter Books

Everywhere. (1990). By Bruce Brooks. New York: HarperCollins. A ten-year-old boy feels helpless when his grandfather, his best friend, has a heart attack. A friend arrives, bringing hope and teaching lessons in courage.

Chapter Books

Bridge to Terabithia. (1972). By Katherine Paterson. New York: Avon. Jess and Leslie create a secret kingdom and a wonderful friendship. However, tragedy strikes and Jess must learn to cope with an enormous loss.

Climb or Die. (1994). By Edward Myers. New York: Hyperion. Danielle and her brother, Jake, rely on her knowledge of mountaineering and their desire to survive as they seek help following a car accident. Fast-paced plot rich with adventure and suspense.

Earthquake at Dawn. (1992). By Kristiana Gregory. New York: Harcourt Brace. Daisy, traveling with a famous photographer, survives the 1906 San Francisco earthquake. This book presents a fictional account of photographer Edith Irvine's experiences during this cataclysmic event.

The Fear Place. (1994). By Phyllis Reynolds Naylor. New York: Atheneum. Doug has sworn never to climb the ridge again and face that paralyzing fear, despite the teasing of his older brother, Gordon. They fight constantly, until an emergency leaves the boys alone in the mountains and Doug must come to terms with both his fear and his relationship with his brother.

Frozen Fire. (1977). By James Houston. New York: Aladdin. A young boy struggles to find his father, lost in a storm in the Canadian artic. Supported by an Inuit friend, he battles weather, starvation, and attacks, in order to complete his search.

Hatchet. (1987). By Gary Paulsen. New York: Macmillan. Brian Robeson's plane crashes in the Canadian wilderness and he's forced to survive on his own. Excellent book to hook reluctant readers.

Iceberg Hermit. (1974). By Arthus J. Roth. New York: Four Winds. Seventeen-year-old Allan faces overwhelming odds when he is shipwrecked on an Arctic iceberg in 1757, with a polar bear cub as his only companion.

Incident at Hawk's Hill. (1971). By Allan Eckert. New York: Dell. A shy six-year-old boy wanders from home and takes refuge in a badger's burrow. Based on a true incident, this novel tells a remarkable tale of survival.

Island of the Blue Dolphins. (1960). By Scott O'Dell. New York: Dell. Based on true events, the book tells the story of a young girl who's left alone on an island in the Pacific. She learns to build a shelter, find food, and survive.

Julie of the Wolves. (1972). By Jean Craighead George. New York: HarperCollins. When Julie/Miyax runs away, she becomes lost on the Alaskan tundra and is eventually adopted by a pack of wolves.

Night of the Twisters. (1984). By Ivy Ruckman. New York: HarperCollins. Two boys and a baby, trapped in a basement during a tornado, must rely on their own resources in order to cope with the catastrophe.

A Place of Lions. (1991). By Eric Campbell. San Diego:Harcourt Brace Javonovich. A young boy and his father survive an airplane crash and struggle to survive in the African desert. Nearby, an old lion tries to maintain his leadership in the pride and the two stories become entertwined.

The River. (1991). By Gary Paulsen. New York: Delacorte. Brian Robeson from *Hatchet* has been asked to return to the wilderness where he had crashed two years ago to show researchers how he survived. Disaster strikes and Brian is forced once more to rely on his wits and judgment.

The True Confessions of Charlotte Doyle. (1990). By Avi. New York: Orchard. Charlotte Doyle boards a sailing ship in 1832, not knowing that her life will be forever changed. She befriends the captain but soon learns that the crew hates him, and she is forced to take a stand.

Voyage of the Frog. (1989). By Gary Paulsen. New York: Dell. In this book, David is swept out to sea in a sailboat and learns some hard lessons about survival and about himself.

Weasel. (1991). By Cynthia deFelice. New York: Avon. When their father doesn't come back from hunting, Molly and Nathan know something is wrong. The puzzle they begin to piece together unfolds as they become involved in a struggle to find and save their father.

Windcatcher. (1991). By Avi. New York: Avon. Tony lets his curiosity, rumors of sunken treasure, and a mysterious couple lead him into danger.

Winter Camp. (1993). By Kirkpatrick Hill. New York: Margaret K. McElderry Books. In this sequel to *Toughboy and Sister*, a brother and sister learn to survive a harsh Alaskan winter by relying upon their Athabascan heritage.

2. B. Reaching Out to Others

Picture Books

Chester's Way. (1988). By Kevin Henkes. New York: Greenwillow. Chester and Wilson are inseparable . . . two of a kind. Then Lily moves into the neighborhood and their friendships take a delightful turn.

Miss Rumphius. (1982). By Barbara Cooney. New York: Viking. Miss Rumphius is determined to do three things in her life: go to far away places, live by the sea, and in some way make the world more beautiful.

Sam Johnson and the Blue Ribbon Quilt. (1983). By Lisa Campbell Ernst. New York: Mulberry. When Sam's wife goes on a trip, he discovers that he really enjoys sewing. However, no one takes him seriously when he tries to join the Women's Quilting Club, so he starts his own.

Somebody Loves You, Mr. Hatch. (1991). By Eileen Spinelli. Illustrated by Paul Yalowitz. New York: Macmillan. Mr. Hatch works quietly at the shoelace factory and keeps to himself. When a box of chocolates is delivered to his door on Valentine's Day, he realizes that he must have a friend and begins to reach out to others.

Picture Books for Older Readers

Beethoven Lives Upstairs. (1994). By Barbara Nichol. Illustrated by Scott Cameron. New York: Orchard. Mr. Beethoven, an eccentric musician, lives in Christoph's house. Through letters to his uncle, Christoph changes his resentment toward and embarassment about the boarder.

Easy Chapter Books

Stay Away from Simon. (1985). By Carol Carrick. Illustrated by Donald Carrick. New York: Clarion. Lucy and her younger brother are forced to examine their fears and their feelings about Simon, a mentally handicapped boy, when he follows them home from school.

Chapter Books

Breaking Free. (1994). By Louann Gaeddert. New York: Atheneum. In 1800, twelve-year-old Richard is sent to his uncle's farm in upper New York state. He discovers that his uncle keeps two slaves and Richard helps them both to freedom.

Bus People. (1993). By Rachel Anderson. New York: Holt. Six interwoven stories bring to life the personalities of disabled children who ride the same bus to their special school.

Dear Mr. Sprouts. (1991). By Errol Broome. New York: Knopf. Written as a series of letters between Australian pen pals, this book chronicles the unlikely friendship between a young boy and girl.

Goodnight, Mr. Tom. (1981). By Michelle Magorian. New York: HarperCollins. As World War II is about to begin, Willie Beach is sent from his abusive mother in London to live with a gruff old man in the country. The friendship between the boy and the man provides the heart of this memorable book. MR

Words of Stone. (1993). By Kevin Henkes. New York: Puffin. Blaze spends the summer with his father and grandmother, trying to come to terms with his mother's death. When he meets Joselle, he learns her mother has abandoned her. Together, they learn to cry and laugh.

2. C. Respecting Animals and Nature

Picture Books

The Great Kapok Tree. (1990). By Lynne Cherry. San Diego: Harcourt Brace Jovanovich. A man enters the rain forest to chop down a Kapok tree. As he rests, he falls asleep and the animals come to whisper why he should not destroy their home.

Owl Moon. (1987). By Jane Yolen. Illustrated by John Schoenherr. New York: Philomel. In this poetic book, a father and his child savor the quiet beauty of the moonlit woods as they go owling.

Prince William. (1992). By Gloria Rand. Illustrated by Ted Rand. New York: Holt. Denny finds a baby seal covered with oil from the oil spill in Prince William Sound in Alaska.

Rain Forest Secrets. (1990). By Arthur Dorros. New York: Scholastic. This picture book describes the animals, people, and plant life in the rain forest. Dorros includes a list of places to write for more information. IB

The Tenth Good Thing About Barney. (1971). By Judith Viorst. New York: Macmillan. At his cat's funeral, a young boy tries to think of ten good things about Barney, but he can think of only nine.

Toby. (1994). By Margaret Wild. New York: Ticknor and Fields. Toby is an old dog, sick and going blind. The story of Toby is paired with glimpses of his owner, Sara, who's getting older, too.

Picture Books for Older Readers

A River Ran Wild: An Environmental Story. (1992). By Lynne Cherry. New York: Harcourt Brace. This true story traces the history of the Nashua River from the beginning of time through the pollution of the modern era to successful efforts to save the river. IB

Boat Ride with Lillian Two Blossom. (1988). By Patricia Polacco. New York: Philomel. When William and Mabel meet Lillian Two Blossom, an elderly woman, they are terrified. Their fears vanish when she begins to tell them the story of the wind, the rain, and the sky.

Come Back, Salmon. (1992). By Molly Cone. Photographs by Sidnee Wheelwright. San Francisco: Sierra Club. The students of Jackson Elementary in Everett, Washington take on the challenge to clean up a polluted stream, stock it with salmon, and preserve it for the return of the salmon. IB

Easy Chapter Books

No One is Going to Nashville. (1983). By Mavis Jukes. Illustrated by Lloyd Bloom. New York: Knopf. Sonia wants to be a veterinarian. Her stepmother proves an ally when she wants to keep a stray dog.

Stone Fox. (1980). By John Reynolds Gardiner. Illustrated by Marcia Sewell. New York: HarperCollins. Little Willy faces the seemingly impossible task of defeating Stone Fox in a dogsled race in order to save his grandfather's farm.

Chapter Books

Forest. (1993). By Janet Taylor Lisle. New York: Orchard. Amber stumbles onto a forest community and unwittingly sets off a war between the animal inhabitants and humans.

The Incredible Journey. (1961). By Sheila Burnford. Two dogs and a cat travel over 200 miles to return to the people they love. Consider pairing this book with the movie, *Homeward Bound*.

Lostman's River. (1994). By Cynthia DeFelice. New York: Macmillan. When Ty and his family settle in the Florida Everglades in 1906, they encounter vicious hunters who pose a threat to the Everglades. Ty's efforts to protect the environment mix with his fear of the hunters. MR

My Side of the Mountain. (1959). By Jean Craighead George. New York: Dutton. Sam Gribley leaves home and lives for a year in a hollowed out tree. Although his first attempts at survival are feeble, Sam learns how to eat, clothe himself, and make some friends. Told in a journal, this classic is filled with specific details of survival.

On the Far Side of the Mountain. (1990). By Jean Craighead George. New York: Penguin. In this sequel to *My Side of the Mountain*, Sam Gribley returns to the wild with his younger sister, Alice, and his falcon, Frightful. When Frightful and Alice disappear, Sam sets out to find them and faces some tough decisions.

Rescue Josh McGuire. (1991). By Ben Mikaelsen. New York: Hyperion. When Josh's older brother dies, his father becomes angry and drinks too much. After his father kills a mother bear, Josh flees with her cub and their survival becomes intertwined.

The Talking Earth. (1983). By Jean Craighead George. New York: HarperCollins. Billie Wind's journey into the Florida Everglades teaches her about herself, her Mikasuki Indian heritage, and her responsibility for the earth.

Where the Red Fern Grows. (1961). By Wilson Rawls. New York: Bantam. Billy works and saves enough to buy two hound dogs, Old Dan and Little Ann. What a memorable team they make. Interesting book to pair with *Shiloh*.

3. ROOTS AND RELATIONSHIPS

3. A. Family Issues

Picture Books

At the Crossroads. (1991). By Rachel Isadora. New York: Scholastic. A close-knit group of brothers, sisters, and their friends in a South African township wait patiently throughout the day and long into the night to welcome their fathers home.

A Chair for My Mother. (1982). By Vera B. Williams. New York: Greenwillow. A young girl saves her money to buy a chair for her mother after everything they own is destroyed in a fire.

Julius, the Baby of the World. (1990). By Kevin Henkes. New York: Greenwillow. Lily isn't impressed with her new brother Julius. Her parents think Julius is the baby of the world; Lily thinks he's disgusting . . . until Cousin Garland comes to visit.

Koala Lou. (1988). By Mem Fox. Illustrated by Julie Vivas. New York: Harcourt Brace Jovanovich. More than anything, Koala Lou wants to hear her mother say, "I love you."

Mama, Do You Love Me? (1991). By Barbara Joosse. Illustrated by Barbara Lavallee. San Francisco: Chronicle. An Inuit mother reassures her child that no matter what happens, she will love her.

Mama One, Mama Two. (1982). By Patricia MacLachlan. Illustrated by Ruth Lercher Bornstein. New York: Harper & Row. A familiar bedtime ritual helps a child understand why she must live with a foster family.

Peter's Chair. (1967). By Ezra Jack Keats. New York: Harper. Peter must overcome his jealousy when his parents give his favorite chair to his baby brother.

The Relatives Came. (1985). By Cynthia Rylant. Illustrated by Stephen Gammell. New York: Bradbury. A station wagon filled with relatives pulls up to the house and the visitors settle in and stay for weeks. Hugs and kisses and illustrations capture the love in this extended family.

Through Moon and Stars and Night Sky. (1990). By Ann Warren Turner. Illustrated by James Graham Hale. New York: Harper & Row. A story for young readers about adoption and a family waiting for a little boy.

Weird Parents. (1990). By Audrey Wood. New York: Penguin. This hilarious book about being embarrassed by one's parents will strike a chord with readers of all ages.

Working Cotton. (1992). By Sherley Anne Williams. Illustrated by Carole Byard. San Diego, CA: Harcourt. This is a simple story of the daily rituals of migrant cotton pickers and the bonds of family love.

You Be Me, I'll Be You. (1990). By Pili Mandelbaum. Brooklyn, NY: Kane/Miller. In this book about appreciating differences, Anna likes the color of her father's white skin and he likes her warm brown skin.

Picture Books for Older Readers

Aunt Flossie's Hats (and Crab Cakes Later). (1991). By Elizabeth Fitzgerald Howard. Illustrated by James Ransome. New York: Clarion. Once a week, Sarah and Susan visit their great-great-aunt Flossie who brings out boxes and boxes of hats. Aunt Flossie tells the family history through each hat.

Brown Angels: An Album of Pictures and Verse. (1993). By Walter Dean Myers. New York: HarperCollins. Accompanying his personal collection of turn-of-the-century photographs, Myers celebrates the lives of African American children. P

Brown Honey in Broomwheat Tea. (1993). By Joyce Carol Thomas. Illustrated by Floyd Cooper. New York: HarperCollins. Soft illustrations showcase this collection of poetry featuring family members, love, and roots. P

Chicken Sunday. (1992). By Patricia Polacco. New York: Philomel. Three children decide they must buy a beautiful Easter hat in Mr. Kodinski's store window for Miss Eula. When they are wrongly accused of throwing eggs at Mr. Kodinski's shop, they discover a way to earn money and establish their innocence.

Henry's Baby. (1993). By Mary Hoffman. Illustrated by Susan Winter. New York: Dorling Kindersley. All the boys in Henry's class can do something special and Henry feels left out. All he has is a baby brother, who helps make him special, too.

Honey I Love. (1978). By Eloise Greenfield. Illustrated by Leo and Diane Dillon. New York: Crowell. This collection of poetry touches upon families, love, and belonging. P

Mrs. Katz and Tush. (1992). By Patricia Polacco. New York: Bantam. Larnel becomes friends with his neighbor, Mrs. Katz. Together they take care of a cat named Tush and discover that their histories as African American and Jewish people have much in common.

My Rotten Redheaded Older Brother. (1994). By Patricia Polacco. New York: Simon & Schuster. Patricia is utterly frustrated because her older brother, Richard, can do everything better than she can. Despite their conflicts, a surprise event brings the two closer together.

Nathaniel Talking. (1988). By Eloise Greenfield. Illustrated by Jan Spivey Gilchrist. New York: Black Butterfly Children's Books. These poems and raps are written in Nathaniel's voice about being nine, missing his mama who died, making friends, and being part of a family. Soft charcoal illustrations enhance the mood of this book. P

Night on Neighborhood Street. (1991). By Eloise Greenfield. Illustrated by Jan Spivey Gilchrist. New York: Dial. Families and neighborhoods, from the tender to the rough, come to life in this collection of poetry. P

The Pain and the Great One. (1974). By Judy Blume. Illustrated by Irene Trivas. Scarsdale, NY: Bradbury. The first half of this book is written from the point of view of the older sister about her younger brother (the Pain). The second half tells the brother's side of the story about his sister (the Great One).

Pass It On: African–American Poetry for Children. (1993). Selected by Wade Hudson. Illustrated by Floyd Cooper. New York: Scholastic. This is a collection of poems about play, families, history, and dreams. P

The Table Where Rich People Sit. (1994). By Byrd Baylor. Illustrated by Peter Parnall. New York: Scribner's. Mountain Girl calls a family meeting to talk about how her family doesn't have enough money. Once they start adding up the value of things like sunsets and the feel of the wind, Mountain Girl realizes they are rich in many ways.

Easy Chapter Books

Arthur, for the Very First Time. (1980). By Patricia MacLachlan. New York: HarperCollins. Arthur learns about himself and his eccentric family during a summer visit with relatives.

Julian, Dream Doctor. (1990). By Ann Cameron. Illustrated by Ann Strugnell. New York: Random House. Julian and his brother Huey try to find the perfect birthday present for Dad, with amusing results.

Maybe Yes, Maybe No, Maybe Maybe. (1993). By Susan Patron. New York: Orchard. PK feels stuck between her older sister, Megan, who's rapidly turning into a teenager and her younger sister, Rabbit. Both sisters love to hear PK tell stories during Rabbit's bathtime. A gentle tale about families, growing up, and the power of stories.

More Stories Julian Tells. (1986). By Ann Cameron. Illustrated by Ann Strugnell. New York: Knopf. More episodes in the life of Julian, his family, and friends.

Sarah, Plain and Tall. (1985). By Patricia MacLachlan. New York: HarperCollins. After Mama dies, Papa puts an ad in the paper for a wife and receives a letter from Sarah from Maine. She comes for a month and Papa and the two children come to know and love her.

Skylark. (1994). By Patricia MacLachlan. New York: HarperCollins. In this sequel to *Sarah, Plain and Tall,* Patricia MacLachlan continues the story of Sarah, Papa, Anna, and Caleb as they struggle physically and emotionally to survive a drought.

Yang the Youngest and His Terrible Ear. (1992). By Lensey Namioka. New York: Dell. The youngest child in a family of musicians, Yang struggles to reconcile his father's wishes that he become a violinist with his own desire to play baseball.

Chapter Books

Baby. (1993). By Patricia MacLachlan. New York: Delacorte Press. In this book about love and death, a family finds a baby left with a note on their doorstep. They are afraid to love her, knowing her mother will return . . . but they can't help themselves.

The Barn. (1994). By Avi. New York: Orchard. In 1855, Ben is brought home from school because his father is ill. Always hopeful, Ben is sure that if he and his brother and sister can build the barn his father wanted, somehow it will keep his father alive.

Child of the Owl. (1977). By Laurence Yep. New York: HarperCollins. When she is sent to live with her grandmother in San Francisco, Casey learns about her Chinese heritage and about being proud of who she is.

Cousins. (1990). By Virginia Hamilton. New York: Scholastic. When tragedy strikes, Cammy discovers that she must make peace with herself and with her family, especially her cousin, her lifelong rival.

A Family Apart. (1987). By Joan Lowery Nixon. New York: Bantam. Six children, whose mother cannot care for them, head west on the Orphan Train to be adopted by new families. This book is the first in a series about how the Children's Aid Society sent 100,000 children from New York City to families on the frontier between 1850 and 1920.

A Forever Family. (1992). By Roslyn Banish. New York: HarperCollins. Eight-year-old Jennifer Jordan-Wong finds a family of her own after living for several years as a foster child.

Here's to You, Rachel Robinson. (1993). By Judy Blume. New York: Orchard. Rachel must learn to accept her brother and deal with her own feelings when he returns home after being expelled from boarding school.

I Am Lavina Cumming. (1993). By Susan Lowell. Minneapolis, MN: Milkweed Editions. Following her mother's death in 1905, ten-year-old Lavina leaves the Arizona Territory and travels alone by train to California. She experiences homesickness, a new school, and a catastrophic earthquake as her future takes shape.

Jacob Have I Loved. (1980). By Katherine Paterson. New York: HarperCollins. Caroline is pampered and loved by all. Her twin, Louise, turns to their father and the sea to find her own identity and come to terms with her jealousy. MR

Journey. (1991). By Patricia MacLachlan. New York: Dell. Journey and his sister have been left with their grandparents. He tries to make sense of his mother's abandonment by looking through family photographs. By taking his own photographs, Journey makes discoveries about his mother and his family.

Mama, Let's Dance. (1991). By Patricia Hermes. Boston: Little, Brown. Determined to remain a family, three children survive the unexpected departure of their mother. A greater challenge ensues as they struggle to manage without adult assistance.

Risk n' Roses. (1990). By Jan Slepian. New York: Scholastic. Skip is tired of taking care of her disabled younger sister and longs to become friends with the dangerous Jean. As Jean teases Mr. Kaminsky beyond the point of fun, Skip has to make some difficult choices.

Shizuko's Daughter. (1993). By Kyoko Mori. New York: Holt. Yuki's life turns upside down when her mother dies and she must now live with a father she doesn't know. She learns to rely on her inner strength and find her place in a new family.

3. B. Generations Learning from One Another

Picture Books

Abiyoyo. (1986). By Pete Seeger. Illustrated by Michael Hays. New York: Scholastic. A young boy and his father creatively and courageously save their community from a giant.

Abuela. (1991). By Arthur Dorros. Illustrated by Elisa Klevan. New York: Dutton. A little girl speaks in both English and Spanish about her abuela, her grandmother. She imagines flying over New York City with her abuela.

Abuela's Weave. (1993). By Omar S. Castaneda. Illustrated by Enrique O. Sanchez. New York: Lee & Low. A young girl draws on her courage to help her grandmother sell their weavings in a Guatemalan market.

All the Places to Love. (1994). By Patricia MacLachlan. Illustrated by Mike Wimmer. New York: HarperCollins. Eli's family shares all the places they love around their home.

Annie and the Old One. (1971). By Miska Miles. Illustrated by Peter Parnall. Boston: Little, Brown. A Navaho child plots to unravel the rug her mother is weaving, hoping to forestall her grandmother's death.

Cornrows. (1979). By Camille Yarbrough. Illustrated by Carole Byard. New York: Coward-McCann. As she braids her granddaughter's hair into cornrows, a grandmother explains their tradition and symbolism.

Grandad Bill's Song. (1994). By Jone Yolen. Illustrated by Melissa Bay Mathis. New York: Philomel. A boy and his family share their memories of what they did on the day Grandad Bill died.

Grandaddy and Janetta. (1994). By Helen V. Griffith. Illustrated by James Stevenson. New York: Greenwillow. Jenetta and her grandaddy share simple joys that young children will appreciate.

Grandma According to Me. (1992). By Karen Magnuson Beil. Illustrated by Ted Rand. New York: Delacorte. Soft watercolors capture the tender relationship between a child and her grandmother.

Grandpa's Face. (1988). By Eloise Greenfield. Illustrated by Floyd Cooper. New York: Philomel. A little girl sees her grandfather practicing for a role in a play and misunderstands his angry expression.

How Does It Feel to Be Old? (1979). By Norma Farber. Illustrated by Trina Schart Hyman. New York: Penguin. Realistic drawings enhance this series of poems about being old and the relationship between a young girl and her grandmother. P

The Keeping Quilt. (1988). By Patricia Polacco. New York: Simon & Schuster. This book tells the story of a quilt that's been passed down in Polacco's own family. The quilt plays a special role in weddings, births, birthdays, and funerals.

Knots on a Counting Rope. (1987). By Bill Martin, Jr. and John Archambault. Illustrated by Ted Rand. New York: Scholastic. As they sit around a campfire, a Navaho grandfather recounts the events of his grandson's birth, helping the boy understand that his blindness is a strength.

Laura Charlotte. (1990). By Kathryn O. Galbraith. Illustrated by Floyd Cooper. New York: Philomel. Soft illustrations enrich this book about a stuffed elephant that belonged to a little girl, then her daughter and granddaughter.

My Grandma Leonie. (1987). By Bijou le Tord. New York: Bradbury Press. A young girl reminisces about the simple pleasures she and her grandmother shared.

My Grandson Lew. (1974). By Charlotte Zolotow. Illustrated by William Pene du Bois. New York: Harper & Row. A tender book for young readers about missing a grandfather he dies.

My Great-Aunt Arizona. (1992). By Gloria Houston. Illustrated by Susan Condie Lamb. New York: HarperCollins. Arizona was born in a log cabin and dreamed of the faraway places she would go. She grew up to be a teacher and she taught students and their children and grandchildren.

Nana Upstairs, Nana Downstairs. (1973). By Tomie de Paola. New York: Penguin. Poignant story of Tommy's relationship with his grandmother and great-grandmother and his acceptance of death.

Now One Foot, Now the Other. (1981). By Tomie de Paola. New York: Putnam's. Bobby's grandfather, Bob, taught him to walk as a baby. When Grandfather Bob has a stroke, Bobby must teach his grandfather to walk again.

Our Granny. (1994). By Margaret Wild. Illustrated by Julie Vivas. Boston: Houghton Mifflin. This book describes how grannies can live in different places, have different jobs, look different, and even kiss differently.

The Quilt Story. (1985). By Tony Johnston. Illustrated by Tomie dePaola. New York: Putnam's. A simple picture book about a quilt that's passed down from generation to generation.

Sitti's Secrets. (1994). By Naomi Shihab Nye. Illustrated by Nancy Carpenter. New York: Four Winds. Mona often thinks of her grandmother who lives half a world away in Palestine. She re-lives their visit and the special language she and her grandmother create to communicate with each other.

Storm in the Night. (1988). By Mary Stolz. Illustrated by Pat Cummings. New York: Harper & Row. Grandfather soothes Thomas's fears of a thunderstorm with tales of his own childhood and long-ago storms.

Through Grandpa's Eyes. (1980). By Patricia MacLachlan. Illustrated by Deborah Ray. New York: HarperCollins. His blind grandfather helps a small boy learn about himself and the world around him.

When I Am Old with You. (1990). By Angela Johnson. Illustrated by David Soman. New York: Orchard. A child imagines the future when he and his grandfather will be old together.

Wilfrid Gordon McDonald Partridge. (1985). By Mem Fox. Illustrated by Julie Vivas. New York: Kane/Miller. Wilfrid lives next door to an old people's home where he has many friends, but his best friend is Miss Nancy. When Wilfrid learns she has lost her memory, he sets out to find it for her.

William's Doll. (1972). By Charlotte Zolotow. Illustrated by William Pene du Bois. New York: Scholastic. When William says he wants a doll, his family tries to interest him in basketball and trains. Only his grandmother understands and buys him a doll, telling William's family it's so he can learn to be a good father.

Picture Books for Older Readers

Grandpa's Slide Show. (1987). By Deborah Gould. Illustrated by Cheryl Harness. New York: Lothrop, Lee & Shepard. Grandpa loves to let his grandsons help during family slide shows. When Grandpa dies, it's hard for the boys to come to terms with his death, yet the healing process begins when they put on another slide show.

The Memory Box. (1992). By Mary Bahr. Illustrated by David Cunningham. Morton Grove, IL: Albert Whitman. Gramps tells Zach he'd like to start a memory box that the two of them can fill with memories and special things. As they begin to fill the box, Zach learns that his grandfather has Alzheimer's disease.

The Old, Old Man and the Very Little Boy. (1992). By Kristine L. Franklin. Illustrated by Terea D. Shaffer. New York: Atheneum. A little boy learns that the elders in his African village once were young, too.

The Patchwork Quilt. (1985). By Valerie Flournoy. Illustrated by Jerry Pinkney. New York: Dial. Tanya helps her grandmother sew a quilt made of pieces of material from the family's clothes. The project draws the family together.

Sunshine Home. (1994). By Eve Bunting. Illustrated by Diane de Groat. New York: Clarion. A moving story of a boy and his parents who pay a visit to his grandmother in a nursing home.

The Village of Round and Square Houses. (1986). By Ann Grifalconi. Boston: Little, Brown. A grandmother in the Cameroons tells her young granddaughter the story of how their culture came to be.

The Wednesday Surprise. (1989). By Eve Bunting. Illustrated by Donald Carrick. New York: Clarion. On Wednesdays, Anna teaches her grandmother how to read as a surprise for her father's birthday.

Easy Chapter Books

Blackberries in the Dark. (1985). By Mavis Jukes. Illustrated by Thomas B. Allen. New York: Dell. Austin and his grandmother struggle to fill the void left by his grandfather's death.

The Canada Geese Quilt. (1989). By Natalie Kinsey-Warnock. Illustrated by Leslie W. Bowman. New York: Dell. As ten-year-old Ariel awaits the arrival of the family's new baby, she feels left out. Grandma helps by teaching Ariel to make a baby quilt, but suffers a stroke before the quilt is finished. Ariel discovers strength through her Grandma's many lessons of love.

The Hundred Penny Box. (1975). By Sharon Bell Mathis. Illustrated by Leo and Diane Dillon. New York: Puffin. Michael's great-great-aunt has a box filled with one penny from each year of her life. At 100 years old, she can tell stories about each penny. When Michael's mother wants to throw away the box, Michael decides he has to save it.

Chapter Books

Finding Buck McHenry. (1984). By Alfred Slote. New York: HarperCollins. Jason believes that the school custodian is really a famous baseball player who seems to ignore his own glorious past. As he tries to convince Mack Henry to return to the game as a coach, Jason learns about friendship and responsibility.

Jericho. (1994). By Janet Hickman. New York: Greenwillow. Twelve-year-old Angela's summer visit weaves the past and present together as she helps care for GrandMin, who is feeble and forgetful. Through flashbacks, episodes of GrandMin's life contrast the generations.

Missing May. (1992). By Cynthia Rylant. New York: Orchard. Summer misses May when she dies, but she also worries about May's husband, Ob, who misses May as much or even more. Her friend, Cletus, believes in the spirit world. Will there be a way to reach May somehow?

Take a Chance, Gramps! (1990). By Jean D. Okimoto. Boston: Little, Brown. Jane is having trouble making friends. In addition, she's worried about her grandfather who's been depressed ever since her grandmother died. To her surprise, both problems look less bleak when she takes her grandfather to a senior citizen's dance.

Thank You, Jackie Robinson. (1974). By Barbara Cohen. Illustrated by Richard Cuffar. New York: Lothrop, Lee & Shepard. A boy brings a treasured gift, a baseball autographed by Jackie Robinson, to his friend, an elderly man at the end of his life.

Toning the Sweep. (1993). By Angela Johnson. New York: Orchard. When Emily and her mother go to the desert to pack their grandmother up to take her to the hospital, she decides to take a camcorder to capture the people and places in the desert she loves.

The War with Grandpa. (1984). By Robert Kimmel Smith. New York: Delacorte. When Peter's grandfather moves into their house, he "takes over" Peter's room. Peter is furious and declares war. As the battle between them escalates, Peter learns some lessons about family, love, and war. The book is written in first person as a writing assignment for Peter's fifth grade teacher.

3. C. Challenges of Poverty

Picture Books

The Boy Who Wanted a Family. (1980). By Shirley Gordon. Illustrated by Charles Robinson. New York: Dell. A young boy and his new mother get to know one another during the one-year waiting period before his adoption is final.

Danny and the Kings. (1993). By Susan Cooper. Illustrated by Jos. A. Smith. New York: Margaret K. McElderry Books. Danny really wishes his mom would get a Christmas tree, but there's no money. He almost has one, but just as he thinks his wish won't come true, a truck driver provides the magic of Christmas.

Fly Away Home. (1991). By Eve Bunting. Illustrated by Ronald Himler. New York: Clarion. A moving story of a homeless boy and his father who live in an airport. They move from one airline terminal to another, trying not to be noticed.

Space Travellers. (1992). By Margaret Wild. Illustrated by Gregory Rogers. New York: Scholastic. Zac and his mother, Mandy, must sleep in the park because they have no home.

Tight Times. (1979). By Barbara Shook Hazen. Illustrated by Trina Schart Hyman. New York: Viking Press. This simple picture book offers the perspective of a young child when he learns his father has lost his job and times get even tighter.

Easy Chapter Books

The Family Under the Bridge. (1958). By Natalie Savage Carlson. Illustrated by Garth Williams. New York: Scholastic. A mother hides her three children under a bridge when she cannot care for them. They discover an elderly man already living there, and together they build new lives.

Jim Ugly. (1992). By Sid Fleischman. Illustrated by Jos. A. Smith. New York: Greenwillow. Jake and his mongrel dog, Jim Ugly, search the old West for clues to the disappearance of Jake's father.

Randall's Wall. (1991). By Carol Fenner. New York: Macmillan. Jean Worth Neary befriends Randall, an unkempt boy, who is ostrasized by his classmates. In the process, she discovers much about the poverty of his home situation.

Under the Hawthorne Tree. (1990). By Marita Conlon-McKenna. New York: Penguin. Set in Ireland in the 1840s, three children face the Great Famine alone and in fear of being sent to the workhouse. Desperate to survive, they battle starvation and illness as they travel to distant Castletaggert in search of relatives they've never met.

Chapter Books

Afternoon of the Elves. (1989). By Janet Taylor Lisle. New York: Orchard. Sara-Kate Connolly secretly takes care of her mentally ill mother. She builds a wall of mystery and toughness around herself that her classmate and neighbor find intriguing.

Against the Storm. (1990). By Gaye Hicyilmaz. New York: Dell. This survival story is set in Turkey, where eleven-year-old Mehmet is befriended by a streetwise young orphan. Through his help and Mehmuts own strength, he learns to survive in the city.

Cave Under the City. (1986). By Harry Mazer. New York: Harper & Row. Twelve-year-old Tolly must take care of his younger brother after his father leaves to find work and his mother becomes sick. This story takes place in New York City during the Depression.

Chive. (1993). By Shelly Barre. New York: Simon & Schuster. Chive's family loses their farm and he and his father end up living on the street. When Terry's mother brings Chive home one night for dinner, they become friends. . . of a sort. The book is told from the perspective of both boys.

Family Pose. (1989). By Dean Hughes. New York: Atheneum. A boy runs away from a foster home and lives on the streets until he can start over as part of a real family.

Home: A Collaboration of Thirty Distinguished Authors and Illustrators of Children's Books to Aid the Homeless. (1992). Edited by Michael J. Rosen. New York: HarperCollins. This collection of poems and short pieces celebrates many types of families and homes. Thirty authors and illustrators donated the proceeds from this book to an organization to aid the homeless. P

Home at Last. (1992). By David DeVries. New York: Bantam Doubleday. Billy faces the challenge of fitting in with a farm family when he is sent away from the New York City streets. When faced with a crisis, he discovers that he does belong after all.

The Leaves in October. (1991). By Karen Ackerman. New York: Dell. After her father loses his job, Livvy and her brother go with him to live in a shelter for the homeless. He promises that when the leaves turn red in October, they'll have a house, but Livvy begins to have doubts.

The Loner. (1963). By Ester Wier. New York: Scholastic. This book tells of a homeless young boy without a family, or even a name, and an older woman who takes him into her home.

Make Lemonade. (1993). By Virginia Euwer Wolff. New York: Holt. Saving money for college, fourteen-year-old LaVaughn takes a job babysitting for Jolly, a proud teenage mother with two children. Their unlikely alliance helps LaVaughn and Jolly find a path to maturity. MR

Maniac Magee. (1990). By Jerry Spinelli. New York: HarperCollins. After the death of his parents, Jeffrey (Maniac) Magee goes to live with his aunt and uncle. He is miserable and leaves their home to live on his own. The Newbery medal winner is written almost as a legend.

Monkey Island. (1991). By Paula Fox. New York: Greenwillow. Eleven-year-old Clay finds himself on the streets after his father leaves home and his mother disappears. He is befriended by two homeless men. This graphic, almost harsh, story gives the reader a realistic sense of what life on the streets might be like.

My Fabulous New Life. (1993). By Sheila Greenwald. New York: Harcourt Brace. Allison must confront the poverty and homelessness she encounters in her new neighborhood when she moves from California to New York City.

Shakedown Street. (1993). By Johnathan Nasaw. New York: Delacorte. Caro and her mother finally find a community on the streets of San Francisco after living in one cult after another.

Slake's Limbo. (1974). By Felice Holman. New York: Scholastic. Thirteen-year-old Aremis Slake is viewed by everyone as worthless. While running away from bullies, he finds a hole in the subway wall that becomes his home for 121 days. He struggles to survive and find inner strength.

Street Child. (1994). By Berlie Doherty. New York: Orchard. Jim, an orphan in London in the mid-1860s, escapes to the street after his mother dies in a workhouse. He discovers chaos and slavery, as well as courage and friendship.

When the Road Ends. (1992). By Jean Thesman. New York: Avon. Though technically not homeless, a group of foster children and an older, slightly confused woman find themselves living in a cabin at the end of a road near a secluded lake. Together they learn to care for and trust one another.

The Wild Children. (1983). By Felice Holman. New York: Puffin. Based on events in Russia's history, a group of hungry children, whose families have been taken by the police, roam the streets in packs. These children survive the harsh winter by stealing, sharing, and depending on their wit and courage.

3. D. Immigration and New Beginnings

Picture Books

Grandfather's Journey. (1993). By Allen Say. Boston: Houghton Mifflin. The story of one man who moves back and forth between Japan and America, always missing one country when he is in the other.

Hoang Anh: A Vietnamese-American Boy. (1992). By Diane Hoyt-Goldsmith. Photographs by Lawrence Migdale. New York: Holiday House. In words and photographs, Hoang Anh tells about his life as an immigrant in the United States. IB

How Many Days to America? A Thanksgiving Story. (1988). By Eve Bunting. Illustrated by Beth Peck. New York: Clarion. As they journey from their Caribbean island homeland to America, a group of refugees finds cause for celebration.

I Hate English! (1989). By Ellen Levine. Illustrated by Steve Bjorkman. New York: Scholastic. When Mei-Mei moves to New York, she refuses to speak English until a teacher helps her find a way to communicate.

Onion Tears. (1991). By Diana Kidd. Illustrated by Lucy Montgomery. New York: Orchard. A young girl escapes the horrors of Vietnam but must now face the challenge of fitting in with her new American life.

Peppe the Lamplighter. (1993). By Elisa Bartone. Illustrated by Ted Lewin. New York: Lothrop, Lee & Shepard. Peppe's large family lives in Little Italy and he is happy to help them with his job as a lamplighter. His father is not pleased about his job until Peppe helps rescue his sister.

Who Came Down that Road? (1992). By George Ella Lyon. Illustrated by Peter Catalanotto. New York: Orchard. When a mother and her child speculate about who came down a long road, they imagine all of the travelers back through time.

Picture Books for Older Readers

The Great Migration: An American Story. (1993). By Jacob Lawrence. New York: HarperCollins. Told through the vivid paintings of one of America's finest contemporary artists, this story chronicles the lives of African Americans who left the rural South for the hope of the North at the time of the First World War. IB

Where Did Your Family Come From? A Book About Immigrants. (1993). By Melvin Berger and Gilda Berger. Illustrated by Robert Quackenbush. New York: Ideals Publishing Corporation. Four families who have immigrated to America face real-life challenges: obtaining citizenship, adapting to a new community, and making friends. IB

Easy Chapter Books

Long Way to a New Land. (1981). By Joan Sandin. New York: Harper & Row. A Swedish family makes the long journey to America in 1868 to escape famine in their homeland.

Make a Wish, Molly. (1994). By Barbara Cohen. Illustrated by Jan Naimo Jones. New York: Doubleday. In this companion to *Molly's Pilgrim*, Molly learns about American birthday parties, friendships, and more about her own family heritage and special traditions.

Molly's Pilgrim. (1983). By Barbara Cohen. Illustrated by Michael J. Deraney. New York: Bantam. Molly's family moves to America from Russia to escape religious persecution. When her American classmates make fun of her, Molly finds the courage to help them learn a lesson in acceptance.

Sarah, Also Known as Hannah. (1994). By Lillian Hammer Ross. Illustrated by Helen Cogancherry. Morton Grove, IL: Albert Whitman. Twelve-year-old Sarah must use her sister's name and passport as she leaves the Ukraine for America.

Chapter Books

Across America on an Emigrant Train. (1993). By Jim Murphy. New York: Clarion. The story of Robert Louis Stevenson's arduous journey from his home in Scotland to Monterey, California in 1879. This informational book is based on his actual journal and weaves in fascinating historical facts. IB

The Best Bad Thing. (1983). By Yoshiko Uchida. New York: Atheneum. When bad things begin to happen, Rinko learns to view the world from a different perspective. Sequel to *A Jar of Dreams*.

Dragon's Gate. (1993). By Laurence Yep. New York: HarperCollins. A Chinese boy flees to America after an accidental killing. There he works with his uncle and father, building a railroad tunnel through the Sierra Nevada mountains in 1867.

Dragonwings. (1975). By Laurence Yep. New York: HarperCollins. A Chinese boy, sent to American in the early 1800s, helps his father attain his dream of building a flying machine.

Immigrant Kids. (1980). By Russell Freedman. New York: Dutton. This documentary glimpse of immigrant children around the turn of the century includes photographs of everyday life. IB

A Jar of Dreams. (1981). By Yoshiko Uchida. New York: Aladdin. Rinko, a first-generation Japanese-American girl growing up in California during the Depression, feels different from her friends. She struggles to fit in until her aunt comes from Japan and helps her find a new outlook.

Journey of the Sparrows. (1991). By Fran Leeper Buss with Daisy Cubias. New York: Dell. After struggling to come to America, a family of Salvadoran refugees begins to find a new home.

Letters from Rifka. (1992). By Karen Hesse. New York: Henry Holt. In a series of letters to her cousin, a young Jewish girl describes her family's flight out of Russia in 1919.

The Star Fisher. (1991). By Laurence Yep. New York: Scholastic. Joan Lee and her Chinese-American family open a laundry in West Virginia in the 1920s. Even though she was born in America and speaks English, she faces the challenges of prejudice.

4.   WIDENING PERSPECTIVES

4. A. Personal Explorations

Picture Book

Dancing with the Indians. (1991). By Angela Shelf Medearis. Illustrated by Samuel Byrd. New York: Holiday House. An African American family attends a celebration of their Seminole Indian neighbors who sheltered an ancestor long ago.

Learning to Swim in Swaziland: A Child's–Eye View of a Southern African Country. (1993). By Nila K. Leigh. New York: Scholastic. Nila's family moves to Swaziland and she writes postcards to her class. This book was written by Nila, now in fourth grade. IB

Picture Books for Older Readers

Dancing Teepees: Poems of American Indian Youth. (1989). Edited by Virginia Driving Hawk Sneve. Illustrated by Stephen Gammell. NY: Holiday House. The writings of young American Indian poets. P

Less than Half, More than Whole. (1994). By Kathleen and Michael Lacapa. Illustrated by Michael Lacapa. Flagstaff, AZ: Northland. A young boy realizes he's not like his friend who states, "I'm all Indian . . . you're only half or less than half." A visit to his grandfather on the reservation helps him understand he's really "more than whole."

Mufaro's Beautiful Daughters. (1987). By John Steptoe. New York: Scholastic. This version of Cinderella from the Kaffir people of Zimbabwe honors a daughter's truth and integrity.

Post Card Passages. (1994). By Susan Joyce. Molalla, OR: Peel Productions. Great-Aunt Gladys writes postcards from her travels around the world. The pages of this book include her postcard notes, photographs, and drawings of her trips around the world from 1953 to 1967.

Soul Looks Back in Wonder. (1993). Edited and illustrated by Tom Feelings. New York: Dial. A beautifully-illustrated collection of powerful poems by and about African Americans. P, MR

Under the Moon. (1994). By Dyan Sheldon. Illustrated by Gary Blythe. New York: Penguin. Paintings tell the story of Jenny, who finds an arrowhead and sleeps outdoors, dreaming of the Rosebud Sioux people who lived nearby long ago.

The Very Last First Time. (1985). By Jan Andrews. Illustrated by Ian Wallace. Vancouver, B.C.: Douglas & McIntyre. Going under the ice to gather mussels alone for the first time, a young Inuit girl must rely on herself in order to return safely.

Chapter Books

Rising Voices: Writings of Young Native Americans. (1992). Selected by Arlene B. Hirschfelder and Beverly R. Singer. New York: Charles Scribner's. A collection of poems and essays in which young Native Americans speak of their identity, their families and communities, rituals, and the harsh realities of their lives. P, MR

Sign of the Beaver. (1983). By Elizabeth George Speare. Boston: Houghton Mifflin. A young boy is left alone to guard his family's cabin in the wilderness. He learns to survive with the help of a native American boy and his family.

Voices from the Fields: Children of Migrant Farmers Tell Their Stories. (1993). By S. Beth Atkin. Boston: Joy Street Books. Photographs, poems, and interviews with children reveal the hardships and hopes of Latino migrant farm workers and their families. IB

4. B. Justice and Prejudice

Picture Books

Angel Child, Dragon Child. (1983). By Michele Maria Surat. Illustrated by Vo-Dinh Mai. Milwaukee, WI: Raintree. Hoa suffers from the teasing of her classmates until one of her tormentors finds out her mother is still in Vietnam. He rallies the school to help raise money to bring Hoa's mother to the United States.

Picture Books for Older Readers

Dear Willy Rudd. (1993). By Libba Moore Gray. Illustrated by Peter Fiore. New York: Simon & Schuster. Miss Elizabeth sits on her porch and thinks back fifty years. She writes a letter to Willie Rudd, the black housekeeper who raised her, telling her all the things she regrets.

Friends from the Other Side. (1993). By Gloria Anzaldua. Illustrated by Consuelo Mendez. New York: Children's Book Press. A young girl confronts the neighbors' prejudice against her friend, a boy who illegally entered this country from Mexico to find work.

Teammates. (1990). By Peter Golenbock. Illustrated by Paul Bacon. New York: Harcourt Brace Jovanovich. This biography of Jackie Robinson, Pee Wee Reese, and the Brooklyn Dodgers owner tells the story of breaking the color barrier in major league baseball. Watercolors accompany original photographs to highlight this story. IB

Easy Chapter Books

The Friendship and *The Gold Cadillac.* (1987). By Mildred D. Taylor. New York: Dial. In *The Friendship*, the issue of race arises, jeopardizing the friendship between two men. *The Gold Cadillac* tells the story of a black family that proudly drives their new gold Cadillac across the country. The farther South they travel, the deeper the suspicions and hatred they encounter.

Journey to Jo'burg: A South African Story. (1985). By Beverly Naidoo. New York: Lippincott. When their young sister becomes seriously ill, Naledi and Tiro set off to Johannesburg to fetch their mother home from her job.

Mississippi Bridge. (1990). By Mildred Taylor. Illustrated by Max Ginsburg. New York: Bantam. When black passengers are forced off a bus to make room for white passengers, a young observer learns a powerful lesson from tragedy.

Chapter Books

The Cay. (1969). By Theodore Taylor. New York: Avon. Phillip is on a ship that sinks but he survives. The only other survivor is an old black man named Timothy and Phillip is forced to confront his prejudice. When Phillip loses his vision, he learns from Timothy about survival and himself.

Let the Circle Be Unbroken. (1981). By Mildred Taylor. New York: Dial. In this sequel to *Roll of Thunder, Hear My Cry*, the Logan family continues to struggle with injustice while maintaining their strong family connection.

The Pool Party. (1993). By Gary Soto. New York: Delacorte   . While helping his father and grandfather work as gardeners in Fresno, California, ten-year-old Rudy sees some differences between his family and the wealthy families that live nearby.

Roll of Thunder, Hear My Cry. (1976). By Mildred Taylor. New York: Puffin. This story is set in Mississippi during the Depression. Cassie Logan faces the horror of racism and hatred. The strength and importance of family are central to this story.

Timothy of the Cay. (1993). By Theodore Taylor. New York: Harcourt Brace. This prequel-sequel to *The Cay* follows Phillip's rescue from the tiny Caribbean island he shared with Timothy and continues with the operation Phillip hopes will restore his sight. The chapters about Phillip's recovery alternate with chapters that explain Timothy's life before the shipwreck that brought them together.

4. C. Heroes and Heroines

Picture Books

Alvin Ailey. (1993). By Andrea Davis Pinkney. Illustrated by Brian Pinkney. New York: Hyperion. The story of Alvin Ailey's artistic journey as he begins his own dance company in New York. IB

Harriet and the Promised Land. (1968, 1993). By Jacob Lawrence. New York: Simon & Schuster. Famed painter, Jacob Lawrence, tells the remarkable story of Harriet Tubman. IB

Swamp Angel. (1994). Anne Isaacs. Illustrated by Paul Zelinsky. New York: Dutton. Swamp Angel, the greatest woodswoman in Tennessee, single-handedly rescues settlers from the fierce bear, Thundering Tarnation. Textured illustrations painted in oil on wood veneers.

Picture Books for Older Readers

Dear Benjamin Banneker. (1994). By Andrea Davis Pinkney. Illustrated by Brian Pinkney. New York: Harcourt Brace. Benjamin Banneker overcame many personal and social obstacles to become recognized as an astronomer in the 18th century. IB

El Chino. (1990). By Allen Say. Boston: Houghton Mifflin. The story of Bill Wong, a Chinese-American who became a famous bullfighter in Spain, is captured in this biography. IB

Ida B. Wells-Barnett: A Voice Against Violence. (1991). By Patricia C. McKissack & Frederick McKissack. Illustrated by Ned Ostendorf. New York: Enslow. This biography chronicles the life of Ida Wells-Barnett, a former slave who spent her life trying to improve race relations. IB

John Henry. (1994). By Julius Lester. Illustrated by Jerry Pinkney. New York: Dial. The spirit of legendary folk hero John Henry exists in this text based on a black folk ballad. Detailed illustrations and descriptive language tell of Henry's superhuman feats.

Easy Chapter Books

Rosa Parks: My Story. (1992). By Rosa Parks with Jim Haskins. New York: Penguin. Rosa Parks recounts the story of her life, including the Montgomery bus boycott, a pivotal event in the Civil Rights movement. IB

Chapter Books

Champions: Stories of Ten Remarkable Athletes. (1993). By Bill Littlefield. Illustrated by Bernie Fuchs. New York: Little, Brown. This book features ten essays about successful athletes who have proved their worth despite extraordinary circumstances. Athletes of both genders and diverse cultures are highlighted. IB

Eleanor Roosevelt: A Life of Discovery. (1993). By Russell Freedman. New York: Clarion. This biography reads like a novel and presents the amazing accomplishments and personality of Eleanor Roosevelt. IB

Franklin Delano Roosevelt. (1990). By Russell Freedman. New York: Scholastic. Using original photographs, Freedman captures an honest glimpse into the public and private life of FDR. IB

Freedom's Children: Young Civil Rights Activists Tell Their Own Stories. (1993). By Ellen Levine. New York: G. P. Putnam's. This provocative collection includes African American teenagers' personal accounts of civil rights and desegregation in the 1950s and 1960s. IB, MR

From Slave to Civil War Hero: The Life and Times of Robert Smalls. (1994). By Michael L. Cooper. New York: Lodestar. An historical account of Robert Smalls' life, telling of his path from slavery to Civil War military hero to state legislator for South Carolina. IB

Lincoln: A Photobiography. (1987). By Russell Freedman. New York: Scholastic. An award-winning account of Lincoln's youth and presidency enhanced through photographs and original documents. IB

Lost Star: The Story of Amelia Earhart. (1988). By Patricia Lauber. New York: Scholastic. This biographical account of the first woman to fly across the Atlantic traces her life from childhood to her mysterious disappearance in 1937. IB

Mr. Lincoln's Drummer. (1995). By G. Clifton Wisler. New York: Dutton. Willie Johnston, too young to enlist as a Union soldier, proved his worth as a drummer boy and a hero. Based on a true story, Willie's courageous exploits during the Civil War earned him the Congressional Medal of Honor.

So Young to Die: The Story of Hannah Senesh. (1993). By Candice Ransom. New York: Scholastic. Eighteen-year-old Hannah Senesh left her home in Hungary to fight for a Jewish homeland. Four years later, she joined the British Air Force. During her military service she took part in courageous rescue missions behind German lines during World War II. An inspiring true story. IB

Starting Home: The Story of Horace Pippin, Painter. (1993). By Mary E. Lyons. New York: Scribner's. This book recounts the life of African American folk artist, Horace Pippin. IB

Visions: Stories About Women Artists. (1993) By Leslie Sills. Morton Grove, IL: Albert Whitman. Artists Mary Cassatt, Leonora Carrington, Betye Saar, and Mary Frank are highlighted in this collection of biographies. IB

4. D. Exploration and Westward Expansion: Multiple Perspectives

Picture Books for Older Readers

Cassie's Journey: Going West in the 1860's. (1988). By Brett Harvey. Illustrated by Deborah Kogan Ray. New York: Holiday House. Lured by the promise of gold, Cassie and her family travel by covered wagon from Illinois to California. Their journey is based on actual accounts and women's diaries from the late 1800s.

Custer's Last Battle. (1969, 1992). By Paul Goble. New York: Pantheon. This is Goble's first book, written because he was unable to find a children's book that captured the Sioux perspective of the Battle of Little Big Horn. The story is told in the words of a fictional Sioux youth present at the battle.

Daily Life in a Covered Wagon. (1994). By Paul Erickson. Washington, D.C.: Preservation Press. In 1853, the Larkin family travel to Oregon in a covered wagon. This informational book includes photographs of their actual journal, items from the wagon, and a detailed description of daily life on the westward journey. IB

Death of the Iron Horse. (1987). By Paul Goble. New York: Macmillan. The true story of how a group of Cheyenne fighters attacked and derailed a train intruding on their land in 1867. IB

My Prairie Year: Based on the Diary of Elenore Plaisted. (1986). By Brett Harvey. Illustrated by Deborah Kogan Ray. New York: Holiday House. Adventures of living on the Dakota prairie in 1889 are captured through a nine-year-old's eyes and told through her notebook. The details and drama of pioneer life are captured in narrative prose and sweeping sketches.

Easy Chapter Books

Save Queen of Sheba. (1981). By Louise Moeri. New York: Dutton. After their wagon train has been attacked by Sioux, King David and his younger sister, Queen of Sheba, set out to find their parents. The book reflects King David's growing understanding of other perspectives.

Chapter Books

Beyond the Divide. (1983). By Kathryn Lasky. New York: Macmillan. An Amish girl and her father brave the perils of overland travel when they leave Pennsylvania for the West in 1849. MR

Bonanza Girl. (1962, 1993). By Patricia Beatty. New York: Morrow. A widow brings her children to the gold rush country of Idaho, searching for a new life.

Bound for Oregon. (1994). By Jean Van Leeuwen. New York: Dial. Fictionalized account of Mary Ellen Todd's family journey from Arkansas to Oregon in 1852. This novel captures pioneering spirit and courage through hardship and adversity.

I am Regina. (1991). By Sally M. Keehn. New York: Dell. When Regina is captured during the French and Indian War, she clings to her identity as she takes on a new life and name as Tskinnak.

Jericho's Journey. (1993). By G. Clifton Wisler. New York: Lodestar. Leaving Tennessee for Texas in 1852, Jericho discovers that growth has more to do with courage than with size.

Legend Days. (1984). By Jamake Highwater. New York: Harper & Row. Amana, an eleven-year-old Northern Plains Indian, is abandoned in the wilderness when smallpox devastates her tribe. She endures as a legend with courage and prowess, even as she witnesses the disintegration of her people's traditions. MR

Sing Down the Moon. (1970). By Scott O'Dell. Boston: Houghton Mifflin. A Navaho girl resists as the army forces her people to move from their homeland to Fort Sumner in 1864.

Thunder Rolling in the Mountains. (1992). By Scott O'Dell and Elizabeth Hall. Boston: Houghton Mifflin. Chief Joseph's daughter tries to help the Nez Perce escape to Canada rather than be forced to leave their Wallowa Mountains home.

4. E. Cultural Conflicts

Picture Books

How My Parents Learned to Eat. (1984). By Ina R. Friedman. Illustrated by Allen Say. Boston: Houghton Mifflin. Trying to honor each other's customs but not knowing how, a Japanese woman and an American sailor struggle to learn about each other's culture.

Sami and the Time of the Troubles. (1992). By Florence Parry Heide and Judith Heide Gilliland. Illustrated by Ted Lewin. New York: Clarion. Set in contemporary Lebanon, Sami's everyday life is interrupted when warfare comes to his neighborhood. As he and his family hide, he tries to understand how his life has changed.

Smoky Night. (1994). By Eve Bunting. Illustrated by David Diaz. New York: Harcourt Brace. This story of two families during the Los Angeles riots is enhanced by illustrations rich in texture.

Picture Books for Older Readers

Encounter. (1992). By Jane Yolen. Illustrated by David Shannon. New York: Harcourt Brace Jovanovich. Haunting illustrations and well-researched text present another side of the Columbus story from the perspective of the Taino people.

Rebel. (1994). By Allan Baillie. Illustrated by Di Wu. New York: Ticknor & Fields. Based on an actual incident in Rangoon, a young boy rebels and saves his village from a general's attempt to take over. This book deals with issues of tyranny and "saving face."

Chapter Books

Catherine Called Birdy. (1994). By Karen Cushman. New York: Clarion. A strong female character struggles with coming of age during medieval times. This book is rich with true bits of daily life during this time period. MR

A Circle Unbroken. (1988). By Sollace Hotze. New York: Clarion. Rachel discovers that she was captured as a child by a band of Sioux Indians and raised as the chief's daughter. She returns to her birth family as Kata Wi, adjusting with great difficulty because of her longing for her Sioux family. MR

The Forty-Third War. (1989). By Louise Moeri. Boston: Houghton Mifflin. When twelve-year-old Uno Ramirez is forced to serve in a Central American revolutionary army, he must find the courage to survive. MR

Guests. (1994). By Michael Dorris. New York: Hyperion. A coming-of-age book about Moss, who flees his native village when his parents invite strangers, Pilgrims, to a harvest meal.

Haveli. (1993). By Suzanne Fisher Staples. New York: Knopf. Shabanu submits to the customs of her people in Pakistan and marries the rich older man to whom she was pledged against her will. Now Shabanu becomes the victim of his family's blood feud and the malice of his other wives. Sequel to *Shabanu: Daughter of the Wind.* MR

Kiss the Dust. (1991). By Elizabeth Laird. New York: Penguin. To escape Iraqi forces, thirteen-year-old Tara must flee with her family over the border into Iran. There they face an uncertain future because of her father's involvement with the Kurdish resistance movement. MR

Morning Girl. (1992). By Michael Dorris. New York: Hyperion. As told in the words of a twelve-year-old girl and her brother, the Taino people faced many changes and challenges when the first European immigrants arrived in 1492.

Night Journey. (1981). By Kathryn Lasky. Illustrated by Trina Schart Hyman. New York: Puffin. Ignoring her parents' wishes, Rachel encourages her grandmother to recount her escape from Russia.

The Road from Home: The Story of an Armenian Girl. (1979). By David Kherdian. New York: Puffin. The author tells his mother's true story as a child in Turkey before the government began to deport its Armenian citizens.

Shabanu: *Daughter of the Wind.* (1989). By Suzanne Fisher Staples. New York: Knopf. At the age of eleven, Shabanu is pledged in marriage to an older man in order to bring prestige to her desert-dwelling family. She must decide whether to accept the decision or risk the consequences of going against her family and culture. MR

Waiting for the Rain. (1987). By Sheila Gordon. New York: Bantam. Two young men—one black, one white—struggle to remain friends through racial tensions in South Africa. MR

The Wall. (1991). By Elizabeth Lutzeier. New York: Holiday House. Hannah must hide the fact that her mother was killed trying to cross the Berlin Wall. This book captures the tensions and events connected with the Berlin Wall. MR

Zlata's Diary. (1994). By Zlata Filipovic. New York: Viking. Through her diary, Zlata Filipovic recounts the mounting horror as her country, the former Yugoslavia, dissolves into ethnic conflict. IB

4. F. Challenges of War

Revolutionary War

Picture Books

Katie's Trunk. (1992). By Ann Turner. New York: Macmillan. When the rebels come, Katie's family runs into the woods but she runs back into the house. Based on a true incident, she hides in a trunk and hopes she won't be discovered.

Chapter Books

The Fighting Ground. (1984). By Avi. New York: Lippincott. In 1778, Jonathon is longing to fight the British. He's thirteen and runs away to fight. Within 24 hours, his feelings about war have totally changed.

Jump Ship to Freedom. (1981). By James Collier & Christopher Collier. New York: Dell. Daniel and his mother are slaves, although by law they should be free. Daniel steals the papers for his freedom, but is caught and sent to the West Indies.

My Brother Sam is Dead. (1974). By James Collier & Christopher Collier. New York: Four Winds. Sam Meeker's father is still loyal to the British, but his brother runs off to fight with the American soldiers.

War Comes to Willy Freeman. (1983). By James Collier & Christopher Collier. New York: Delacorte. When Willy Freeman's father is killed during the Revolutionary War, she must disguise herself as a boy to rescue her mother, imprisoned in New York City.

Who Is Carrie? (1984). By James Collier & Christopher Collier. New York: Dell. Carrie is a slave who knows nothing about her name or her past. While working in various homes, she eavesdrops on famous leaders and presidents, catching a glimpse of both the history of early America and her own past.

Civil War and Slavery

Picture Books

Aunt Harriet's Underground Railroad in the Sky. (1992). By Faith Ringgold. New York: Crown. Aunt Harriet tells the story of slavery and the Underground Railway while Cassie follows from station to station. The last few pages contain factual information and a map.

Cecil's Story. (1991). By George Ella Lyon. New York: Orchard. Cecil worries about whether his father will come back from the Civil War and bravely tries to be the man of the house.

Follow the Drinking Gourd. (1988). By Jeanette Winter. New York: Knopf. The song, "Follow the Drinking Gourd," leads escaping slaves to freedom in the North.

Picture Books for Older Readers

Nettie's Trip South. (1987). By Ann Turner. Illustrated by Ronald Himler. New York: Macmillan. Based on a real diary of the author's relative, Nettie writes her impressions of her trip South and her horror and revulsion at seeing a slave auction.

Now Let Me Fly: The Story of a Slave Family. (1993). By Dolores Johnson. New York: Macmillan. The story begins in Africa and follows a family to a slave plantation, where the family soon is torn apart.

Pink and Say. (1994). By Patricia Polacco. New York: Philomel. Pink, a former slave, and Say, a Michigan farm boy, are both members of the Union Army. While Pink rescues Say in battle, both endure harm from marauders, capture by Confederates, and suffer injustice due to the Civil War.

Sweet Clara and the Freedom Quilt. (1993). By Deborah Hopkinson. New York: Knopf. Clara dreams of fleeing North to freedom. She discovers how to find her way and help others escape as she sews a quilt to map the route north.

Easy Chapter Books

Thunder at Gettysburg. (1991). By Patricia Gauch. New York: Bantam. When the Battle of Gettysburg comes right through her back yard, Tillie must come face to face with her own terror in order to help those around her.

Chapter Books

Across Five Aprils. (1964). By Irene Hunt. Chicago: Follett. The story of the tragic involvement of Matthew Creighton's family in the Civil War, with loved ones fighting on both the Confederate and Union sides.

The Boys' War. (1990). By Jim Murphy. New York: Clarion. Many soldiers on both sides of the Civil War were only twelve or thirteen. In this book, the author provides firsthand accounts of these young soldiers and a glimpse of the daily glory and horror of war. IB,

Brady. (1987). By Jean Fritz. New York: Puffin. No one trusts Brady to keep a secret. He suspects his neighbor and father have something to do with helping runaway slaves and wants to help, but knows no one will trust him. A book about the Underground Railway, fear, and courage.

Bull Run. (1993). By Paul Fleischman. New York: HarperCollins. Told from multiple perspectives on both sides, this account of the first battle of the Civil War vividly depicts the destruction of war.

Cezanne Pinto: A Memoir. (1994). By Mary Stolz. New York: Knopf. Cezanne Pinto escapes slavery through the Underground Railroad in the company of a remarkable woman. He travels to the West and becomes a cowboy. Cezanne's memoirs are based on true events in history.

Charley Skedaddle. (1987). By Patricia Beatty. New York: Morrow. Charley leaves New York and joins the Union Army as a drummer, full of enthusiasm. However, when he actually encounters fighting, Charley is terrified and runs away (skedaddles) into the Blue Ridge Mountains. Charley meets an old woman and learns much about war and about himself.

A Girl Called Boy. (1982). By Belinda Hermence. New York: Clarion. Boy is disgusted with her father's interest in history and can't imagine how anyone would let themselves become a slave. However, when she steps across a stream and finds herself back in the 1850s, she learns firsthand the challenges and struggles of her people during the Civil War.

The House of Dies Drear. (1968). By Virginia Hamilton. New York: Macmillan. A house once used to shelter escaping slaves causes an African-American family to search the past.

Jayhawker. (1991). By Patricia Beatty. New York: Morrow. Lije Tutley works as an abolitionist raider and spy to free slaves in Missouri.

The Long Road to Gettysburg. (1992). By Jim Murphy. New York: Clarion. Told from the perspectives of a Northern and a Southern soldier, this non-fiction account of the Battle of Gettysburg illustrates the chaos and horror of war. IB

Many Thousand Gone: African Americans from Slavery to Freedom. (1993). By Virginia Hamilton. Illustrated by Leo and Diane Dillon. New York: Knopf. Vivid illustrations enhance tales of slaves who followed the quest for freedom via the Underground Railroad.

Nightjohn. (1993). By Gary Paulsen. New York: Delacorte. Set in the 1850s, twelve-year-old Sarney endures life as a young slave. Danger and potential hope arrive when an escaped slave, Nightjohn, teaches her how to read. MR

Out from this Place. (1988). By Joyce Hansen. New York: Walker. In this sequel to *Which Way Freedom?*, Easter tries to find Obi, who has run away from slavery to fight in the Civil War on the Union side.

Red Cap. (1991). By G. Clifton Wisler. New York: Penguin. A young Union soldier shows remarkable courage when captured and imprisoned at Andersonville.

The Root Cellar. (1981). By Janet Lunn. New York: Scribner's. Twelve-year-old Rose is packed off to live with unknown relatives on a farm in Canada. There she ventures into the root cellar and emerges in another century, where she experiences events during the Civil War.

Shades of Gray. (1989). By Carolyn Reeder. New York: Macmillan. Will is filled with anger when his family is killed and he's sent to live with an uncle who refused to fight in the war. Used to city life, Will learns about living and working on a farm and about the meaning of love and courage.

Slave Dancer. (1973). By Paula Fox. Scarsdale, NY: Bradbury. A thirteen-year-old boy is kidnapped by the crew of an Africa-bound ship, where he is forced to play music for its human cargo. A graphic and haunting tale. MR

Sojourner Truth: Ain't I a Woman? (1992). By Patricia McKissack & Frederick McKissack. New York: Scholastic. An informational book about a slave named Isabella who was born in New York in 1797. She lived in the North, but wasn't freed until she was 30. Choosing the name Sojourner Truth, she became an abolitionist and activist for the rights of blacks and women. IB

Steal Away. (1992). By Jennifer Armstrong. New York: Orchard. Susannah is an orphan who is sent to live on a plantation in the South but longs to run home to the north. Bethlehem is a slave who Susannah tries to befriend and they decide to run north together. The book tells of their tenuous friendship, their journey north to Vermont, and their reunion much later in Canada.

Undying Glory: The Story of the Massachusetts 54th Regiment. (1991). By Clinton Cox. New York: Scholastic. The true story of a Union regiment of African-American soldiers and their courage in the face of overwhelming odds. IB

Which Way Freedom? (1986). By Joyce Hansen. New York: Walker. Obi runs away from slavery to join the Union Army during the Civil War, facing certain death at the hands of the Confederate soldiers if he is captured.

With Every Drop of Blood. (1994). By James Lincoln Collier and Christopher Collier. New York: Delacorte. A Southern boy finds himself captured by a Union soldier of about the same age.

World War II and Korean War

Picture Books

Baseball Saved Us. (1993). By Ken Mochizuki. Illustrated by Dom Lee. New York: Lee & Low. The story of the harsh conditions at an internment camp during World War II and how baseball gave the Japanese-Americans something positive in a terrible situation.

The Bracelet. (1993). By Yoshiko Uchida. New York: Philomel. Emi discovers the enduring power of friendship when she loses the bracelet given to her by a friend before her family was taken to an internment camp during World War II.

Let the Celebrations Begin! (1991). By Margaret Wild. Illustrated by Julie Vivas. New York: Orchard. Based on true facts, this touching story tells of women in a concentration camp who made toys for the children.

The Lily Cupboard. (1992). By Shulamith Levey Oppenheim. Illustrated by Ronald Himler. New York: HarperCollins. A simple book of a young Jewish girl who is hidden by a family during World War II. Miriam has a secret cupboard where she hides when German soldiers are near.

A Picture Book of Anne Frank. (1993). By David A. Adler. Illustrated by Karen Ritz. New York: Holiday House. A powerful picture book version of Anne Frank's story for younger readers. IB

Sadako. (1993). By Eleanor Coerr. Illustrated by Ed Young. New York: Putnam's. This picture book tells the story of Sadako's struggle to survive the effects of the atom bomb dropped on Hiroshima years before.

Picture Books for Older Readers

Faithful Elephants: A True Story of Animals, People and War. (1988). By Yukio Tsuchiya. Translated by Tomoko Tsuchiya Dykes. Illustrated by Ted Lewin. Boston: Houghton Mifflin. A haunting true story of the zookeepers in Tokyo who had to kill all the animals when bombs began to fall. Most difficult of all was watching the death of the elephants they loved.

Rose Blanche. (1985). By Roberto Innocenti and Christophe Gallaz. New York: Stewart, Tabori & Chang. Roberto Innocenti's simple text and haunting oil paintings capture the growing understanding of a German girl during World War II. Rose Blanche became the name of a group of German citizens who protested the war.

Easy Chapter Books

The Big Lie. (1992). By Isabella Leitner. New York: Scholastic. Isabella Leitner tells her family's true story of courage and survival during the Holocaust. IB

Sadako and the Thousand Paper Cranes. (1977). By Eleanor Coerr. New York: Dell. Sadako must battle leukemia and cling to hope for recovery and peace. Her folding of paper cranes has become a symbol for peace around the world.

Chapter Books

Anne Frank: Beyond the Diary. (1992). By Ruud van der Rol and Rian Verhoeven. New York: Viking. This powerful account of Anne Frank's life includes many original photographs of Anne, her diary, and the attic where her family hid. IB

The Champion. (1993). By Maurice Gee. New York: Simon & Schuster. The lives of a twelve-year-old boy and his friends will never be the same after an African-American soldier arrives in their New Zealand hometown during World War II.

Daniel's Story. (1993). By Carol Matas. New York: Scholastic. Daniel and his family must find the courage to survive the horror of the Holocaust "for all those who couldn't." Published in conjunction with the exhibit, "Daniel's Story: Remember the Children" at the United States Holocaust Museum in Washington, D.C.

The Devil's Arithmetic. (1988). By Jane Yolen. New York: Viking Kestrel. Hannah opens the door during her family's Passover celebration and finds herself in Poland in 1940. The Nazi soldiers are coming and Hannah tries to warn her family, but no one believes her. An incredible novel providing an inside glimpse into the concentration camps of World War II and the courage of the Jewish people. MR

Echoes of the White Giraffe. (1993). By Sook Nyul Choi. Boston: Houghton Mifflin. As Sookan adjusts to life in the refugee camp in Pusan, she clings to her hope that the civil war will end and her family will be reunited in Seoul. Sequel to *Year of Impossible Goodbyes.* MR

The Eternal Spring of Mr. Ito. (1985). By Sheila Garrigue. Ontario, Canada: Maxwell Macmillan. A young girl and an elderly gardener must save a 200-year-old bonsai tree after the Japanese bombing of Pearl Harbor.

Farewell to Manzanar. (1973). By Jeanne Wakatsuki Houston and James D. Houston. New York: Bantam. A true story of the internment of Japanese-American citizens during World War II. MR, IB

The Hidden Children. (1993). By Howard Greenfield. New York: Ticknor & Fields. Howard Greenfield tells the stories of thirteen men and women who were hidden as children during World War II. A powerful book for older readers about courage and the horrors of war. IB

I Am an American: A True Story of Japanese Internment. (1994). By Jerry Stanley. New York: Crown. Japanese internment comes to life through stories of real people whose lives were displaced and disregarded. A no-nonsense view of history. MR, IB

Journey Home. (1978). By Yoshiko Uchida. New York: Atheneum. When they are released from an internment camp, a Japanese-American girl and her family must rebuild their lives. Sequel to *Journey to Topaz.*

Journey to Topaz. (1971). By Yoshiko Uchida. Berkeley, CA: Creative Arts Book Company. A Japanese-American family is forcibly sent to an internment camp in Utah following the bombing of Pearl Harbor at the start of World War II.

Kim/Kimi. (1987). By Hadley Irwin. New York: Margaret K. McElderry Books. In an internment camp during World War II, Kimi Yogushi searches for her family's roots and tries to understand her own place in society.

Never to Forget: The Jews of the Holocaust. (1976). By Milton Meltzer. New York: HarperCollins. This book offers eyewitness accounts through letters, diaries, journals, and memoirs of those who experienced the terror and grief of the Holocaust. MR, IB

Number the Stars. (1989). By Lois Lowry. New York: Dell. This Newbery Award winner tells the story of Ellen Rosen, a Jewish girl who comes to live with Annemarie's family in Copenhagen during World War II. Annemarie must come face to face with bravery and fear.

Rosie's Tiger. (1994). By Anna Myers. New York: Walker. Rosie, awaiting the return of her brother from the Korean war, discovers that he's bringing his Korean wife and their son to America. This novel portrays Rosie's initial jealousy and eventual acceptance.

Snow Treasure. (1942). By Marie McSwigan. New York: Scholastic. Appearing to "play in the snow," a team of courageous children smuggles Norwegian gold out from under the guns of German soldiers during World War II.

Stepping on the Cracks. (1991). By Mary Downing Hahn. New York: Avon. Margaret and Elizabeth are proud of their brothers who are overseas fighting during World War II. They learn the complexities of war when they discover a neighbor has run away from the war and is hiding in the woods. All of them are forced to confront their feelings about truth and love and war.

Under the Blood Red Sun. (1994). By Graham Salisbury. New York: Delacorte. Tomikazu Nakaji's biggest concerns are baseball, homework, and the local bully until life with his Japanese family in Hawaii changes drastically after the bombing of Pearl Harbor in 1941. MR

Year of Impossible Goodbyes. (1991). By Sook Nyul Choi. Boston: Houghton Mifflin. Sookan and her family survive the Japanese occupation of Korea, only to face overwhelming hardship at the hands of the Communist government that follows. When they escape to the South, they must leave everything behind. MR

The Vietnam War and Southeast Asia

Picture Books

The Lotus Seed. (1993). By Sherry Garland. Illustrated by Tatsuro Kiuchi. San Diego: Harcourt Brace Jovanovich. When she must flee her homeland, a Vietnamese girl carries with her a lotus seed as a reminder of an emperor's courage.

The Wall. (1990). By Eve Bunting. New York: Clarion. A boy and his father visit the Vietnam Veterans Memorial to find his grandfather's name.

Easy Chapter Books

The Wall of Names. (1991). By Judy Donnelly. New York: Random House. An easy chapter book for younger readers with facts about the Vietnam War and the Vietnam Veterans Memorial. IB

Chapter Books

The Clay Marble. (1991). By Minfong Ho. New York: Farrar, Straus & Giroux. As Dara's family flees the advance of Khmer Rouge soldiers in Cambodia, she becomes separated from them in the chaos.

Goodbye Vietnam. (1992). By Gloria Whelan. New York: Random House. The seemingly impossible dream of escaping Vietnam for Hong Kong and freedom challenges a refugee family's courage and perseverance.

Little Brother. (1985). By Allan Baillie. New York: Penguin. Vithy must survive the Cambodian jungle and the Khmer Rouge soldiers to rescue his older brother.

Park's Quest. (1988). By Katherine Paterson. New York: Puffin. Park struggles to understand his father's death in the Vietnam War. His search for answers eventually leads him to acceptance and growth.

Song of the Buffalo Boy. (1992). By Sherry Garland. New York: Harcourt Brace. Loi flees Ho Chi Minh City to escape society's scorn for her Amerasian heritage and to find her American father.

5.   SPARKING THE IMAGINATION

5. A. Tales and Twists

Traditional Tales

Beauty and the Beast. (1989). Retold and illustrated by Jan Brett. New York: Clarion.

Jack and the Beanstalk. (1991). By Steven Kellogg. New York: Trumpet.

The Princess and the Pea. (1982). Adapted and illustrated by Janet Stevens. New York: Scholastic.

Rapunzel. (1982). Retold by Barbara Rogasky, illustrated by Trina Schart Hyman. New York: Holiday.

Saint George and the Dragon. (1984). Retold by Margaret Hodges, illustrated by Trina Schart Hyman. Boston: Little, Brown.

Snow White. (1974). Retold by Paul Heins, illustrated by Trina Schart Hyman. Boston: Little, Brown.

The Twelve Dancing Princesses. (1990). Retold and illustrated by Ruth Sanderson. Boston: Little, Brown.

Less Familiar or New Tales

Dear Mili. (1988). By Wilhelm Grimm, newly translated by Ralph Manheim, illustrated by Maurice Sendak. New York: Farrar, Straus and Giroux.

Dove Isabeau. (1989). By Jane Yolen, illustrated by Dennis Nolan. New York: Harcourt Brace Jovanovich.

The Enchanted Wood. (1991). By Ruth Sanderson. Boston: Little, Brown.

Gawain and the Green Knight. (1994). By Mark Shannon, illustrated by David Shannon. New York: Putnam's.

Heckedy Peg. (1987). By Audrey Wood, illustrated by Don Wood. New York: Harcourt Brace Jovanovich.

The King's Equal. (1992). By Katherine Paterson, illustrated by Vladimir Vagin. New York: HarperCollins.

The Kitchen Knight. (1990). Retold by Margaret Hodges, illustrated by Trina Schart Hyman. New York: Holiday.

The Loathsome Dragon. (1987). Retold by David Wiesner & Kim Kahng, illustrated by David Wiesner. New York: Putnam's.

Tam Lin. (1990). By Jane Yolen, illustrated by Charles Mikolaycak. New York: Harcourt Brace Jovanovich.

Young Guinevere. (1993). By Robert D. San Souci, illustrated by Jamichael Henterly. New York: Doubleday.

Cinderella Versions

Cinderella. (1985). By Charles Perrault, retold by Amy Ehrlich, illustrated by Susan Jeffers. New York: Dial.

Cinderella. (1988). By Charles Perrault, translated and illustrated by Diane Goode. New York: Alfred Knopf.

The Egyptian Cinderella. (1989). By Shirley Climo, illustrated by Ruth Heller. New York: Thomas Crowell.

The Korean Cinderella. (1993). By Shirley Climo, illustrated by Ruth Heller. New York: HarperCollins.

Moss Gown. (1987). By William Hooks, illustrated by Donald Carrick. New York: Clarion.

Mufaro's Beautiful Daughters: An African Tale. (1987). By John Steptoe. New York: Lothrop, Lee & Shepard.

Princess Furball. (1989). Retold by Charlotte Huck, illustrated by Anita Lobel. New York: Greenwillow.

The Rough-Face Girl. (1992). By Rafe Martin and David Shannon. New York: Putnam's.

The Talking Eggs. (1989). By Robert San Souci, illustrated by Jerry Pinkney. New York: Dial.

Yeh-Shen: A Cinderella Story from China. (1982). Retold by Ai-Ling Louie, illustrated by Ed Young. New York: Philomel.

Twists or Variations on Tales

The Cowboy and the Black-Eyed Pea. (1992). By Tony Johnston, illustrated by Warren Ludwig. New York: Putnam's.

Deep in the Forest. (1976). By Brinton Turkle. New York: Dutton.

Each Peach Pear Plum. (1978). By Janet and Allan Ahlberg. New York: Viking Penguin.

A Frog Prince. (1989). By Alix Berenzy. New York: Henry Holt.

The Frog Prince Continued. (1991). By Jon Scieszka. New York: Viking Penguin.

The Giant's Toe. (1986). By Brock Cole. Toronto, Canada: Farrar, Straus and Giroux.

Jim and the Beanstalk. (1970). By Raymond Briggs. New York: Coward-McCann.

The Jolly Christmas Postman. (1991). By Janet and Allan Ahlberg. Boston: Little, Brown.

The Jolly Postman or Other People's Letters. (1986). By Janet and Allan Ahlberg. Boston: Little, Brown.

Once Upon a Golden Apple. (1991). By Jean Little and Maggie de Vries. New York: Viking.

The Paper Bag Princess. (1980). By Robert Munsch, illustrated by Michael Martchenko. Toronto, Canada: Annick Press.

Pondlarker. (1990). By Fred Gwynne. New York: Simon & Schuster.

Princess Smartypants. (1986) and *Prince Cinders.* (1987). By Babette Cole. New York: Putnam's.

The Principal's New Clothes. (1989). By Stephanie Calmenson, illustrated by Denise Brunkus. New York: Scholastic.

Roald Dahl's Revolting Rhymes. (1983). By Roald Dahl. New York: Bantam Doubleday Dell.

Ruby. (1990). By Michael Emberley. Boston: Little, Brown.

Sleeping Ugly. (1981). By Jane Yolen, illustrated by Diane Stanley. New York: Coward-McCann.

The Stinky Cheese Man and Other Fairly Stupid Tales. (1992). By Jon Scieszka, illustrated by Lane Smith. New York: Viking.

The Three Little Javelinas. (1992). By Susan Lowell. Flagstaff, AZ: Northland Publishing.

The Three Little Wolves and the Big Bad Pig. (1993). By Eugene Trivizas, illustrated by Helen Oxenbury. New York: Maxwell Macmillan.

The True Story of the 3 Little Pigs! (1989). By Jon Scieszka, illustrated by Lane Smith. New York: Viking.

5. B. Fantasy and Magic Journeys

Picture Books

Jumanji. (1981) By Chris van Allsburg. Boston: Houghton Mifflin. When Peter and Judy find a game at the park, they think it will be great fun. However, when they roll the dice and a *real* lion appears, they discover that the game was more of an adventure than they expected.

Liang and the Magic Paintbrush. (1980). By Demi. New York: Holt. Everything Liang paints with his magic paintbrush comes alive, which leads to many adventures and problems. Perfect to pair with the novel based on this tale, *A Brush with Magic* (Brooke, 1993).

The Rainbabies. (1992). By Laura Krauss Melmed. Illustrated by Jim LaMarche. New York: Lothrop, Lee & Shepard. A childless couple finds a dozen tiny babies in the grass to love and protect until they are given a child of their own.

The Sweetest Fig. (1993). By Chris van Allsburg. Boston: Houghton Mifflin. Monsieur Bibot receives two magical figs that will make his dreams come true. He dreams of wealth, but his dog has a different vision.

The Walloping Window-blind. (1994). By Charles E. Carryl. Adapted and illustrated by Jim LaMarche. New York: Lothrop, Lee & Shepard. This classic poem is brought to life with LaMarche's whimsical illustrations of young children's adventures aboard a magical ship.

The Widow's Broom. (1992). By Chris van Allsburg. Boston: Houghton Mifflin. A widow keeps a witch's old broom until her neighbors decide it's wicked.

Picture Books for Older Readers

(see list of fairy tale versions and twists)

The Tempest. (1994). By William Shakespeare. Retold by Bruce Coville. Illustrated by Ruth Sanderson. New York: Doubleday. Shakespeare tells the tale of the Duke of Milan and his daughter who are stranded on an island with the spirit Ariel and the monster Caliban. Coville's adaptation and Sanderson's illustrations bring this tale of magic to life for young readers.

Easy Chapter Books

Bright Shadow. (1985). By Avi. New York: Macmillan. Morwenna is unexpectedly given the last five wishes in the world to keep or use. She uses four to save others, then runs away to decide how best to use the last wish.

The Farthest-Away Mountain. (1976). By Lynne Reid Banks. New York: Avon. Dakin embarks on a dangerous journey to fulfill her three desires: to visit the farthest away mountain, to meet a gargoyle, and to find a prince.

Charlie and the Chocolate Factory (1964), and *Charlie and the Great Glass Elevator* (1972). By Roald Dahl. New York: Knopf. Charlie is lucky enough to discover an entry ticket into Mr. Willy Wonka's mysterious chocolate factory. His adventure begins with a tour into the world of chocolate and ends when he is launched into space in the great glass elevator.

The Gold Dust Letters. (1994). By Janet Taylor Lisle. New York: Orchard. Angela's investigation into the mysterious letters from her fairy godmother helps take her mind off her strained relationship with her father.

James and the Giant Peach. (1961). By Roald Dahl. James Henry Trotter is an unhappy orphan who travels across the ocean with giant insects in a giant peach.

The Knights of the Kitchen Table (1991), *The Not So Jolly Roger* (1991), *The Good, the Bad, and the Goofy* (1992), and *Your Mother Was a Neanderthal* (1993). By Jon Scieszka. New York: Viking. A magic book transports the Time Warp Trio to wild adventures in King Arthur's court, a desert island, the Wild West, and prehistoric times.

The Mouse and the Motorcycle (1965), *Runaway Ralph* (1970), and *Ralph S. Mouse* (1982). By Beverly Cleary. New York: Morrow. A reckless young mouse named Ralph makes friends with a boy, discovers the joys of motorcycling, and becomes a peace maker.

Wizard's Hall. (1991). By Jane Yolen. New York: Harcourt Brace Jovanovich. A young apprentice wizard saves his training hall by trusting and believing in himself.

Chapter Books

Behind the Attic Wall. (1983). By Sylvia Cassedy. New York: Avon. Maggie hears ghostly voices in the unfriendly house of her great aunt. Instead of finding fear, however, she discovers a magic that awakens her capacity to reach out to others.

Beauty: A Retelling of the Story of Beauty and the Beast. (1978). By Robin McKinley. New York: HarperCollins. McKinley's skill as a weaver of stories rounds out this classic tale of how Beauty's love for the Beast releases him from a magic spell. This version has well-rounded characters whose insights and changes give this fairy tale a new twist.

The Black Cauldron (1965), *The Book of Three* (1964), *The Castle of Llyr* (1966), *Taran Wanderer* (1967), and *The High King* (1968). By Lloyd Alexander. New York: Holt, Rinehart and Winston. A fantasy tale series about the imaginary kingdom of Prydian and the young defender, Taran, who goes in search of his birthright and the truth about himself.

The Boggart. (1993). By Susan Cooper. New York: Macmillan. When her family returns home after visiting their inherited castle in Scotland, twelve-year-old Emily discovers that they have been accompanied by a boggart, an invisible and mischievious creature.

A Brush with Magic. (1993). By William Brooke. Illustrated by Michael Koelsch. New York: HarperCollins. An orphan with a magic paintbrush travels to the court of the emperor of China to find fortune and true love.

The Castle in the Attic (1985) and *The Battle for the Castle* (1993). By Elizabeth Winthrop. New York: Bantam. William receives a gift of a castle. When he picks up a knight, it comes alive! In the second book in the series, William is the one who enters into the medieval world of dragons, wizards, and magic.

The Dark is Rising (1973), *Greenwitch* (1974), *The Gray King* (1975), and *Silver on the Tree* (1977). By Susan Cooper. New York: Macmillan. Will Stanton discovers that he is the last of the Old Ones destined to seek the magical Signs that will eventually enable the Old Ones to triumph over the evil forces of the Dark.

Dealing with Dragons (1990), *Searching for Dragons* (1991), *Calling on Dragons* (1993), and *Talking to Dragons* (1985). By Patricia Wrede. New York: Harcourt Brace Jovanovich. Cimorene, an unconventional and spunky princess, joins a witch, a king, a dragon, and a host of other characters in battles against evil wizards.

Dinotopia: A Land Apart from Time. (1992). By James Gurney. Fantasy-lovers will be fascinated by the meticulous details of Professor Denison's descriptions and drawings of the lost island of Dinotopia.

Dragon's Milk (1989) and *Flight of the Dragon's Kyn* (1993). By Susan Fletcher. New York: Macmillan. Kaeldra possess the power to understand dragons. She uses this power to try to save lives and to mediate a fierce rivalry between King Orrik and his jealous brother Rog.

The Hobbit (1938, 1966), *The Fellowship of the Rings* (1965), *The Two Towers* (1965), and *The Return of the King* (1965). By J.R.R. Tolkien. Boston: Houghton Mifflin. The adventures of the well-to-do hobbit, Bilbo Baggins, who lived comfortably in his home until a wandering wizard granted his wish and started him down a long road filled with adventures and magic.

The Indian in the Cupboard (1981). New York: Avon. *The Return of the Indian* (1986) and *The Secret of the Indian* (1989). New York: Bantam Doubleday. *The Mystery of the Cupboard* (1993). New York: Morrow. By Lynne Reid Banks. A boy and his friend become entangled in adventure and discovery when a plastic toy Indian comes alive and their lives become intertwined.

The Lion, the Witch and the Wardrobe (1950), *Prince Caspian* (1951), *The Voyage of the Dawn Treader* (1952), *The Silver Chair* (1953), *The Horse and His Boy* (1954), *The Magician's Nephew* (1955), and *The Last Battle* (1956). By C.S. Lewis. New York: Macmillan. Four British children find their way through the back of a wardrobe into the magic land of Narnia and begin a series of adventures in a magical kingdom.

Lost Magic. (1993). Amoss, Berthe. New York: Hyperion. In the Middle Ages, orphaned Ceridwen learned the art of herbal healing and gained the protection of the local lord, only to lose it when she is accused of witchcraft.

Redwall (1986), *Mossflower* (1988), *Mattimeo* (1990), *Mariel of Redwall* (1991), *Salamandestron* (1992), *Martin the Warrior* (1993), and *The Bellmaker* (1995). By Brian Jacques. New York: Philomel. Lengthy but engrossing books about a peaceful community of woodland animals at Redwall Abbey and the constant struggle and adventures with evil creatures such as Slagar the Fox, Cluny the Scourge, and Tsarmina the Wildcat. Wonderful language and fast-paced adventures.

Mrs. Frisby and the Rats of NIMH (1971). New York: Atheneum. Sequels by Jane Conly. *Racso and Rats of NIMH* (1986) and *R-T, Margaret and the Rats of NIMH* (1990). New York: Harper. By Robert C. O'Brien. A secret community of rats has learned to read and write and create an underground world. Animals and humans learn lessons of courage and bravery in this three-part series of adventures.

A Rat's Tale. (1986). By Tor Sieidler. Illustrated by Fred Marcellino. New York: Farrar, Straus & Giroux. Montague, an artistic young rat, lives beneath the streets of New York City. He thinks he can do nothing to save his friends from extermination until he comes to understand his family and himself.

A Taste of Smoke. (1993). By Marion Dane Bauer. New York: Clarion. As Caitlan plans a camping trip in the woods of Northern Minnesota, she doesn't foresee the complications ahead, including a visit by the ghost of a boy who died in a fire a hundred years ago.

A Telling of the Tales: Five Stories (1990). By William Brooke. New York: Harper & Row. *Untold Tales* (1992). New York: HarperCollins. Humorous retellings of classic tales from today's perspective: Cinderella, Sleeping Beauty, Paul Bunyan, John Henry, and Jack and the Beanstalk, The Frog Prince, Snow White, and Beauty and the Beast.

Tom's Midnight Garden. (1958). By Philippa Pearce. New York: Dell. When the grandfather clock strikes thirteen, Tom steps outside the house into another century and a complex story of discovery.

Tuck Everlasting. (1975). By Natalie Babbitt. New York: Farrar, Straus & Giroux. The Tuck family has found the secret of eternal life; however, they are confronted with an agonizing situation when they discover that a young girl and a malicious stranger now share their secret.

The Wainscott Weasel. (1993). By Tor Sieidler. Illustrated by Fred Marcellino. New York: HarperCollins. Bagley, a young weasel, is smitten with Wendy and tries to save her life.

A Wrinkle in Time (1962), *A Wind in the Door* (1973), and *A Swiftly Tilting Planet* (1978). By Madeleine L'Engle. New York: Farrar, Straus and Giroux. Meg Murray and her unusual family become involved with forces of good and evil through a series of adventures in which they travel through space.

The Wizard of Oz. (1900, 1982). By L. Frank Baum. New York: Holt, Rinehart & Winston. The classic story of Dorothy, who is transported by a cyclone to the land of Oz and must seek out a great wizard in order to return home to Kansas.

6.   MEETING AUTHORS AND ILLUSTRATORS

A. Books About Authors/Illustrators (listed by author/illustrator)

Aardema, Verna (1992). *A Bookworm Who Hatched.* Katonah, NY: Richard C. Owen. (picture book)

Andronik, Catherine M. (1993). *Kindred Spirit: A Biography of L. M. Montgomery, Creator of Anne of Green Gables.* New York: Atheneum.

Asher, Sandy. (1987). *Where Do You Get Your Ideas? Helping Young Writers Begin.* New York: Walker.

Blair, Gwenda. (1981). *Laura Ingalls Wilder.* New York: Putnam's.

Bruce, Harry. (1992). *Maud: The Life of L. M. Montgomery.* New York: Bantam.

Buchan, Elizabeth. (1987). *Beatrix Potter: The Story of the Creator of Peter Rabbit.* New York: Penguin.

Byars, Betsy. (1991). *The Moon and Me.* Englewood Cliffs, NJ: Julian Messner.

Campbell, Patricia. (1985). *Presenting Robert Cormier.* Boston: Twayne.

Carpenter, Angelica. (1990). *Frances Hodgson Burnett: Beyond the Secret Garden.* Minneapolis, MN: Lerner.

Cleary, Beverly. (1988). *A Girl from Yamhill: A Memoir.* New York: Dell.

Collins, David. (1989). *Country Artist: A Story About Beatrix Potter.* Minneapolis, MN: Carolrhoda.

Collins, David. (1989). *To the Point: A Story About E. B. White.* Minneapolis, MN: Carolrhoda.

Copeland, Jeffrey. (1993). *Speaking of Poets: Interviews with Poets Who Write for Children and Young Adults.* Urbana, IL: National Council of Teachers of English.

Cummings, Pat. (Ed.). (1992). *Talking with Artists.* New York: Bradbury.

Dahl, Roald. (1986). *Going Solo*. New York: Viking Penguin.

Dahl, Roald. (1984). *Boy*. New York: Penguin.

Daly, John. (1989). *Presenting S. E. Hinton*. New York: Dell.

Duncan, Lois. (1982). *Chapters: My Growth as a Writer*. New York: Little, Brown.

Dunkle, Margaret. (Ed.). (1987). *The Story Makers*. Melbourne, Australia: Oxford University Press.

Fox, Mem. (1992). *Dear Mem Fox, I Have Read All Your Books Even the Pathetic Ones and Other Incidents in the Life of a Children's Book Author*. New York: Harcourt Brace Jovanovich.

Fox, Mem. (1993). *Radical Reflections: Passionate Opinions on Teaching, Learning, and Living*. New York: Harcourt Brace.

Fritz, Jean. (1982). *Homesick: My Own Story*. New York: Dell.

Fritz, Jean. (1992). *Surprising Myself*. Katonah, NY: Richard C. Owen. (picture book)

Gallo, Donald. (Ed.). (1990). *Speaking for Ourselves: Autobiographical Sketches by Notable Authors of Books for Young Adults*. Urbana, IL: National Council of Teachers of English.

Gallo, Donald. (Ed.). (1992). *Authors' Insights: Turning Teenagers into Readers and Writers*. Portsmouth, NH: Heinemann.

Gallo, Donald. (Ed.). (1993). *Speaking for Ourselves, Too: More Autobiographical Sketches by Notable Authors of Books for Young Adults*. Urbana, IL: National Council of Teachers of English.

Gherman, Beverly. (1992). *E. B. White: Some Writer*. New York: Atheneum.

Goble, Paul. (1994). *Hau kola: Hello Friend*. Katonah, NY: Richard C. Owen. (picture book)

Greenwood, Barbara & McKim, Audrey. (1987). *Her Special Vision: A Biography of Jean Little*. Toronto: Irwin.

Hearne, Betsy. (Ed.). (1993). *The Zena Sutherland Lectures 1983–1992*. New York: Clarion.

Hopkins, Lee Bennett. (1993). *The Writing Bug*. Katonah, NY: Richard C. Owen. (picture book)

Hopkins, Lee Bennett. (1987). *Pass the Poetry, Please!* New York: Harper & Row.

Howe, James. (1993). *Playing with Words*. Katonah, NY: Richard C. Owen. (picture book)

Hunter, Mollie. (1976). *Talent is Not Enough: Mollie Hunter on Writing for Children*. New York: Harper & Row.

Hurwitz, Johanna. (1989). *Astrid Lindgren: Storyteller to the World*. New York: Viking Penguin.

Hyman, Trina Schart. (1981). *Trina Schart Hyman: Self-Portrait*. New York: Addison–Wesley. (picture book)

Kiefer, Barbara. (Ed.). (1991). *Getting to Know You: Profiles of Children's Authors Featured in Language Arts 1985–1990*. Urbana, IL: National Council of Teachers of English.

Kovacs, Deborah & Preller, James. (1991). *Meet the Authors and Illustrators: 60 Creators of Favorite Children's Books Talk About Their Work*. New York: Scholastic.

Kovacs, Deborah & Preller, James. (1993). *Meet the Authors and Illustrators: 60 Creators of Favorite Children's Books Talk About Their Work, Volume Two*. New York: Scholastic.

Lasky, Kathryn & Knight, Maribah. (1993). *Searching for Laura Ingalls*. Photographs by Christopher G. Knight. New York: Macmillan.

Lee, Betsy. (1981). *Judy Blume's Story*. New York: Dillon.

Little, Jean. (1987). *Little by Little: A Writer's Education*. New York: Penguin.

Little, Jean. (1990). *Stars Come Out Within*. New York: Viking.

Lloyd, Pamela. (1987). *How Writers Write*. Portsmouth, NH: Heinemann.

Marcus, Leonard. (1991). *Margaret Wise Brown: Awakened by the Moon.* Boston: Beacon Press.

Martin, Rafe. (1992). *A Storyteller's Story.* Katonah, New York: Richard C. Owen. (picture book)

Meltzer, Milton. (1988). *Starting from Home: A Writer's Beginnings.* New York: Viking Penguin.

Naylor, Phyllis Reynolds. (1987). *How I Came to Be a Writer.* New York: Macmillan.

Norby, Shirley & Ryan, Gregory. (1988). *Famous Children's Authors: Book One.* Minneapolis, MN: T.S. Denison.

Norby, Shirley & Ryan, Gregory. (1989). *Famous Children's Authors: Book Two.* Minneapolis, MN: T.S. Denison.

Paterson, Katherine. (1981). *Gates of Excellence: On Reading and Writing Books for Children.* New York: Dutton.

Paterson, Katherine. (1989). *The Spying Heart: More Thoughts on Reading and Writing Books for Children.* New York: Dutton.

Paulsen, Gary. (1993). *Eastern Sun, Winter Moon.* New York: Harcourt Brace Jovanovich. (for adults)

Peck, Richard. (1991). *Anonymously Yours: A Memoir.* Englewood Cliffs, NJ: Simon & Schuster.

Peet, Bill. (1989). *Bill Peet: An Autobiography.* Boston: Houghton Mifflin.

Polacco, Patricia. (1994). *Firetalking.* Katonah, NY: Richard C. Owen. (picture book)

Rees, David. (1984). *Painted Desert, Green Shade.* Boston: Horn Book.

Roginski, Jim. (1985). *Beneath the Covers.* Littleton, CO: Libraries Unlimited.

Rylant, Cynthia. (1992). *Best Wishes.* Katonah, NY: Richard C. Owen.

Rylant, Cynthia. (1989). *But I'll Be Back Again: An Album.* New York: Orchard.

Soto, Gary. (1992). *Living Up the Street: Narrative Recollections.* New York: Dell.

Taylor, Judy. (1992). *Letters to Children from Beatrix Potter.* New York: Warne.

Taylor, Judy. (1990). *Beatrix Potter's Letters.* New York: Warne.

Taylor, Judy. (1988). *Beatrix Potter 1866–1943: The Artist and Her Work.* New York: Warne.

Uchida, Yoshiko. (1991). *The Invisible Thread: A Memoir by the Author of The Best Bad Thing.* Englewood Cliffs, NJ: Messner.

Weidt, Maryann. (1989). *Presenting Judy Blume.* Boston: Twayne.

Yolen, Jane. (1992). *A Letter from Phoenix Farm.* Katonah, New York: Richard C. Owen. (picture book)

Zemach, Margot. (1979). *Self-Portrait: Margot Zemach.* Reading, MA: Addison-Wesley.

Zinsser, William (Ed.). (1990). *Worlds of Childhood: The Art and Craft of Writing for Children.* Boston: Houghton Mifflin.

7.   READING FOR PROFESSIONAL GROWTH

7. A. Professional Books on Literature Circles and Response

Applebee, Arthur. (1978). *The Child's Concept of Story.* Chicago: University of Chicago Press.

Atwell, Nancie. (1987). *In the Middle: Writing, Reading, and Learning with Adolescents.* Portsmouth, NH: Heinemann.

Atwell, Nancie. (1990). *Coming to Know: Writing to Learn in the Intermediate Grades.* Portsmouth, NH: Heinemann.

Atwell, Nancie. (1990). *Workshop 2: Beyond the Basal.* Portsmouth, NH: Heinemann.

Avery, Carol. (1993). *And with a Light Touch: Learning about Reading, Writing, and Teaching with First Graders.* Portsmouth, NH: Heinemann.

Benedict, Susan & Carlisle, Lenore. (Eds.). (1992). *Beyond Words: Picture Books for Older Readers and Writers.* Portsmouth, NH: Heinemann.

Burke, Eileen M. (1990). *Literature for the Young Child.* Boston: Allyn & Bacon.

Cullinan, Bernice. (Ed.). (1987). *Children's Literature in the Reading Program.* Newark, DE: International Reading Association.

Cullinan, Bernice. (Ed.). (1992). *Invitation to Read: More Children's Literature in the Reading Program.* Newark, DE: International Reading Association.

Cullinan, Bernice. (Ed.). (1993). *Fact and Fiction: Literature Across the Curriculum.* Newark, DE: International Reading Association.

Daniels, Harvey. (1994). *Literature Circles: Voice and Choice in a Student-Centered Classroom.* York, ME: Stenhouse.

Feeley, Joan, Strickland, Dorothy & Wepner, Susan. (Eds.). (1991). *Process Reading and Writing: A Literature-Based Approach.*

Fisher, Bobbi. (1991). *Joyful Learning: A Whole Language Kindergarten.* Portsmouth, NH: Heinemann.

Glazer, Joan. (1986). *Literature for Young Children.* New York: Merrill.

Goodman, Kenneth. (1986). *What's Whole in Whole Language? A Parent/Teacher Guide to Children's Learning.* Portsmouth, NH: Heinemann.

Hagerty, Pat. (1992). *Readers' Workshop: Real Reading.* New York: Scholastic.

Hall, Susan. (1990). *Using Picture Storybooks to Teach Literary Devices.* Phoenix, AZ: Oryx Press.

Harris, Violet. (Ed.). (1993). *Teaching Multicultural Literature in Grades K–8.* Norwood, MA: Christopher-Gordon.

Harste, Jerome, Short, Kathy & Burke, Carolyn. (1988). *Creating Classrooms for Authors: The Reading-Writing Connection.* Portsmouth, NH: Heinemann.

Hart-Hewins, Linda & Wells, Jan. (1990). *Real Books for Reading.* Portsmouth, NH: Heinemann.

Hickman, Janet & Cullinan, Bernice. (Eds.). (1989). *Children's Literature in the Classroom: Weaving Charlotte's Web.* Norwood, MA: Christopher-Gordon.

Hickman, Janet. (Ed.). (1994). *Children's Literature in the Classroom: Extending Charlotte's Web.* Norwood, MA: Christopher-Gordon.

Holland, Kathleen, Hungerford, Rachael & Ernst, Shirley. (1993). *Journeying: Children Responding to Literature.* Portsmouth, NH: Heinemann.

Hornsby, David, Parry, Jo-Ann & Sukarna, Deborah. (1992). *Teach On: Teaching Strategies for Reading and Writing Workshops.* Portsmouth, NH: Heinemann.

Hornsby, David, Sukarna, Deborah, & Parry, Jo-Ann. (1986). *Read On: A Conference Approach to Reading.* Portsmouth, NH: Heinemann.

Huck, Charlotte, Hepler, Susan & Hickman, Janet. (1987). *Children's Literature in the Elementary School.* Fourth edition. Chicago, IL: Holt, Rinehart & Winston.

International Reading Association. (1991). *Kids' Favorite Books: Children's Choices 1989–1991.* Newark, DE: International Reading Association.

International Reading Association. (1992). *Teens' Favorite Books: Young Adults' Choices 1987–1992.* Newark, DE: International Reading Association.

Lukens, Rebecca. (1990). *A Critical Handbook of Children's Literature.* Fourth edition. Glenview, IL: Scott, Foresman.

Lynch, Patricia. (1986). *Using Big Books and Predictable Books.* New York: Scholastic.

Meinbach, Anita Meyer, Rothlein, Liz & Fredericks, Anthony D. (1995). *The Complete Guide to Thematic Units: Creating the Integrated Curriculum*. Norwood, MA: Christopher-Gordon.

Moir, Hughes, Cain, Melissa, & Prosak-Beres, Leslie. (Eds.). (1992). *Collected Perspectives: Choosing and Using Books for the Classroom*. Norwood, MA: Christopher-Gordon.

Monseau, Virginia & Salvner, Gary. (1992). *Reading their World: The Young Adult Novel in the Classroom*. Portsmouth, NH: Heinemann.

Moss, Joy. (1984). *Focus Units in Literature: A Handbook for Elementary School Teachers*. Urbana, IL: National Council for Teachers of English.

Moss, Joy. (1994). *Using Literature in the Middle Grades: A Thematic Approach*. Norwood, MA: Christopher-Gordon.

O'Brien-Palmer, Michelle. (1993). *Book-talk: Exciting Literature Experiences for Kids*. Kirkland, WA: MicNik Publications.

O'Brien-Palmer, Michelle. (1994). *Read and Write*. Kirkland, WA: MicNik Publications.

Peterson, Ralph & Eeds, Maryann. (1990). *Grand Conversations: Literature Groups in Action*. New York: Scholastic.

Purves, Alan & Monson, Dianne. (1984). *Experiencing Children's Literature*. Glenview, IL: Scott, Foresman.

Rief, Linda. (1991). *Seeking Diversity: Language Arts with Adolescents*. Portsmouth, NH: Heinemann.

Rosenblatt, Louise. (1978). *The Reader, the Text, the Poem: The Transactional Theory of the Literary Work*. Carbondale, IL: Southern Illinois University Press.

Rosenblatt, Louise. (1983). *Literature as Exploration*. Fourth edition. New York: The Modern Language Association of America.

Roser, Nancy & Frith, Margaret (Eds.). (1983). *Children's Choices: Teaching with Books Children Like*. Newark, DE: International Reading Association.

Routman, Regie. (1988). *Transitions: From Literature to Literacy*. Portsmouth, NH: Heinemann.

Routman, Regie. (1991). *Invitations: Changing as Teachers and Learners K-12*. Portsmouth, NH: Heinemann.

Rudman, Masha. (Ed.). (1993). *Children's Literature: Resource for the Classroom*. Norwood, MA: Christopher-Gordon.

Russell, David. (1994). *Literature for Children: A Short Introduction*. (2nd Edition). New York: Longman.

Short, Kathy Gnagey & Pierce, Kathryn Mitchell. (Eds.) (1990). *Talking About Books: Creating Literate Communities*. Portsmouth, NH: Heinemann.

Somers, Albert B. & Worthington, Janet Evans (1979). *Response Guides for Teaching Children's Books*. Urbana, IL: National Council of Teachers of English.

Stewig, John Warren & Sebesta, Sam Leaton. (1989). *Using Literature in the Elementary Classroom*. Urbana, IL: National Council of Teachers of English.

Temple, Charles & Collins, Patrick. (1992). *Stories and Readers: New Perspectives on Literature in the Elementary Classroom*. Norwood, MA: Christopher-Gordon.

Tunnell, Michael & Ammon, Richard. (1993). *The Story of Ourselves: Teaching History through Children's Literature*. Portsmouth, NH: Heinemann.

Wollman-Bonilla, Julie. (1991). *Response Journals: Inviting Students to Think and Write about Literature*. New York: Scholastic.

Wood, Karen & Moss, Anita. (Eds.). (1992). *Exploring Literature in the Classroom: Content and Methods*. Norwood, MA: Christopher-Gordon.

Author and Title Index

Aardema, Verna, 116
Abijoyo (Seeger), 29, 36
Adler, David, 114
Afternoon of the Elves (Lisle), 71, 78, 163
Alcott, Louisa May, 1
Alexander, Lloyd, 6, 151, 217
Allard, Harry, 34, 114
All the Magic in the World (Hartmann), 139
Anansi the Spider (McDermott), 116
Andersen, Hans Christian, 117-117
Archambault, John, 29, 49, 50
Art Lesson, The (de Paola), 28, 37
Avi, 90, 173

Babbitt, Natalie, 137, 217
Babe: The Gallant Pig (King-Smith), 221
Baby (MacLachlan), 193
Barre, Shelley, 80, 155
Bauer, Caroline Feller, 20
Baum, L. Frank, 1
Beatty, Patricia, 164
BFG, The (Dahl), 7
Black Cauldron, The (Alexander), 151, 217
Blume, Judy, 64
Boggart, The (Cooper), 119
Book of Three, The (Alexander), 6
Borrowers, The (Norton), 119, 120, 213
Boy (Dahl), 7, 99
Brett, Jan, 32
Bridge to Terabithia (Paterson), 9, 88, 217
Briggs, Raymond, 50
Brown, Marcia, 115
Bulla, Clyde Robert, 95
Bunting, Eve, 75, 156

Cages (Kehret), 219
Cave Under the City (Mazer), 78
Charley Skedaddle (Beatty), 164
Cherry, Lynne, 123
Chive (Barre), 80, 155
Chocolate Fever (Smith), 59
Christopher, John, 119, 217
Circle Unbroken, A (Holtze), 150
City of Gold and Lead (Christopher),, 217
Cleary, Beverly, 64
Clifton, Lucille, 8
Clown of God, The (de Paola), 50

Come Back, Salmon (Cone), 125
Cone, Molly, 125
Conrad, Pam, 118
Cookie's Week (Ward), 13, 15, 20, 44, 46
Cooper, Susan, 118, 119
Cricket in Times Square, The (Solden), 136

Dahl, Roald, 7, 99, 213
Dark is Rising, The (Cooper), 118
Dealing with Dragons, (Wrede), 150, 217
Dear Mr. Henshaw, (Cleary), 64
DeFelice, Cynthia, 150
De Paola, Tomie, 18, 28, 37, 42, 46, 50
Doctor DeSoto (Steig), 119
Dream Wolf (Goble), 115

Ernst, Lisa Campbell, 32
Estes, Eleanor, 212
Everett Anderson's Goodbye (Clifton), 8

Family Apart, A (Nixon), 211
Family Pose (Hughes), 202-203
Fantastic Mr. Fox (Dahl), 7
Fighting Ground, The (Avi), 90, 91, 173
Filipovic, Zlata, 99
Fitzhugh, Louise, 213
Fleischman, Sid, 212, 213
Fly Away Home (Bunting), 75, 156, 157, 159
Fox, Paula, 77, 78, 202
Fraser, Kathleen, 140
Frog Prince, The, 116
Frog Prince Continued, The (Scieszka), 60

Gág, Wanda, 205, 206
Gardiner, John Reynolds, 59, 132, 140
Gelman, Rita, 15
George, Jean Craighead, 62, 64, 65
Ghost-Eye Tree (Martin & Archambault), 29, 49
Giver, The, (Lowry), 118, 119, 161-162
Goble, Paul, 115
Goldilocks, 116
Grandfather's Journey (Say), 41
Great Gilly Hopkins, The (Paterson, 122-123

Hansel and Gretel, 116
Harold and the Purple Crayon (Johnson), 37
Harriet the Spy (Fitzhugh), 213
Hartmann Wendy, 139
Hatchet (Paulsen), 62, 63, 217
Henkes, Kevin, 118
Hesse, Karen, 91
Hill, Kirkpatrick, 8
Holm, Anne, 164
Holman, Felice, 71
Holtze, Sollace, 150
Howe, James, 147
Howliday Inn (Howe), 147
How to Eat Fried Worms (Rockwell), 213
Hughes, Dean, 202
Hundred Dresses, The (Estes), 212
Hyman, Trina Schart, 99

In the Year of the Boar and Jackie Robinson (Lord), 9
Island, The (Paulsen), 131

Jacques, Brian, 119
James and the Giant Peach (Dahl), 7, 213
Jim and the Beanstalk (Briggs), 50
Johnson, Angela, 18
Johnson, Crocket, 37
Julie of the Wolves (George), 64

Kehret, Peg, 219
Kid in the Red Jacket, The (Park), 74
King-Smith, Dick, 221
Knots on a Counting Rope (Martin & Archambault), 50
Kraus, Robert, 15, 19, 44, 50, 169
Kuskin, Karla, 140
Leaving Morning, The (Johnson), 18
LeGuin, Ursula, 118
L'Engle, Madeleine, 119-120
Leo the Late Bloomer (Kraus), 15, 17, 50, 169
Letters from Rifka (Hesse), 19
Lights on the River (Thomas), 205
Lindgren, Astrid, 119
Lion to Guard Us, A (Bulla), 75
Lisle, Janet Taylor, 71, 78, 163
Little Fir Tree, The (Anderson), 118
Little Old Lady Who Wasn't Afraid of Anything, The (Williams), 29, 33
Little Red Riding Hood, 115, 116
Little Women (Alcott), 1
Livingston,, Myra Cohn, 140
Lobel, Arnold, 33

Loner, The (Weir), 78
Lon Po Po (Young), 115, 117
Lord, Bette Bao, 91
Lowry, Lois, 91, 118, 119, 161, 164

Macaulay, David, 201, 203
MacLachlan, Patricia, 43, 193
Maniac Magee (Spinelli), 59, 78, 219
"Marbles" (Fraser), 140
Martin, Bill Jr., 29, 49, 50
Matilda (Dahl), 7
Mazer, Harry, 78
McDermott, Gerald, 116
McSwigan, Marie, 212, 213
Millions of Cats (Gag), 205, 206
Miss Nelson Has a Field Day (Allard), 34
Miss Nelson is Missing, (Allard), 34, 114
Mitten, The (Brett), 32
Monkey Island (Fox), 77, 78, 202
More Spaghetti I Say (Gelman), 15
Moser, Barry, 156
Mouse Soup (Lobel), 33
Mrs. Katz and Tush, (Polacco), 30
Mufaro's Beautiful Daughters (Steptoe), 116, 141
Myers, Walter Dean, 219
My Mom Travels a Lot (Bauer), 20
My Side of the Mountain (George), 62, 65

Nana Upstairs, Nana Downstairs (de Paola), 46
Nancy Drew mysteries, 1
Naylor, Phyllis Reynolds, 4, 9, 136, 152, 205, 211, 223
Nettie's Trip South (Turner), 59
Nightjohn (Paulsen), 193
Night of the Twisters (Ruckman), 5, 72, 74
Nixon, Joan Lowry, 217
North to Freedom (Holm), 164
Norton, Mary, 119, 213
Now One Foot, Now the Other (De Paola), 18, 42, 46, 50
Number the Stars (Lowry), 91, 121, 122, 164

O'Dell, Scott, 91
Owen (Henkes), 118
Owl Moon (Yolen), 58

Park, Barbara, 74
Paterson, Katherine, 9, 88, 122, 217
Paulsen, Gary, 62, 63, 131, 153, 193, 217
Pearce, Philippa, 119

Picture Biography of Anne Frank, A (Adler), 114
Pink and Say (Polacco), 8
Pippi Longstocking (Lindgren), 119
Polacco, Patricia, 8, 30
Polly Vaughn (Moser), 156, 158
Popcorn Days and Buttermilk Nights (Paulsen), 153-154

Redwall (Jacques), 119
Relatives Came, The (Rylant), 114
River Ran Wild, A (Cherry), 123, 125
Rockwell, Thomas, 213
Roll of Thunder, Hear My Cry (Taylor), 107, 154, 29
Ruckman, Ivy, 5, 72, 74
"Rules" (Kuskin), 140
Rylant, Cynthia, 114

Sam Johnson and The Blue Quilt (Ernst), 32
Say, Allen, 41
Scieszka, Jon, 31, 50, 52
Scorpions (Myers), 219
Sebestyen, Ouida, 91
Seeger, Pete, 29, 36
Selden, George, 136
Sendak, Maurice, 119
Shiloh (Naylor), 4, 9, 136-137, 205, 211, 223
Ship (Macaulay), 201
Sing Down the Moon (O'Dell), 91
Slake's Limbo (Holman), 71
Smith, Robert Kimmel, 59
Snow Treasure (McSwigan), 212, 213
Spinelli, Jerry, 59, 78, 219
Stafford, Kim, 141
Steig, William, 119
Steptoe, John, 116, 141
Stone Fox (Gardiner), 59, 132-133, 140
"Street Song" (Livingston), 140

Tales of a Fourth Grade Nothing (Blume), 64
"Talking" (Viorst), 140
Taylor, Mildred, 107, 154, 217
Tenth Good Thing About Barney, The (Viorst), 28
Thesman, Jean, 71
Thomas, Jane Resh, 205

Three Billy Goats Gruff, The (Brown), 115
Three Little Pigs, The, 116, 117
Through Grandpa's Eyes (MacLachlan), 43
Tin Soldier, The (Andersen), 118
Tom's Midnight Garden (Pearce), 119
Toughboy and Sister, (Hill), 8
Trina Schart Hyman: Self-Portrait (Hyman), 99
True Story of the 3 Little Pigs!, The (Scieszka), 31, 52
Tub People, The (Conrad), 118
Tuck Everlasting, (Babbitt), 137, 217
Turner, Ann, 59

Velveteen Rabbit, The (Williams), 118
Viorst, Judith, 28, 140

Ward, Cindy, 13, 15, 20, 44, 46
Weasel (DeFelice), 150
We Got Here Together (Stafford), 141
When the Road Ends (Thesman), 71
Where The Wild Things Are (Sendak), 119
Whipping Boy, The (Fleischman), 212, 213
White Mountains, The (Christopher), 119, 217
Whose Mouse Are You? (Kraus), 15, 44
Why Mosquitoes Buzz in People's Ears (Aardema), 116
Wier, Ester, 78
Wild Christmas Reindeer (Brett), 32
Williams, Linda, 40
Williams, Marjorie, 118
William's Dell (Zolotow), 18, 19
Wizard of Earthsea, A (Le Guin), 118
Wizard of Oz, The (Baum), 1
Words by Heart (Sebestyen), 91
Wrede, Patricia, 150, 219
Wrinkle in Time, A (L'Engle), 119-120
Yolen, Jane, 58
Zlata's Diary: A Child's Life in Sarajevo (Filipovic), 99
Zolotow, Charlotte, 18, 19

General Index

ABC book, 144
Accordion book, 144
Achievement testing, 202, 207-208
Adoff, Arnold, 203
Aesthetic stance to literature, 6
Anecdotal notes, 168-173, 193, 194
Artistic and dramatic response,
    assessing, 188, 190, 192-194
    intermediate students, 192-'94
    primary students, 190
Art of Teaching Writing, The
    (Calkins), 30
Arts, and meaning making, 153-166
    cooking, 158
    dance, 157
    implications for classroom,
    161-165
    poetry, 157-159
    visual art, 158-159
Assessment and evaluation, 8, 167-
    198
    artistic and dramatic response,
    188, 190, 192-194
    extensive reading, 175-178
    oral response, 168-174
    participation, 178-185
    portfolios, 194,-195, 197
    written response, 185-188
    See also Authentic assessment
Assessment and Evaluation in
    Whole Language Programs
    (Harp), 168, 169
Atwell, Nancie, 61, 213, 218
Au, Kathryn, 4
Authentic assessment, 200
    achievement testing, 207-208
    and extended reading, 202-
    203
    in literature circles, 201-202
    reader response, 202, 203-206
    See also Assessment and
    Evaluation
Autobiographies, student, 99

Beyond Words: Picture Books for
    Older Readers and Writers
    (Benedict & Carlisle), 59
Booktalk, 101-102

Calkins, Lucy, 30
Cambourne, Brian, 7, 14, 218, 220
Character web, 73
Children and Books (Sutherland &
    Arbuthnot), 126

Children's Literature in the Elemen-
    tary School (Huck, Heppler, &
    Hickman), 216
Children's Literature in the Reading
    Program (Cullinan), 216
Choice, and student involvement, 7,
    22, 28, 39, 61, 62
Choosing books, 113-126
    fantasy, 117-120
    informational, 123, 125-126
    realistic fiction, 121-123
    traditional literature, 114-117
    See also Selecting books
Choral reading, 140
Class constitution, 100
Collaboration among students, 6-7
Commemorative stamp, 144, 150
Compliment Box, 100
Conferences, 66
Constructivist model of literacy, 4
Conversations, 98-99
Cooking, as response to literature,
    158
Creating Classrooms for Authors:
    The Reading—Writing
Connection (Harste, Short, &
    Burke), 31, 72, 218
Creative Drama in the Classroom
    (McCaslin), 139, 219
Critical Handbook of Children's
    Literature, A (Lukens), 126
Cube, 144

Dance, as response to literature, 157
Davis, F., 207
Debriefing, 57, 65, 106-108, 183
Developmental reading continuum,
    195, 196
Dialogue, 5
Diary, 73, 134, 144
Dillon, Diane and Leo, 116
Diorama, 144, 150
Discussion groups, 17-18, 30-33,
    39, 62-65, 74, 89, 92
Drama, as response to literature,
    153-154
DRTA (directed reading thinking
    activity), 214

Efferent stance to literature, 6
Essentials of Children's Literature
    (Lynch-Brown & Tomlinson),
    126
Evocation, 204, 206
Extended reading, 202-203

Extension, 67
        projects, 142-148, 217
Extensive reading, 5
Extensive reading, assessing, 175-
        178
        reading conferences, 175, 178,
        179
        reading logs, 175, 176, 177

Fantasy
        selecting, 117-119
        structure of, 119-120
Feedback to students, 138
Flannel board story, 144
Focus of discussion, 9
Fox, Mem, 6, 9
*Frames of Mind: The Theory of
        Multiple Intelligence*
        (Gardner), 155
Freedman, Russell, 203
Fritz, Jean, 203

Gammell, Stephen, 114
Gardner, Howard, 155
Giblin, James Cross, 203
Gifted readers, 199
Gift From The Sea (Lindbergh), 98
Goodland, John, 99
Grand Conversations: Literature
        Circles in Action (Peterson &
        Eeds), 16, 30, 72, 168, 178,
        215, 216,
Group dynamics, 103-108
        clarifying, 105
        debriefing/self-reflection, 106-
        108
        empathetic and reflective
        listening, 104-105
        facilitating, 104

Harris, Violet, 8
Harwayne, Shelley, 140
*Home: A Collaboration of Thirty
        Distinguished Authors and
        Illustrators of Children's
        Books to Aid the Homeless*
        (Rosen), 79
Homeless, The (Jenkes), 80

Illustration, as journal response, 73,
        134
Improvisation, 141
Independent reading, 28-29, 57, 66
        promoting, 45
Individualized Reading, 207
Intensive reading, 5
Interaction among students, 6-7
Interview, 73, 134

*In the Middle: Writing, Reading,
        and Learning with Adoles-
        cents* (Atwell), 61, 213, 218
*Invitations: changing as Teachers
        and Learners K-12*
        (Routman), 86, 102, 135

Jackdaw, 144, 151
Journal prompts, 19, 109
Journal response, 29-30, 73, 92,
        133-137
Journal writings, 18-20
Journeyline, 144

Kauffman, Gloria, 31
Kettel, Ray, 75

Lamme, Linda, 199
Lasting Impressions (Harwayne),
        140
Lauber, Patricia, 203
Letter, as journal response, 73, 134
Lewis, C.S., 138
Lindbergh, Anne Morrow, 98
Literacy development, 42-45
Literature circles,
        adapting to classroom, 91, 92
        assessment and evaluation,
        167-198
        authentic assessment in, 201-
        202
        benefits of, 110-111
        choosing books, 113-126
        defined, 2-3
        and emergent readers, 27-54
        extensions, 67
        in first grade, 13-25
        goals for, 15
        guidelines for assessing, 208-
        209
        and intermediate readers, 71-
        80
        rationale for, 3-8
        and response, 41-52
        sample of, 75-80
        and teaching reading, 8-10,
        55-69
        teaching strategies, 21-23
Literature response, 20-21

Main idea belt, 144, 151
Map, 144
Marshall, James, 114
Matthews, Cindy, 168
Maturity in Reading, Its Nature and
        Appraisal (Gray & Rogers),
        202
McCaslin, Nellie, 219
Meltzer, Milton, 203

Mime, 139-140, 145
Mind map, 64, 65, 73, 134
Mini-lessons, 4, 57-61, 134, 135, 173-174
    and authors' craft, 58-59
    based on students' needs, 60-61
    procedural, 57-58
    skill and strategy, 58
    student-led, 137-138, 218-219
Miscue analysis, 194
Moss, Elaine, 209
Multicultural literature, 7-8
Mural, 145
Music, a response to literature, 155
Musical accompaniment, 145
Music and movement, 141

No Place To Be: Voices of Homeless Children (Berck) 80, 202
Norton, Donna, 3

Open-ended questions, 51-52
Oral response, assessing, 168-174
    anecdotal notes, 168-169
    mini-lessons, 173-174
Ownership, 7, 22-23

Pamphlet, 73, 134
Paragraph, as journal response, 134
Parental involvement, 16-17, 24
Participation, assessing, 178-185
    peer evaluation, 182-183
    retrospective self-evaluation, 183-184
    self-evaluation with intermediate students, 180-182, 183, 184
    self-evaluation with primary students, 178, 180, 181
Peer evaluation, 182-183
Peer interviews, 100
Personal memoirs, 99
Poetry
    as journal response, 73, 135
    as response to literature, 154, 157-158, 165
Pop-up, 73, 135
Pop-up book, 145
Portfolio Assessment in the Reading-Writing Classroom (Tierney, Carter, & Desai), 168
Portfolio Portraits (Graves & Sunstein), 168, 195, 220, 222
Portfolio reflections, 195, 197
Portfolios, and evaluation, 194-195, 197

"Post-it" notes, 169-170, 171
Practical Aspects of Authentic Assessment: Putting the Pieces together (Hill & Ruptic), 167, 195
Prediction, as reading strategy, 21
Prelutsky, Jack, 203
Puppet show, 145

Range of books, 23
Read-alouds, 48, 132
"Read between the lines" strategy, 4
Reader response, 6, 202, 203-206
Readers Theatre, 140-141, 145, 153
Reading and the performing arts,
    choral reading, 140
    improvisation, 141
    mime, 139-140
    music and movement, 141
    Readers Theatre, 140-141, 145
    Story Theatre, 140
    teacher's role, 140
Reading conferences, 175, 178, 179, 193
Reading folder, 66
Reading log, 66, 175, 176, 177, 193
Reading Process and Practice: From Socio-Psycholinguistic to Whole Language (Weaver), 72
Reading strategies, students', 33
Reading workshop
    debriefing, 57, 65
    independent reading and conferences, 57, 66
    literature circle discussions, 62-65
    literature circle extensions, 67
    literature study choices, 61-62
    management issues, 66
    mini-lessons, 57-61
    scheduling, 55-56
    structure, 56-57
Read-On: A conference Approach to Reading (Harnsby, Sukarna, & Parry), 30, 214
Reflection, 205, 206
Repeated readings, 21-22
Response projects, 34-38
Response questions, 77, 83
Response to literature, 41-52, 108-110
Retelling, 193
Retrospective self-evaluation, 183-184
Riddle character book, 145
Rief, Linda, 220

Ritz, Karen, 114
Rosenblatt, Louise, 4, 6, 9, 204
Routman, Regie, 4, 102
Running records, 193
Scaffolding, 97-111, 220
Scheduling, 15, 55-56, 92, 215-216
Scrapbook, 145
*Seeking Diversity: Language Arts
    with Adolescents* (Rief), 220
Selecting Books, 44-45, 46-48, 92.
    See also Choosing books
Self-evaluation
    intermediate students, 180-
    182, 183, 184
    primary students, 178, 180,
    181
    retrospective, 183-184
Self-portraits, 100
Short, Kathy, 31
Sign systems, 155
Sketch-to-Stretch, 73, 135, 137
Smith, Karen, 9
Song, 145
Status-of-the-class, 57, 61-62, 69
Story banner, 145
Story or character quilt, 146
Story Theatre, 140, 146
Story wheel, 146, 152
Student's role during literature
    study, 10
Summary/reaction, 73, 135
Summer reflections, 99

Tableaux, 146
Talking About Books (Smith), 9
Talk Show, 146

Taxonomics for assessing response,
    206
Teacher's observations, purposes of,
    110
Teacher's role during literature
    circles, 10, 216
Text analysis, 203-204
Timeline, 73
Traditional literature
    selecting, 114-116
    structure of, 116-117
Transactional theory, 202

*Using Picture Storybooks to Teach
    Literary Devices* (Hall), 59

Venn Diagram, 73, 74, 135
Visual art, as response to literature,
    154, 158-159, 162, 163
Vygotsky, Lev, 6

*Whole Story, The: Natural Learning
    and the Acquisition of
    Literacy in the Classroom*
    (Cambourne), 14, 218, 220
Written response, 51
Written response, assessing, 185-
    188
    growth over time, 185-186
    of intermediate students, 188,
    191
    of primary students, 187-188,
    189, 190
Writing, and the visual arts, 132-
    138